Academy Zappa

Proceedings of the First International Conference of Esemplastic Zappology (ICE-Z)

edited by
Esther Leslie and Ben Watson

Academy Zappa

Proceedings of the First International Conference of Esemplastic Zappology (ICE-Z)

edited by
Esther Leslie and Ben Watson

First published in 2005
by SAF Publishing

SAF Publishing Ltd.
149 Wakeman Road, London.
NW10 5BH
ENGLAND

email: info@safpublishing.com
www.safpublishing.com

ISBN 0 946719 79 9

A CIP catalogue record for this book is available from the British Library

Printed in England by the Cromwell Press, Trowbridge, Wiltshire

This volume is dedicated to the memory of

Dominique Jeunot

Président des Fils de l'Invention
who died unexpectedly in his sleep
on the night of 26 December 2004
leaving this building entirely too soon
goodbye friend

ICE-Z THANKS: Distant cousins & far-flung speakers; Gamma & Elena Giacomini, Than McBride, Rowan & Max Watson for providing beds, floors and Martian Embassies for delegates; George & Aristotle Eugeniou at Theatro Technis; Eleanor Crook for moustache sculpture; the fabulous digital documentarists Liam Massey and Bruno Le Tohic; Working Men's College for the data projector; Roy & Café Brasil at the Working Men's College; Evil Dick & the Banned Members; Jonathan Goslan, Ian Stonehouse and Simon Prentis for the PA; Rachel at the College Bar; *The Psychoanalytic Quarterly* for permission to reprint Romantic Love Songs data; the editors of *Naked Punch* for permission to reprint Daniel DiPaolo's "The Negative Dialectics of *Arf*-Enlightenment"; Dave Hallbery and Mick Fish at SAF.

Table of Contents

Illustrations

Photographs at ICE-Z taken by:
Esther Leslie, Liam Massey, Bruno Le Tohic

Academy Zappa

Proceedings of the First International Conference of Esemplastic Zappology (ICE-Z)

Introduction

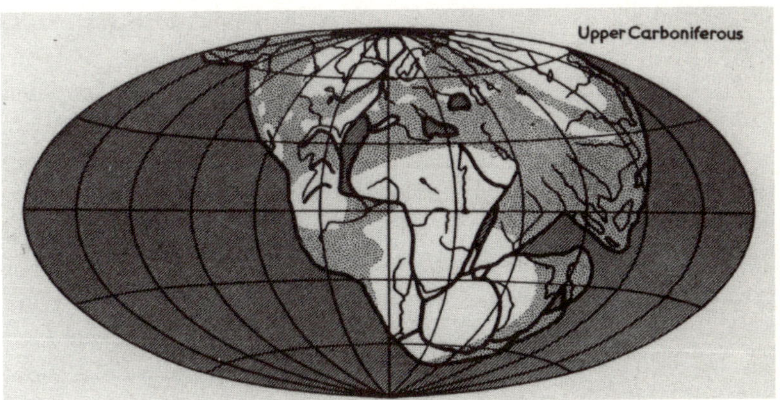

Fig 1: Undrifted Continents

The Zappa Fan Today

The mass culture industry today is a global phenomenon. Rupert Murdoch pushes the tentacles of his tits'n'tattle empire into the new, capital-friendly China; Universal Music execs, reeling at the hyberbolic afflatus of their company name, quaff champagne and demand back massages as they fly first class across the Atlantic to inflict the likes of Jamie Cullum on unsuspecting audiences; an anthropologist in Leipzig worries that David Beckham is overrated and that football has been corrupted by the star system; the blockbuster *Spider-Man 2*—already a blockbuster before anyone's seen it—debuts simultaneously all over the world as film, toy, fast-food theme and computer game; Mr Bean's assault on Buckingham Palace is greeted with gales of laughter and deafening applause in an Armenian cinema; coconut milk is shipped in cans to London from Penang, Malaysia, with the information that it is 'ideal for a wide variety of dishes, including seafood, meat, poultry, sauces, salads, cakes, biscuits, scones, curries, desserts, cocktails, tea and coffee'.

Under the pressure of the globalized market, any singular thing must become universal. We too, as suppliers of that universal commodity—labour power—have become international phenomena, and strain towards the universal: there has never been so much working abroad, whether "legal" and protected by US troops (as in Iraq), or illegal and harassed by customs officers and policemen (as in the UK).

How does the Frank Zappa fan fit into this? The answer proposed by the International Conference of Esemplastic Zappology (ICE-Z) is that the Zappa fan must become *universal* too. We must find out what everyone else out there is thinking, must organise internationally, resuscitate old hopes for a United Mutations and an Intercontinental Absurdities. After all, it is only because current conditions deny our geological-time clocks that we don't recognise that all lands were once—quite literally—united. In 1966, the same year that *Freak Out!* was issued, Dover Publications in New York published a book about continental drift. Reality is more absurd than you think.

> North America at one time lay alongside Europe and formed a coherent block with it and Greenland, at least from Newfoundland and Ireland northwards. This block was first broken up in the later Tertiary, and in the north as late as the Quaternary, by a forked rift at Greenland, the sub-blocks then drifting away from each other. Antarctica, Australia and India up to the beginning of the Jurassic lay alongside southern Africa and formed together with it and South America a single large continent, partly covered by shallow water. This block split off into separate blocks in the course of the Jurassic, Cretaceous and Tertiary, and the sub-blocks drifted away in all directions ... In the westward drift of both Americas, their leading edges were compressed and folded by the frontal resistance of the ancient Pacific floor, which was deeply chilled and hence a source of viscous drag. The result was the vast Andean range which extends from Alaska to Antarctica.[1]

Such a geophysical reality demands an active imagination, breaking through the skin of business-as-usual with which capitalism shields its dark, atrocious alchemy. Zappologists must respond to the globalization of product with the production of *glow balls of intellectual fire,* ladies and gentlemen, dense clusters of insight, deep-crustal penetrations and fervid exchanges of star dust and sleep motes. We must organise from below, since the topdown view of those in control of the culture industry ignores our proclivities and betrays our interests. They want to make money out of us, and this relentless pressure makes our culture stupid. How to respond to this pressure? How should fans fight back? There is something more to do than place a stapled A4 pamphlet of transcribed interviews with *alumni,* soundmixers and groupies to wilt on the shelves of Helter Skelter in London's Denmark Street (actually, we can't even do that any more, the great rock bookshop has vaporised into an e-entity).

There's a world out there of conscious and unconscious Esemplastic activity. Let's take a look at current institutions and activities which are impossible to imagine without Zappa's music and Zappa's example. The Arf Society. The Zappanale. Les Fils de l'Invention in Paris. Debra Kedabra in Rome. The Idiot Bastard Son Website. The Frank Zappa Family Trust. The Wrong Object. The Muffin Men. Swamp Dogg. When Worlds Collide. Project/Object. The Akashic Ensemble. Gamma in Cantelowes Park and at the Martian Embassy. Evil Dick & the Banned Members. The Marshall-McLuhan-*Finnegans Wake* Reading Club in Los Angeles. The Grandmothers. Alternative TV. The Fall. *The Simpsons.* The Jim & Jack Show. Laurie Harding Associates. Steve Vai. Len Massey's drawing studio. Ian Stonehouse. Amnesia Vivace. Pleasure-Drenching Improvers. *<www.MilitantEsthetix.co.uk>*. The Prime-Time Sublime Community Orchestra. **Who are these people and why do they do what they do?**

Academy Zappa: Proceedings of the First International Conference of Esemplastic Zappology does not promise to list everything that happens today under the name or influence of Zappa, whether trademarked or pirate, celebratory or exploitative, inspired or wack, intellectual or dumb, succulent or fraudulent. But it does attempt to start a *discussion* about why we're here in the first place, what Zappa's evident difference

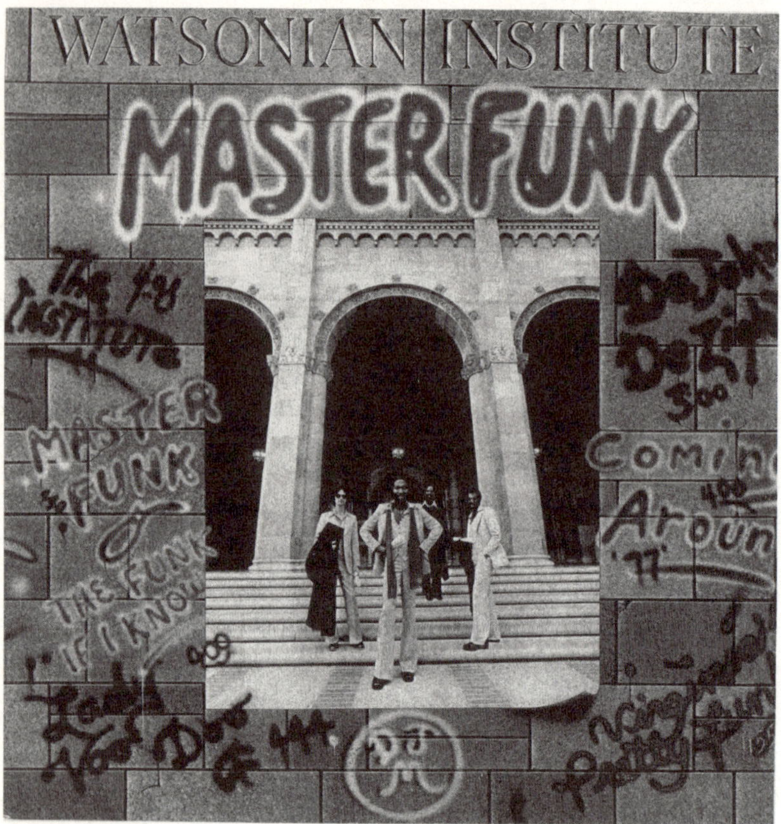

Fig 2: The Watsonian Institute

from regular mass and avantgarde music really is. We're Zappa fans. We love it all, the crackpot completism of *The Torchum Never Stops* Team from an unnamed location in Germany, who in 1991 and 1992 produced four gigantic volumes—with colour illustrations—of every purchasable *object* connected with Zappa; the post-communist completism of Wolfhard Kutz, leading Arf Society member and *impresario* for the Zappanale in Bad Doberan, who is amassing a collection of *every single international Zappa release* (from the Venezuelan *Hot Rats* to the Japanese *Stairway To Heaven* 12"); Roger Carey's band with Jonathan Miller on keyboards playing two sets of Zappa from the Parliament Hill bandstand on Hampstead Heath in the rain in June 2004, replacing John Etheridge's Zappatistas at short notice ("Toads of the

Fig 3: The Ministry of Silly Walks

Short Forest"? *Jeezus*!). We love it all, but we don't think with our love we can change a world we can't *understand*.

That's why this book is called *Academy Zappa*, a way of signalling our distance from mere fan worship (*cf.* Zappo's calendars, bless him). We refuse the deleterious schism which capitalism induces between production and consumption, self-development and entertainment, learning and earning. Though some of our speakers hail from the nether fringes of the academic hierarchy (rather as the heretics of old always numbered in their ranks some turbulent priests and frazzled friars), ICE-Z has no designs upon academic respectability. We've watched the process enveloping novelist Iain Sinclair, and it's not a pretty sight. We funded ICE-Z ourselves for own amusement, in hock to no academic institution or committee. Yes, folks, we're a zappological academic simulacrum, a parody, a concatenation of freakos, a DIY-barbecue with theses based on puns, proof by boogaloo, with canine delegates, grown men in curly eighteenth-century wigs declaiming in French, and DJ Jonathan Goslan playing "Andy" and "Jewish Princess" at a local pub so we can dance in depraved abandon. The institutions *we* aspire to liaise with are the Watsonian Institute and the Ministry of Silly Walks on an anti-war demo near you.

Outside the ivory tower, there's a tendency for the peasantry to associate anyone who reads fat books or uses long words with its glass bead game. Not so. Academic conferences are invariably hobbled by the star system and scholastic reference protocol. Without Slavoj Zizek as a plenary speaker, you're dead as a duck in the dark water (with no *Pudel* to fish you out). Without nods to the weedy tenders of the flame of social science ('As Simon Frith has taught us, young people buy records (Frith, 1978: 19)...' *etc*) or the holy texts of Parisian idealism ('As Jean Baudrillard has taught us, images are the murderers of their own model (Baudrillard, 1983a: 10)...' *etc*), you'll never get your paper published in a refereed journal. ICE-Z didn't care about that rigmarole, and didn't cater to it. We subverted it with our unreasonable and teeming passion for the music of Frank Zappa. A conference where people were allowed to talk about stuff they actually *like*? Outside James Joyce studies, it's unheard of! And we've found the ideal publishers in SAF: when we rang them up, they suggested we meet for a pint, a social ritual no-one in academic publishing seems capable of.

Watson *chez* Zappa

Of course, intellectual and/or verbal comprehension hardly has pride of place in the Zapparian universe. Zappa made *music*, which is concrete philosophy, truth more material and bodily than the concept. He dissed intellectuals and other dead people, and many fans do the same. Yet one of the editors of this volume had the experience of being invited to Zappa's home on Woodrow Wilson Drive in North Hollywood, shortly before his death of prostate cancer in 1993, to read aloud to him his 600-page, Adorno-adorned, abstruse-and-impossible analysis *Frank Zappa: the Negative Dialectics of Poodle Play*. Watson also read at one of Frank's *soirées*, and his work was praised and applauded by the invitees. He was put to work in a downstairs studio with engineer Spencer Chrislu, recording the four original essays which formed the basis of *Poodle Play* for a mooted 3CD spoken-word release.[2] For someone who thought Zappa would sneer at every line and every connection as some English cerebral disease, this was encouragement of a wild kind. The great 'what if' created by Zappa's too-early demise cannot be posthumously denied by fan prejudice. What would the anti-intellectual 'hardcore' fans, whose anti-Watson insults pepper

<alt.fan.frank-zappa>, have made of the lecture tour of US campuses Zappa wanted to organise for Watson? But if Zappology is to progress, it must lose the Ben Watson *imprimatur*, and become *collective*. Our exagmination round his factification for inca-roadside illumination of an output macrostructure warped in process (Democritus: 'the atoms however *swerve*') needs many brains, brawns, generational experiences, class backgrounds and nationalities, or it will become a hobby-horse, stale and ropey.

The Esemplastic method

First, a definition. Apart from its nod to 'plastic', an especially resonant theme in Zappa's early *oeuvre* (see "Who Are The Brain Police?", "You're Probably Wondering Why I'm Here", "Plastic People", "Uncle Bernie's Farm", "Brown Shoes Don't Make It" and Captain Beefheart's "Plastic Factory"), 'Esemplastic' is not a commonly-used term in the Zapparian universe, or indeed in any universe. Why then use it? Because we needed a term that could distinguish the kind of Zappology proposed by ICE-Z from the kind of Zappology engaged in elsewhere. Yes, we love it all, but we also want to change and transmogrify the state of Zappology worldwide. We want to leave a mark. We have a method to promulgate. We think our variety yields more. We like to write! Some people say, Why can't we leave criticism and debate and dialectic behind, and unite everyone in some ecumenical, sentimental, hands-across-the-water, everything-is-healing-nicely zappological get-on-my-cloud hallelujah chorus which smells like that stuff they put in the toilet paper? Such proposals simply put the whole question on the plane of *pity and injured feelings*! They are a direct admission of bankruptcy as regards real arguments of principle and real zappological insights. Thirteen speakers gathered together in Theatro Technis for the purpose of creating zappological **enlightenment**, not of *indulging in mutual compliments and philistine sentimentality*. Our only consideration should be the interest of Zappology, and whether or not what's said contributes materially to the illumination of Zappa's *oeuvre*. 'Yo!' as Lenin said in 1903.[3]

Contrasting Zappologies	
Esemplastic	Empirical
Materialist	Literal
Critical	Slavish
00s	80s
Clusters	Lists
Internationalist	Imperialist
Social Utterance	Private Property
Iconoclastic	Fetishistic
Poodle	Official Product
Playful	Serious
Chadbourne	Vai
Collective	Individualist
Dada	Corporate Logo
Volosinov	Chomsky
Brilliant	Pathetic
Absurd	Absurd
Literal	Idealist
Actual	Virtual
Articulate	Rude
Chomsky	Clinton
Improvised	Bought-in
Contrary	Affirmative
Face-to-face	Newsgroups
Appropriot	Appropriate

The deployment of the word 'Esemplastic' is not just a rhetorical and divisive ruse, however. Our use of it is highly motivated, and the word itself has a significant history. It was coined in 1817 by the poet Samuel Taylor Coleridge in his book *Biographia Literaria*. He began Chapter X with a polemic against those who refuse the unknown or the unexpected. He did this by imagining their response to a word they'd never encountered before, and couldn't look up in Samuel Johnson's *Dictionary of the English Language* (1755, 1773), a book which defined the lingustic norms of Coleridge's epoch (isn't it slightly odd that Zappa, who spent his whole life 'nuking norms'[4], should have created a fan base so vociferously on guard versus contamination by the non-Zappological... everything in there is *contaminated* for fuck's sake!). Like Zappa himself with Harry and Rhonda in *Thing-Fish*, Coleridge ventriloquizes for those he guesses will object to his inventions.

> '*Esemplastic*. The word is not in Johnson, nor have I met with it elsewhere.' Neither have I! I constructed it myself from the Greek words, *εἰς ἓν πλάττειν*, *i.e.* to shape into one; because, having to convey a new sense, I thought that a new term would both aid the recollection of my meaning, and prevent its being confounded with the usual import of the word *imagination*.[5]

Esemplastic Zappology takes a stand versus the mere listing of zappological 'facts', and seeks to understand both the spin Zappa gave them and the social import of that spin. It wants to *situate* Zappa without reducing him to a mere oddity in an already-existing landscape. For us, Zappa's *oeuvre* is like a telescope or microscope, a device which allows us to examine and analyse the world about us. A world not round and flat and fixed and boring, but developing and changing, choc-a-bloc with absurdity and coincidence and poetry as well as money, poverty, war, anti-war, people, animals, ear wax, cheese, Eugene Chadbourne, burgers, drifting incontinence, pumpernickel, mahogany elbows and green things in general. That is why a Zappology exclusively directed towards Zappa the Man would be truly sad and preposterous, like a telescope or microscope bent round to peer at itself, unusable, kept forever in its velvet-lined box, merely fetished and fondled for its ornamental fittings. That's how some fans strike us. Esemplastic Zappology wants to call every vegetable and put the *oeuvre* to work.

For us, 'shaping into one' means the attempt to understand the Whole by looking at the Details. Zappa alerts us to the fact that reality is holographic and fractal: everything's there in the tiniest fragment because we're looking at it and we are the sum product of everything, insect feelers on the event horizon of cosmic history. We see no limit and accept no circumscription in our passionate attempt to descry the gilded sparks and splinters spilling out from the dark poodle which *spritzt.* Esemplasticists won't allow their Esemplastic imaginations to be broken on a rack of particulars. We want to discern the Output Macrostructure. The present-day Esemplasticists refuse to die!

People who talk about Frank Zappa without talking about what's wrong with capitalism, about its deleterious effect on us and the world, about the insolent fraud of television and the reeking atrocity of the arms trade, about global war as a permanent adjunct of a consumer economy, about religion and racism as scandals which prove the untruth and inefficacy of bourgeois reason, about the infinite potential of human cravings versus the draconian law of commodity exchange, about what's subversive about sexual fantasy and what is critical about smut, such people have a corpse in their mouth.

The esemplastic method goes back aeons. Relating the Detail to the Whole is the task of dialectics: understanding the transitions from the Many to the One. In the third century BC, Socrates explained it to Protarchus in these words (well, not quite, forgive the somewhat Victorian aroma of Jowett's rendition):

> We say that the One and the Many become identified in our propositions, and that now, as in time past, they run about together, in every sentence which is uttered. This union of the One and Many will never cease, and is no new phenomenon, but is, I believe, an everlasting quality of propositions which never grows old. When we first taste these subtleties, we're delighted, and fancy we've found a spouting font of wisdom, a cornucopia of canny remarks; in the first enthusiasm of our joy we leave no stone—or rather no thought—unturned, now rolling up the Many into One, and kneading them together, now unfolding and dividing them; we puzzle ourselves first and above all, and then proceed to puzzle our neighbours, whether they're older or younger, or our own age—that makes no difference; neither father nor mother do we spare;

> no human being who has reason is safe from us, *not even our dogs*, and a barbarian would have no chance of escaping us, provided we could find an interpreter.[6]

And of course, a too hurried or slapdash transition from the Detail to the Whole, the Many to the One, is insufficient. The synoptic 'vision' of Flower Power or Rave Culture or Noise—mainlining straight to the Cosmos without mediation—doesn't convince us because it misses out the role of the US military and the CIA in the development of hallucinogens, the cash passed to the gangsters who sold you your E, the opening up of heroin routes since the bombing of Yugoslavia and Afghanistan, the travesty of avantgarde as flattery of nihilistic conformism. Flower Power without Allen Ginsberg's paeans to the joys of social revolution and anal sex becomes a promotional device for the sale of tie-dye T-shirts. We like Zappa's methodology because it grazes without compunction over the whole territory of contemporary life, and considers nothing too off-*piste* or filthy or mundane for comment.

Despite its Coleridgen nomenclature, Esemplastic Zappology has no truck with the academic 'study' of pop culture. The Popsicle Academy buffers itself against the experience of music with so much bulky, fashionable theory it loses its ability to hear. It homes in on bad music like a crap-seeking missile. The spate of 'studies' of Madonna in the late-80s was particularly stupid: knowing, collusive, careerist post-feminism tracing its concepts from the media to academia and back again. The personnel of the Popsicle Academy themselves flit between media consultancy and research fellowship, advertising and sociology, believing they're at some 'cutting edge', but it all looks like advertorial *falafel* to us. They pronounce on youth and sub-cultures, dazzle us with their theoretical imports from Paris—watered down Marxism, domesticated surrealism, recuperated scraps from the situationists—ever keen to find escape routes out of the sinking universities. The academy, once a bastion against the lure of marketing and commercialism, turns inside-out, implodes. Postmodern theories and inter-university competition provide a twin legitimation for trampling on the notion of the academic life; orientation towards the fashionable, rather than the eternally truthful; the rapid deadline, rather than long-researched forages; puff and hype rather than critique. We end up with a pale reflection of magazine chatter, not its nemesis. Those who talk about pop culture with an eye on the stipend... in the immortal words of Rosco Gordon: 'We don't like 'em!'.[7]

Esemplastic Zappology also distances itself from music journalism, which must pander to editorial notions of trends and fads (*saleability*). We hate both the relentless discovery of 'new' rock bands who always sound like the Beatles or the Velvets and the reactionary curatorship of the antique gods of the rock pantheon, the endless regurgitation of stories about drug indulgence and rehab. We are allergic to the day-dream psychosis of those who forever want to read about people who are richer and more famous and more sexually successful than they are (isn't *Mojo* really just a version of *Hello* marketed to rock music victims?). We want to live right now. *Freak Out!* Liberate the *saucissons* and *sauerkraut*, comrades!

From Adorno to Zappa

Neither academia nor journalism has been able to divine the real reason why Zappa's music sinks its hooks so far into our psyches, why his records—even more so than the peaks of Hendrix and Iggy and the Pistols and George Clinton and the Fall and Snoop Doggie Dogg—feels like an entire social and political programme, the only *Aufhebung* of the split between politics and aesthetics of the twentieth century which has resulted in *music* (albums) rather than theory (Guy Debord). To gauge Zappa, you don't need the latest theoretical gabble from Cultural Studies or the latest boy band from London, you need the words of Thomas Mann from *Dr Faustus*. When Zappa drew up the blueprints for the Project/Object in 1961 and 1962, they might have sounded like this:

> Is it a sentimentality to say that music today—which after all stands for everything of any real value in contemporary society—burns to break from its dignified isolation, yearns to become accessible without becoming banal, and to speak a language which even the musically untaught could understand? Sentimentality could never be the right tool. What we need is *sarcasm* and *scorn* and *ridicule*, which—by clearing the air of romanticism, pathos and prophecy, sound-intoxication and literature—could enable us to experience

> the objective and elemental. I'm calling for recognition of music as it actually is: *organisation through time.* A difficult task! For close by lies the trap of false primitivism, and hence a return to the sloughs of romanticism by another route. We must keep our places at the vanguard of intellectual progress, taking off from the most refined aspects of European musical advance, so that the New is made available to everyone. We must put the musicians in charge, allow them freedom to use all these modernist inventions as building blocks, transform the tradition of innovation represented by Beethoven into something experienced from *inside,* rather than something picked-over and manipulated by academics and epigones![8]

First published in 1947 in his novel *Doctor Faustus,* these words were Thomas Mann's transcription of the conversation of Theodor Adorno while in war-exile in Los Angeles. He put them in the mouth of a fictional composer named Adrian Leverkühn. How dare we associate the smut tycoon of rock with a philosopher so difficult most academics can't read him? How dare we not, *Schmütterfänchen*! Life's too short for your stupid limitations and defensive, ministerial restrictions, Mistah Greenaway. How could the best in twentieth-century music *not* be viewed in the light of the best twentieth-century critic? Esemplastic Zappology proceeds from the materialist proposition that Zappa and Adorno existed in the same social universe, and so could respond to the same things and develop parallel arguments—music as an index of truth in a permanent arms economy, musical actuality versus commercial fraudulence, art as a struggle between the forces of manipulation (*Them*) and the forces of self creation (*Us*). *Of course they're different.* That's why we like bringing them together, like chalk and cheese, snorks and Twelve Tone, Black Sabbath and Elliot Carter, "America Drinks" and "Amnerika", numbskull! But peer into the spooky correspondences between Zappa's 'unconscious' imagery and Adorno's pronouncements: the difference between us is not very far, cruising for burgers in Daddy's new car. Locked in the class system's dungeon of despair, the ruling curmudgeons of the separate camps—academia and fanland—may refuse our miscegenation of high and low, our desire to segue Pierre Boulez with the UK Subs, but we say *phooey on them*!

Let's examine some of these correspondences coming fresh at us down the chute, the 'let us speculate' implied by a lettuce sandwich. In his famous press release about the Project/Object (cited by Dominique Jeunot in his paper in this collection and quoted in the appendix), Zappa said one of his sources was 'God (as energy)'. In *Doctor Faustus* the composer Leverkühn, Mann's cipher for Adorno, says:

> Music is energy itself, yet not as idea, rather in its actuality. I call your attention to the fact that this is almost the definition of God.[9]

Zappa's attitude towards divinity was ambivalent. He adored the natural mysticism of children, and said that he didn't think prayer 'in its *truest sense*' was 'anything to scoff at'[10]. He conceded a role to religion as a social practice, but mercilessly satirized its beliefs.

> If you want to stand on the steps of **any building** (or waterslide), all dressed up on a Sunday morning, **for whatever purpose** (a Christian business discussion, perhaps), great—go for it.
>
> If you want to get together in any *exclusive situation* and have people *love* you, **fine**—but to hang all this desperate sociology on the idea of **The Cloud-Guy** who has **The Big Book**, who knows if you've been **bad or good—and CARES about any of it**—to hang it all **on that**, folks, is the *chimpanzee* part of the brain working.[11]

Because it delivers its potential in the here and now, *music* is the preeminent and prehensile weapon against religious promises and blandishments. It gratifies our proclivities in a manner that might be ridiculous, but it's present and correct and material and examinable. Watch the candle flames sway in the cathedral: it's the *breath of the choir* that's doing that.

In Thomas Mann's novel, music is alchemical. Composition is referred to as 'that curiously cabbalistic craft'[12], practiced in 'the hermetic laboratory, the gold-kitchen'. Leverkühn announces:

> I will refine on the *prima materia*, in that I add to it the *magisterium* and with spirit and fire drive the matter through many limbecs and retorts for the refining thereof.[13]

This parallels frequent alchemical reference in Zappa, from "But Who Was Fulcanelli?" (*Guitar*, 1988) to the figure of the mad scientist in his laboratory (Uncle Meat, Ringo Starr composing in *200 Motels*, *Thing-Fish*'s The Evil Prince) torturing, mashing and fusing his materials. The cabbalistic imagination is magical and poetic, it sees marks and signs not as one-to-one correspondents to objects in the 'real' world, but as agents of transformation. It is thus subversive of the authoritarianism of official systems of signification. Poets, arise!

In *Doctor Faustus*, an early climax is provided by a lecture on music by Wendell *Kretschmar*. In his final masterpiece *Civilization Phaze III* (1994) (note the 'Z's), Zappa put the Ensemble Modern's Hermann *Kretzschmar* (note the additional 'Z', *c'est vraiment bizarre!*) inside a piano with rapper Michael Rappaport, his daughter Moon and Turkish arranger Ali Askin to discuss music, their European-African-Californian-Arab backgrounds intimating the cross-wired, universal aspirations of Zappa's music. Such 'coincidences' as this reoccurrence of 'Kretschmar'—Zappa didn't read novels and couldn't understand Adorno—are bizarre, so bizarre they require a radical theory. That theory is Esemplastic Zappology, which insists that genuine music—contingent and holistic at once—is a material practice that renders practical results. There is no way of avoiding Germany's historic role in world music, and if the names of people who transmit that tradition are noted, the same ones crop up. Just as scientists working on the latest data come up with theories like relativity or drifting continents or chaos theory *simultaneously*, so too do composers and musicians and music-theorists who are working on *sound*. Music is not simply a matter of inherited 'styles' clashing and competing in the marketplace: there *are* objectitudes in the stuff of listening, and identical seams may be mined by different parties. The reality of art is objective, not plausible. Provided, that is, that we learn to approach the musical material untramelled by received dogma and academic rulebooks.

In *Doctor Faustus*, Kretschmar holds that music isn't simply about sound. It's also about the signs used to direct the sounds.

> Many a turn of phrase in musician's jargon came not from the acoustic but the visual, the note-picture: for instance, one speaks of *occhiale* because the broken drum-basses, half-notes that are coupled by a stroke through their necks, look like a pair of spectacles;

> or as one calls 'cobbler's patches' (*rosalia*) certain cheap sequences one after another in stages like intervals (he wrote examples for us on the blackboard).[14]

This corresponds to Zappa's fascination with his own initial 'Z', from Roger Price's 'droodle', whose "ZA" shape named *Ship Arriving Too Late to Save a Drowning Witch* (1982) to Clarence Snyder's photograph 'Bethlehem Steel' showing Z-shaped metal staircases leading nowhere, a rebuke to the otherworldly lachrymosity of Led Zeppelin's "Stairway To Heaven" (a photo reproduced on Zappa's 12" release of the song in 1991). As with the Lettrists (the Parisian avantgarde movement which preceded the situationists), this materialism of the letter resists the transcendence of the spirit.

Adrian Leverkühn envisages an art that is dense and compact, shedding the *longueurs* demanded by the bourgeoisie.

> I have heard him say: 'The work of art? It is a fraud. It is something the burgher wishes there still were. It is contrary to truth, contrary to serious art. Genuine and serious is only the very short, the highly consistent musical moment.'[15]

Zappa was coming from the same place. Varèse wrote world-shattering pieces that were incredibly compact in length—"Ionisation" is 4m 50s, "Hyperprism" is 3m 50s—and contain all you need to know about his approach to sound.

> Varèse is much more economical than Stravinsky, I think, and that's a virtue. You see in his music how little bits and pieces of things get repeated in strange ways, and themes emerge from basic material which has not that great a spectrum.[16]

In outlining his theory of creative music, Kretschmar talks about a Seventh-Day Baptist named Johann Conrad Beissel who found that most of the chorals in the hymnbook were

> too forced, complicated, and artificial to serve for his flock. He wanted to do something new and better and to inaugurate a music better answering to the simplicity of their souls[17]

He decided to base his rhythms upon words rather than the metronome.

> Rhythm was now the part of theory which remained to be dealt with by this redoubtable man. He accomplished it with consummate success. He painstakingly followed with the music the cadence of the words, simply by providing the accented syllables with longer notes, and giving unaccented shorter ones. To establish a fixed relation between the values of the notes did not occur to him; and just for that reason he preserved considerable flexibility for his metre.[18]

Ever wondered how Zappa came up with a tune like "This Town is a Sealed Tuna Sandwich"? He let the words dictate the notes. He admired the speech-based soloing of Johnny 'Guitar' Watson, who could say 'son of a bitch' on his guitar, and when he was writing scores for performance by the London Symphony Orchestra told Robin Denselow of *The Guardian*:

> Boulez writes complex rhythms but they are mathematically derived, while the rhythms I have are derived from speech patterns. They should have the same sort of flow that a conversation would have, but when you notate that in terms of rhythmic values, sometimes it looks extremely terrifying on paper.[19]

Zappa's anti-intellectualism isn't opposed to complexity, even that which is written down: but it retains the primacy of oral speech—living utterance—as against the written word. This is equivalent to a commitment to living labour (creativity) versus congealed labour (capital).

In *Doctor Faustus*, Adrian Leverkühn puts it this way:

> Should not one learn all that about suspensions, passing-notes, modulation, preparations and resolution, much better *in praxi* from hearing, experiencing and inventing oneself, than out of a book?[20]

After dissing both classical ('accommodating the entertainment needs of deceased kings and popes') and contemporary academic rules and procedures ('the twelve-tone business'), Zappa says:

> The *Ultimate Rule* ought to be **"If it sounds GOOD to YOU, it's bitchen; and if its sounds BAD to YOU, it's shitty."** The more varied your experience, the easier it is to define for yourself *what you like* and *what you don't like.* American radio listeners, raised on a diet of ________ (*fill in the blank*), have experienced a musical universe so small they cannot begin to *know* what they like.[21]

Like a good dialectician, Zappa combines one argument ("we know what we like") with its opposite ("we don't know enough to know what we like"). Curiosity, which Freud associated with the sexual instinct, is the key to progress and creativity. Sell your soul to the devil. Open the box!

ICE-Z: The Conference

Well, so much for wicked intentions, I hear you say, but what was the conference actually like? Well, *read the papers in this book*! However, for those who'd like a sneak preview before settling down with *Academy Zappa*, a bag of wine gums and a flagon of scrumpy in some shady nook, here is the gist of a report which was sent to *Le Pingouin Ligoté*, organ of Les Fils de l'Invention in Paris, for translation into the tongue of André Breton and Guy Debord by M. Didier Mervelet. The speakers were dealt with in the order they actually spoke (an order which has not been followed in the book). Some of the titles of the papers read differently from the titles in the book. This is because they'd not yet been finalised. However, it seemed better not to back-project consistency on such non-finalisation... (for the order of talks on the day, see Fig. 5).

Yes, on Friday 16 January 2004, the First International Conference of Esemplastic Zappology (ICE-Z) *was* convened in Somers Town, London, at Theatro Technis on Crowndale Road. Seventy-two people (and two dogs) listened intently to thirteen papers by Zappologists from London, Paris, Leipzig, Manchester and Rome, and enjoyed a theatrical presentation by Les Fils de l'Invention: Didier Mervelet,

Fig. 4: Freakmap of Crowndale Road

Véronique Malvoisin and Sylvestre Hannoun presented pages 3-14 of Frank Zappa's *Them Or Us [The Book]* in a delightful French translation. Mlle. Malvoisin—who sports a fetching moustache and imperial for purposes of theatrical illusionism—played Francesco Zappa, the Italian composer who 'flourished' between 1763 and 1788 according to the *Grove Dictionary of Music.* M. Mervelet played the Duke of York, the English blaggard and failed 'cellist. M. Hannoun played Lady Aurora in drag, sporting a very fetching wig.

Hosted by the website *<www.militantesthetix.co.uk>*, ICE-Z also included the exhibition of a garden-centre Venus de Milo *détourné* into a scary moustache by artist Eleanor Crook in her Cheshunt studio whilst listening to high-volume Zappa on CD, and Wanda the Vacuum Speaker, who travelled from Paris to London on the Channel Tunnel (an e-mail from Euro Star to M. Bruno Le Tohic assured Les Fils that Wanda would not be confined to the baggage compartment, but could enjoy the trip with her entourage). Wanda has a built-in CD and her suction hose poots forth weird snatches of dishevelment from the Zappa *oeuvre.* Evil Dick & the Banned Members (whose leader, Richard Hemmings, delivered a paper on Zappa's "Approximate" at the

ICE-Z

International Conference of Esemplastic Zappology

Friday 16 January 2004
Theatro Technis 26 Crowndale Road London NW1 1TT
an event organised by ***Militant Esthetix***

a playbill to fondle, Wanda, as you wonder what enormities of intellectual, "dead-person" entertainment - à la *Thriller* (free Wacko Jacko! free Scott-Heron!) - may be whizzing your way down the poop-chute ... to invite maybe ... (gasp) ... audience participation ...

10.15-12.30

Marco Maurizi (Rome) "Zappa's Cheepnis & the Poverty of Philosophy"
Simon Prentis (Hampstead) "The Torture Never Stops: FZ & the Mental Hygiene Dilemma"
Ben Watson (Somers Town) "Houston ... Forte .. Marcuse: Sin versus Archetype in Zappa"
Esther Leslie "Compliment Any Burger You Put On (Centre-Hinge Sliced)"

12.45-1.30

LUNCH: Brazilian wonders on a platter at the Working Men's College on Crowndale Road £4.50 (or soup/sandwich £2)

1.30-3.00

Jürgen Gispert (Leipzig) "The Conservatism of *Easy Rider*: Zappa's Critique of American Concepts of Freedom"
Sean Bonney (Vauxhall) "A Dagger in the Head of Mojo-Man"
Keston Sutherland (Cambridge) "What's the Ugliest Part of your Market-research Anaclitic-Affect Repertoire? [*Franz Zappa als Anlehnungstypuskritik*]"
Paul Sutton (Queen Mary's) "Bogus Pomp & Bourdieu's Paradox: Zappa & Resentment"

3.15-4.15

Richard Hemmings (Leicester) "Randomness as a Compositional Device"
Dominique Jeuzot (Paris) on "The Secret Meaning of 'Arf': Canine Continuity in the Output Macrostructure"
Stu Calton (Levenshulme) "Water Melon In Easter Hay: the Poverty of the Individual Spirit"

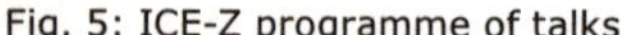

Fig. 5: ICE-Z programme of talks

4.30-5.30

Gamma (Kentish Town) "Poodles: a Zappological reading of *Ulysses*"
Francesco Gentile (Rome) "Xenoarrangements, or, Insane Grafts Day-Dreamed by a Zappa hardcore Fanatic not inclined to exit his Monomaniacal World"
Les Fils de L'Invention (Paris) ***Tableau Vivant*** concerning the baroque composer and 'cellist Francesco Zappa (fl. 1763-88), plus **Wanda the Vacuum Speaker** straight off the EuroStar.

RESPONSIBLE FOR THE CAGED MOUSTACHE: **Eleanor Crook**

EVENING GIG: 7.00pm (prompt start) **Evil Dick & the Banned Members** (Leicester) at the College Arms on Crowndale Road/corner Royal College Street.

8.30 **DJ Jonathan Goslan** spins Zappa vinyl, plus **Chocolate Sandwich**, Les Fils de l'Invention, **the Mad Pride Contingent from the East**, Gamma, film-makers, bemused locals, **Debbie and her Daughter from Somers Town**, xenochronous Derek Bailey, chance encounters, yourSELVES. **Poets arise!**

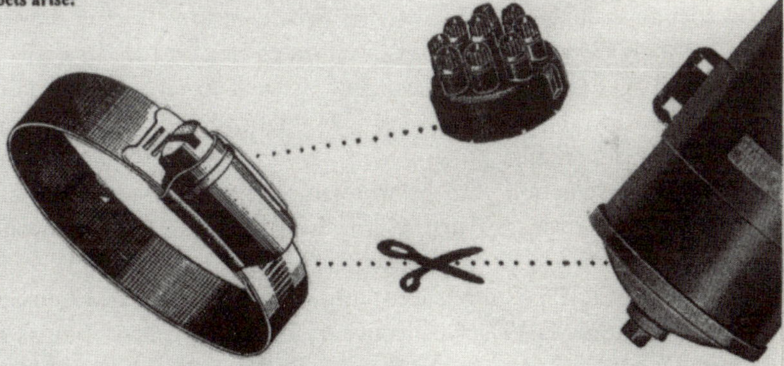

ICE-Z THANKS: Evil Dick & the Banned Members for heroic voluntarism; Jonathan Goslan, Ian Stonehouse, Simon Prentis, Ben Watson for splitting the PA hire fee for the College Bar disco (£120); distant cousins & speakers, all of whom paid their own train/air fares; Gamma & Elenore, Than McBride, Rowan & Max Watson, Ben & Esther for providing beds, floors and Martian Embassies for delegates; George & Aristotle Eugeniou at Theatro Technis; Working Men's College for lending us the data projector; Sina Nocerino of Godwin & Crowndale Estate Office for parking spaces; Eleanor Crook for sculpture; Roy & Café Brasil for lunch; Rachel at the College Bar for music space (and sandwiches).

www.militantesthetix.co.uk

conference) played two outstanding sets in a local pub on Crowndale Road named the College Bar, illustrating Evil's groundbreaking genre of Rock'n'Random. A local 'stumbling man' (a zappological motif Dr. Esther Leslie had remarked on in her analysis of "Kaiser Rolls") played 'air guitar' to Banned Member Gimp Wilkinson's virtuosic guitar stylings. Everyone (including our 'stumbling man') danced the frug, the twist and the funky penguin-in-bondage to Zappa records spun by DJ Jonathan Goslan until 'closing time', the venerable British institution which ensures everyone is in bed with the lights off by midnight.

ICE-Z was staged outside any institutional framework or funding (the availability of Theatro Technis was a favour left over from a Lottery-funded event the previous June). Delegates paid for their own travel and expenses, and were accommodated by London Zappa fans. This autonomy—study motivated by the pleasure principle—resulted in particularly undutiful and pertinent lectures. Driven by Zappa fans' enthusiasms and grievances, the pseudo-scientific 'citationese' of academic sociology and pop studies (where nothing is 'true', however groaningly obvious, until it has been stated in an article in a refereed journal) was jettisoned in favour of the real issues: commercialism, commodification, authorial status, copyright, sound technology, artistic legacy, leadership, group dynamics, social revolt, freedom, ethics, musical construction. The bizarre nature of the 'coincidences' infesting the Output Macrostructure provided a perpetual source of wonder and laughs.

Marco Maurizi (Rome), noted improvising guitarist and Adornoite from the Amnesia Vivace collective, read a paper called 'Zappa's Philosophy of "Cheepnis" & the Poverty of Philosophy'. Signor Maurizi contended that in the song "Spider of Destiny" from the *Hunchentoot* musical, Drakma the Queen of Cosmic Greed 'shows the inner mechanics of Identity Thinking', backed up with a quote from Adorno & Horkheimer's hysterical post-war classic *Dialectic of Enlightenment.* Maurizi's materialist polemic had none of the humourless hostility to the suffering subject characteristic of either Logical Positivism or Stalinized Marxism, and got some laughs, especially when he showed a picture of Jim Morrison being nibbled by a gigantic termite. Maurizi concluded that 'the contingency of human race can be a source of desperation only for those who can't live their *present*', and backed up his assertion by cavorting with wild abandon at the Zappa disco later that night (though it has been reported that he joined Dr. Esther in a 'salad in a pitta bread kebab' *sortie* to Camden High Street, thus failing to witness Evil Dick's second set with the guest appearance by T.H.F. Drenching on Dictaphone, but this rumour has not yet been confirmed).

Simon Prentis (Hampstead), known to Zappa fans as the annotator of the 3CD set *Läther*, gave a talk called 'The Torture Never Stops: FZ & the Mental Hygiene Dilemma'. Mr Prentis's ten years in Japan led him towards the Big Note when he offered to correct the translations of lyrics in Japanese releases of Zappa music. Prentis revealed that prior to discovering Zen Buddhism, the young Zappa wanted to become a Roman Catholic monk, so we owe Zen a vote of thanks. Prentis circulated a 'golden turd' good-luck charm from Japan. His contention that Zappa had no libidinal investment in the smut he portrayed caused a lively discussion among delegates (discussion was later curtailed due to shortage of time and the statistical density of the papers, a deficiency which will need to be addressed at future ICE-Zs). His 'pull your socks up' advice to the world's unhappy and disadvantaged rather reminded this delegate of Samuel Smiles.

Ben Watson (Militant Esthetix, Somers Town) declared he had already spoken and written too much about Zappa, so he instead indulged some sentimental reminiscence about Danny Houston, the freak from Glasgow who inducted him into Zappological delirium. Mr Watson also carried out a close reading of Peter Frampton's chiffon-in-a-wrist-array on the pic-sleeve of his "I'm In You" 7-inch single, claiming that the letters 'F R A' ('Arf!' backwards) may be discerned in the chiffon. However, in the panic of organising for the conference (destoning olives, baking pizzas, pouring wine, billeting delegates on London Zappa fans, accommodating the Banned Members' astonishing capacity for alcohol), he'd forgotten to load up his images onto Esther's laptop for projection.[22] Watson's contention was that Herbert Marcuse and Charles Fort, whose work was widely available in paperback during the revolutionary years following 1968, are both useful in understanding Zappa's scepto-materialist monism. His 'pull your socks down' advice to the world's happy and advantaged rather reminded this delegate of Raoul Vaneigem.

A new carrier of the Zappological flame, **Dr. Esther Leslie** (Birkbeck College, London) read a paper named 'Compliment Any Burger You Put On (Center Hinge Sliced)'. A socio-materialist investigation of "Kaiser Rolls" from *FZ:OZ* revealed that the song was about hamburgers and cars. Since fast food is just as much a product of the capitalist motor-car industry as motorways, pollution, road death, supermarkets, isolated nuclear families, the decay of unitary urbanism (*aka* 'street life') and wars for oil (the hamburger is the meal you can eat with one hand, *i.e. whilst driving*[23]), Dr. Esther's presentation showed that any Zappa song is a microcosm of social forces at work in the United States (and here in Europe too). The discovery of '*hratche-plche*' in the lyrics to "Kaiser Rolls" created a ripple of excitement among those who had listened to the 3CD set *Zappanale #14* issued by the Arf Society, and been psychically tweezed by Gamma's phone message about the disappearance of '*hratche-plche*' between the printing of the lyrics of "Brown Shoes Don't Make It" in *International Times* August-September 1967, and the reissue of *Absolutely Free* on CD. This reminder of *Absolutely Free* and Zappa's back-cover portrayal of a traffic-choked street confirmed Dr. Esther's thesis that the *motor car* is the central problematic in both Zappa and post-war American culture. Or are Zappa and post-war American culture actually THE VERY SAME THING? ICE-Z had begun to wreak havoc on the Kantian separation between art and life. After Dr. Esther's paper, delegates repaired to the Working Men's College on Crowndale Road, where they ate lunch provided by Roy of Café Brasil.

Jürgen Gispert (Leipzig) delivered perhaps the most ambitious paper of the day: 'The Conservatism of *Easy Rider*: Zappa's Critique of Dumb Concepts of Freedom'. Flower Power and Hippiedom's phoney and inadequate rejection of American values proved to be recurrent targets for speakers at ICE-Z. Herr Gispert's anthropological survey was weirdly echoed by **Gamma** (Kentish Town), who later in the day read from John Whiteside Parsons' *Freedom Is A Two-Edged Sword* (1950). Gamma arrived in the afternoon with drinking companions Mick and Martin, plus two dogs including Jake the Poodle (when Jake stares at you with his big brown eyes, you understand why Johan Wolfgang Goethe cast Mephistopheles as a big black poodle in the opening scenes of *Faust*). As we become aware of the material constituents of

Fig. 6: Jake the Poodle

cultural production, self-consciousness about the formation of groups comes to the fore.

The only conference speaker to sport Zappa's moustache and imperial (or is that Johnny Otis's?), Gispert evoked the bizarre image of Frank Zappa reincarnated as German left intellectual. He spoke about the political confrontation that faced Zappa and the Mothers in Berlin in 1968, a crisis written about in "Holiday In Berlin". This tune was—*oddly enough*, as we say in the trade—also part of **Francesco Gentile**'s (Bebra Kadabra, Italy) presentation: 'Xenoarrangements, or, Insane Grafts Day-Dreamed by a Zappa Hard-Core Fanatic not inclined to exit his own Monomaniacal World'. Gispert had never heard the version of the tune with lyrics before (available on the *Tenga na' Minchia Tanta* 'official' bootleg), but the song was quickly etched onto a tape cassette for Gispert to take back to Leipzig for further study (whether or not Gispert still thinks Zappa's line on the revolting students compares to Jürgen Habermas's, we have not yet heard).

Sean Bonney (Vauxhall) delivered 'A Dagger in the Head of *Mojo* Man', a polemic about *Trout Mask Replica* and its place in the canon of classic rock. This was a stirring performance, the high point of the conference for some, although Joe Lancaster (film documentarist of the event) was repelled by what he interpreted as Bonney's 'junkie chic' mannerisms (talking in highly cinematic terms, some delegates called this 'a classic case of projection'). Zappology provides a field for the encounter of painful truths which in other areas of class society remain unstated, or lead to bitter quarrels and fist fights.

Keston Sutherland (Gonville & Caius College, Cambridge) read "What's the Ugliest Part of your Market-Researched Anaclitic-Affect Repertoire? [*Franz Zappa als Anlehnungstypuskritik*]", which interpreted Zappa's *We're Only In It for the Money* as a prophylactic sally versus the regressive tendencies of love-object formation among pop fans (Out To Lunch gazed at the Zappa-face t-shirts worn by some ICE-Z delegates, and wondered if this is really true).

Paul Sutton (Queen Mary's College, London) read 'Bogus Pomp & Bourdieu's Paradox: Zappa & Resentment', a careful but eventually devastating critique of Pierre Bourdieu's inability to deal with aesthetic experience. The polemical uses of Zappology as a bullshit-detector in the academic humanities have rarely been so forcefully (and so elegantly!) demonstrated.

Richard Hemmings (De Montfort University, Leicester) read 'Randomness as Compositional Device: The Treatment of Random Pitches in Frank Zappa's "Approximate"', using a score he'd acquired from Arthur Barrow's website as material evidence. This was a powerful example of practical Zappology, and Hemmings' later performance as Evil Dick showed that he was not talking cheese through his arse.

Dominique Jeunot (Paris) read 'The Secret Meaning of "Arf": Canine Continuity in the Output Macrostructure', a paper which was picked out for praise by Andrew Greenaway on the Idiot Bastard Son website. Greenaway thought other speakers at ICE-Z were guilty of chasing red herrings. It would have been wowie-zowie to see Mr Sutherland and Mistah Greenaway engage in a wrestling match over the issue of *Anlehnungstypus*-neurosis among Zappa fans, but time was running out, and the afternoon became paper after paper with no time for such red herrings.

T.H.F. Drenching (Levenshulme), who had escaped for a day from his life-sentence as Dictaphonist in Derek Bailey's Limescale quintet, read '"Watermelon In Easter Hay": the Poverty of the Individual Spirit', a polemic which produced lively discussion between Gispert, Watson and Les Fils de l'Invention at a post-ICE-Z wine and mashed-potatoes-and-sausages-and-*sauerkraut* party (we're so European!) held

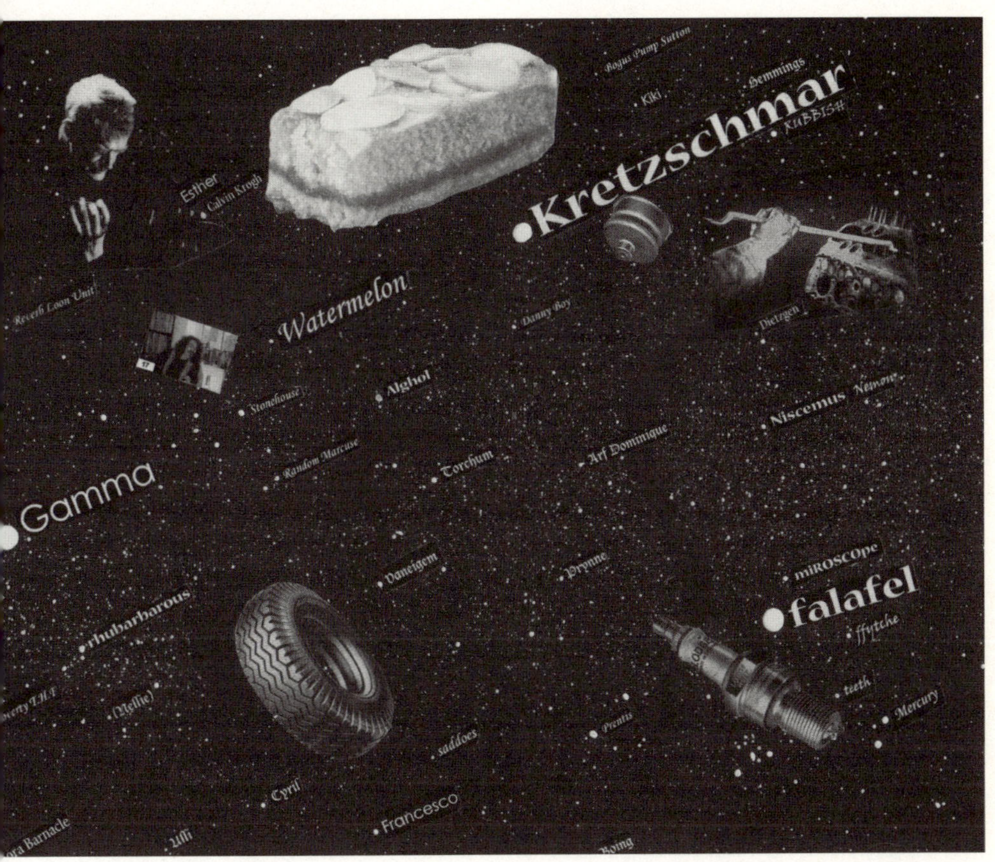

Fig 7: Starmap with Cake

all Saturday at a secret venue on Crowndale Road. Is "Watermelon" a bit of Pink Floydish *kitsch*, or the 'soul' of Frank? Calton's preference for the semantic disintegration of "A Little Green Rosetta" over "Watermelon" was strenuously argued.

In conclusion—at 3.00am on Saturday night in an alcoholic haze—it was decided that the papers at ICE-Z were worthy to be shared with the world, and Ben Watson and Dr. Esther Leslie were entrusted with the task of finding a suitable publisher.

The Esemplasm

In the final analysis, the Zappological Esemplasm is a unity, but a conflictual one, combined and uneven, at once scented and stinky. At the empirical/practical end stand Richard Hemmings and Simon Prentis, the former concerned with notational instruction, the latter with ethical instruction. At the tip of the canine snout stand M. Le Président des Fils de l'Invention, Dominique Jeunot (or sadly stood), and Gamma. Like Mistah Greenaway's, Jake the Poodle's favourite talk was Jeunot's: he stood up to attention and panted, his tongue lolling appreciatively. At the abstract end stand Paul Sutton and Keston Sutherland, the former leaning towards class-consciousness, the latter towards *Anlehnungspsychoanalyse.* During their talks Jake the Poodle fell—rather ostentatiously we thought—asleep. In his attention to the placement of the notes themselves, Francesco Gentile resembled Hemmings, but in his suggestion that we do things to the *oeuvre* rather than merely contemplate it, he resembled Watson. Ben Watson and Esther Leslie constituted the hard left of the conference, closely allied to T.H.F. Drenching, who peppered his communist anti-property polemic with Sutherland's anti-romanticism. Of all the delegates touched by Adorno (wittingly: Watson, Drenching, Sutton, Bonney, Sutherland, Esther, Maurizi/unwittingly: Hemmings, Prentis, Gentile, Gamma, Jake), Maurizi's Adornoism was the most pronounced, sheer Hegelianism mediating his hard-left praxis into philosophical maxims, although his insistence on Zappa's refusal of divine origins brought him into startling congruence with Esther's 'critical thought finds itself always *in medias res*'. Sean Bonney, meanwhile, seemed to think he was at a conference on Captain Beefheart, but his rant against the brain police of musical accessibility was enjoyed by all (apart from Joe).

Every great collection requires an addendum, and we've found the best, in the pages of the journal *Naked Punch* #3 in January 2005 while browsing in the London Review of Books Bookshop on Bury Place, Bloomsbury. Daniel DiPaolo had in fact contacted us in late January 2004, four days after ICE-Z, pigsick that he'd missed it. His essay

'The Negative Dialectics of *Arf*-Enlightenment'—the concentrate of an academic dissertation—contains an intimate quantity of nut-and-bolts musicology, illumined by a strikingly uncluttered appreciation of Frankfurt School tenets. Welcome to the Esemplasm, Dan man.

Zappology is gradually emerging from the sweatbeds & smellpits of rock fandom to take on the bogus and inefficient worlds of spectacular politics and top-down social science. We're moving the Project/Object forward! It's turning Esemplastic, internationalist, dialectical and dialogic. It's the latest anti-discipline discipline. It's open to all comers prepared to speculate openly on a consistently materialist and humanist basis.

Esemplastic Zappology is a practical extension of joy-in-music to other domains, and has a power and *id*-gratification which no other fashion, discipline, cult or intellectual movement can deliver. Esemplastic Zappology allows massive disagreements and social tensions to co-exist, debate and fructify in a field simultaneously sceptical, imaginative, playful and serious. When are *you* going to organise an ICE-Z? We ALL want to come!

Esther Leslie/Ben Watson
1 May 2005

1. Alfred Wegener, *The Origin of Continents and Oceans*, 1929; translated John Biram, New York: Dover, 1966, pp. 19-20.
2. In a recent letter, Gail Zappa has retracted this welcome, insisting that Frank merely thought *Frank Zappa: the Negative Dialectics of Poodle Play* 'preposterous'. This beyond-the-grave, Stalinist rewrite of history hurts, but Frank's death hurt everyone, so I suppose it's to be expected.
3. If this sounds suspiciously like Vladimir, the scourge of the world bourgeoisie, it's because it's based on what V.I. Lenin said at the 1903 Congress of Social Democracy: *Collected Works*, translated Abraham Fineberg and Naomi Jochel, Moscow: Foreign Languages Publishing House, 1961, Vol.5, pp. 25-3.
4. Frank Zappa with Peter Occhiogrosso, *The Real Frank Zappa Book*, New York: Poseidon, 1989, p. 185.
5. Samuel Taylor Coleridge, *Biographia Literaria, Or Biographical Sketches of my Literary Life and Opinions*, 1817; London: J.M. Dent & Sons Ltd, 1975, p. 91.
6. Plato (428-348BC), *Philebus* 16d-16a; translated Benjamin Jowett, London: Sphere, 1970, p. 54. Translation has been amended (third person singular to first person plural) in order to de-gender the discourse and thus make a slave-owner's discourse available to communist proletarians. Although we accept Chris J. Arthur's thesis (*The New Dialectic and Marx's* Capital, Leiden: Brill, 2002) that Marx's dialectic was improvised in order to understand capitalism (*cf.* Marco Maurizi's '*Logik des Zerfalls*' in his paper below), we suspect that the postmodernist assault on Plato's One/Many dialectic (Deleuze and Guattari's 'either or ...

or ... or', which finds its political expression in the anarchism of Antonio Negri's 'multitudes'), is in fact a sentimental and evasive irrationalism seeking a non-social identity.

7. Rosco Gordon, "Cheese and Crackers" (Hayden Thompson), recorded at Sun Studios with Lionel Prevost on sax, James Jones on piano, Philip Walker on electric guitar, Louis Canty on bass and Joe Payne on drums, 25 October 1956. This song obviously sprang to mind because Rosco's name is hidden inside 'micROSCOpe'.
8. Thomas Mann, *Doctor Faustus,* translated H.T. Lowe-Porter, London: Penguin, 1968, p. 310. Translation amended in the interests of Esemplastic Zappology.
9. *Ibid.* p. 79.
10. Frank Zappa with Peter Occhiogrosso, *Op. Cit.,* p. 307.
11. *Ibid,* p. 301.
12. Thomas Mann, *Op. Cit.,* p. 146.
13. *Ibid,* p. 130.
14. *Ibid,* p. 62.
15. *Ibid,* p. 176.
16. Frank Zappa to John Dalton, *Guitar,* June 1979, p. 26.
17. Thomas Mann, *Op. Cit.,* pp. 66-7.
18. *Ibid,* p. 67.
19. Frank Zappa talking to Robin Denselow, 'Father of Invention', *The Guardian,* 11 January 1983.
20. Thomas Mann, *Op. Cit.,* p. 138.
21. Frank Zappa with Peter Occhiogrosso, *Op. Cit.,* p. 188.
22. But luckily, due to the wonders of print craft, they may be viewed in the version of Watson's paper in this book, or in colour on <*www.militantesthetix.co.uk/ice-z/ice-z.htm*>.
23. Eric Schlosser, *Fast Food Nation: What the All-American Meal is Doing to the World,* Harmondsworth: Allen Lane, 2001, p. 17 (for further developments in relation to Chicken McNuggets, the ultimate one-hand, bite-sized drivin' & eatin' version of a chicken, see p. 139).

The Treatment of Random Pitches in Frank Zappa's "Approximate"

Richard Hemmings

Frank Zappa is one of the few composers to experiment with randomness and contribute genuinely new approaches to its use in popular music. Zappa's use of randomness was inspired as much by the Dada movement of the early twentieth century, as the avant-garde New York composers of the 1950s. It played a part in his assault on the limitations of the Top 40 song format and the steadfast rules of formula pop. Before looking in detail at "Approximate", and discussing how Zappa went about notating random pitches, three avant-garde compositions from the twentieth century are worth examining: two aleatoric[1] pieces by Marcel Duchamp—*La Mariée mise à nu par ses celibataires même. Erratum Musical* (1912) and *Erratum Musical* (1913)—and *Intersection I* (1951) by Morton Feldman. Like "Approximate", these compositions randomise pitch as a means of breaking from tradition.

Frank Zappa and Randomness

Zappa motto 'Anything, Any Time, Anywhere—for No Reason at All'[2] is also a summary of the way he deployed randomising strategies in live performances and recordings throughout his career. In concerts, the purpose of embracing chance occurrences, indeterminacy, improvisation and audience participation was to forge a unique experience in contrast to the fully composed sections. It is no coincidence that Zappa appeared on the John Cage tribute CD, *A Chance Operation* (Koch, 1993).

Without Cage, Zappa said, much of what takes place in modern music and art 'would not be possible'.[3] In 1968 Zappa told Sally Kempton of the *Village Voice* that Cage was the inspiration behind an indeterminate piece of music theatre in which Mothers' saxophonist, Motorhead Sherwood, talked banally about souped-up cars, working in an aeroplane factory, and various girlfriends.[3] That Zappa was using Cage's strategies within popular music made them especially resonant since in this context they found a new audience.

Understanding the excitement which unpredictable forms of behaviour could bring to a live event, Zappa encouraged concert audiences to get involved. This often resulted in some form of unplanned mayhem. During a concert at the Royal Albert Hall in 1968, a member of the audience climbed on stage with a trumpet. Possibly making the mistake that free jazz was easy to play, the interloper was left flailing behind when the band joined in. Zappa captured the incident on tape and released it on *Uncle Meat* (1969).[5] Recordings of live events also caught the occasional audience outburst. The unsettled fan, heard shouting from the back of the concert hall at the end of *Burnt Weeny Sandwich* (1970), was a forerunner of the rioting Italian audience Zappa dealt with at the end of the 1982 tour.[6] Unrehearsed, unplanned moments offered performances of the older repertoire a new identity. Before going on tour, Zappa would spend months rehearsing his group to the point of perfection, inserting and removing 'eyebrows' as he saw fit. But when it came to live albums, Zappa was only too happy to include the version with the unexpected 'humour-something': the reveller, the tear-gas grenade, the 'fucked-up' lick.

"Approximate" is indeterminate; that is to say, some of the decisions regarding its performance are left to the musicians. Of course, all notated music is indeterminate to a degree; the fact that scores leave room for interpretation is a mark of this. However, scores that utilise regular notation do not aim to sound completely different at each performance, whereas indeterminate works usually do. Although indeterminacy in music can be traced back as far as C.P.E Bach, it did not really penetrate the art form until the 1950s, when Cage and fellow composers, Morton Feldman, Earle Brown and Christian Wolff began investigating ways of incorporating chance. The idea of allowing pitches to be decided by the performers is also common to jazz. At around the same time, Charles Mingus is known to have created scores that allowed musicians to choose harmonising pitches from a selection. The aim here was to diminish repetition.[6] The initial seeds, however, were sown some thirty years earlier in Switzerland.

Erratum Musical

In his book *Dada: Art and Anti-Art* (1964), Hans Richter tells the story of how Dada painter and collagist Hans Arp supposedly first came to use chance techniques. Dissatisfied with a drawing he had been working on for some time, he ripped it up, allowing the torn pieces of paper to fall to the floor. Later, he noticed that the pattern they formed on the floor seemed to express what he had initially been aiming for.[8] Richter states:

> Chance appeared to us as a magical procedure by which one could transcend the barriers of causality and of conscious volition, and by which the inner eye and ear became more acute, so that new sequences of thoughts and experiences made their appearance. For us, chance was the 'unconscious mind' that Freud had discovered in 1900.[9]

With regards to the development of compositional techniques that incorporate chance, the Dadaist Marcel Duchamp is important. Although he composed only three pieces of music, they contain the origins of the principles later adopted by Cage, and in turn, Zappa. Duchamp scored *Erratum Musical* (1913) based on the following procedure:

> Three people pull notes out of a hat and place them in order on music paper. Each note is sung slowly—the singers follow the same tempo. The text for these random harmonies is the dictionary definition of the verb to print (imprimer): '*Faire une empreinte marquer des traits une figure sur une surface imprimer un sceau sur cire*' (To make an imprint mark with lines a figure on a surface impress a seal on wax).[9]

The piece allows for some interpretational leeway; if pitches turn up outside the singer's range they may be performed approximately. Alongside the incomplete version of *La Mariée mise à nu par ses celibataires même. Erratum Musical* (1912) scored by Duchamp, exists a description of how the piece should be carried out. It can be performed on virtually any instrument. In addition, some peculiar bits of equipment are required: a large funnel, five toy train wagons (open and connected) and numbered balls, one for each timbre or pitch the instruments can produce. The performer assigns a time period to each of the five wagons. The balls are then poured into the funnel and allowed to fall at random into the wagons as they are pulled underneath. Balls that fall outside the wagons are discounted. Upon completion of this task, balls are removed from each wagon, at a rate proportional to the time period allocated to the wagon. Dynamics are left to the performer to decide. The final result is a piece of music in five sections, however, Duchamp allows the process to be repeated any number of times, making it essentially 'unfinishable'.

The sheer banality of these compositions probably accounts for the fact that Duchamp's ideas were slow to be taken up by musicians and composers, especially if one considers that in the same year as *Erratum Musical*, Stravinsky's vibrant *Le Sacre du printemps* (1913) received its premiere performance. Duchamp's attempt to create random music produced, in his own words, 'a very useless performance in any case', but as the 20th century progressed, composers began to break from traditional ideas of what was expected of a piece of music and randomness became increasingly relevant.

Intersection I

In both *La Mariée mise à nu par ses celibataires même. Erratum Musical* (1912) and *Erratum Musical* (1913) pitches are chosen using chance procedures to prevent performers controlling the order they are played. In contrast, Feldman's *Intersection I* places the note choices in the hands of the performers; not a single pitch is defined. Whereas Duchamp was strict about each pitch being heard only once, Feldman opens up the possibilities by allowing note repetition, so that the chance of two identical performances becomes even more unlikely. Scored for large orchestra, the piece only contains four parts: one for wind instruments, one for the brass instruments, one for violins and violas, and one for cellos and basses. Each part indicates three ranges of pitch—high, middle and low—the limits of which are determined by the performers. The simplistic look of the score, free of dynamic markings and fixed durations, belies the difficulty of a successful interpretation, which depends heavily on the skill and imagination of the performers.

Although Feldman provides instructions to play high, middle and low pitches (providing all the information required to generate simple melodic shapes), the piece is essentially an investigation of abstract sound rather than chance melodies. In this it provides an interesting contrast to Zappa's treatment of pitch in "Approximate".

"Approximate"

The first public performance of "Approximate" took place on 10 September 1972 at the Hollywood Bowl, home of the easy-listening 101 Strings Orchestra. Third on the set list, Zappa described it as the most 'far-out'[11] of his pieces to be performed. Four parts are shared between twenty musicians, generating an arrangement in much the same way as Feldman's *Intersection I.* Zappa explained the process to his audience:

> There is one page that is for all instruments in C and F, including percussion. There's another page for all the instruments in E flat and B flat and elsewhere and then there's a bass part and a drum set part, which combine the rhythms of the other two. The only thing that is indicated in the score is the exact rhythm... that is supposed to happen for most of the piece and all players get to choose their own pitches that they play. So... it randomizes a certain bit.[12]

Subsequent versions of "Approximate", performed by various incarnations of Zappa's rock band, have since been released, with one on *Zappa In New York* (1977) and two others in the *You Can't Do That on Stage Anymore* series *Vol.2* and *Vol.4* (1988). There is also a version on the video release *Dub Room Special*.[13] The score, the majority of which omits pitch information, contains the type of rhythms Zappa went on to perfect in pieces like "The Black Page". By removing determination of pitch, the score is open to interpretation by any instrument, allowing an unusual type of flexibility when generating arrangements. Here, a comparison with Duchamp's *La Mariée mise à nu par ses celibataires même. Erratum Musical* (1912) for toy wagons and numbered balls is relevant. In the *Stage Vol.2* version, Zappa turns "Approximate" into movement theatre, his band performing the score with their feet. There is also a version for voice, in which singing the most stomach-warming[14] dissonances would seem to be the prerequisite.

With musicians able to make different pitch choices each time, there exists a greater degree of freedom to explore harmonic possibilities. In later versions, the randomness of "Approximate" seems to become less of a feature. The speed of the 1974 Mothers' rendition indicates that initial random note choices, possibly decided upon during rehearsals, had become fixed parts of the score, there being less noticeable variations between different performances. Arthur Barrow, Zappa's 80s bass player, contests this:

> Like most of his music, Frank was always experimenting and changing things. Perhaps some players picked random notes they stayed with, but I think they mostly stayed random.[15]

Initial investigations, conducted without a score, involved comparing the *Stage Vol.2* version with the *Stage Vol.4* version to differentiate between random and composed pitches. This proved problematic, with both versions structurally at odds and performed at dramatically different speeds. Close listening revealed a number of mutual characteristics. Both versions share an introductory three-and-a-half bar long, reiterated B-flat motif, which instantly establishes itself as the tonal centre. Zappa stated that the fixed pitches were deployed 'for the sake of contrast'[16], but the effect they have is much greater, since they contain some of the longest durations in the piece.[17] The majority of the random pitches occur in jittery groups of semiquaver tuplets, which move too fast to establish any tonal stability. Despite this, there are moments in both versions that sound distinctly like descending sequences[18]; the *Stage 2* version even sounds like it contains repeated phrases.

When Zappa told his audience that the piece was randomised a 'certain bit', he was talking about the degree of randomness: the dichotomy between the pitches with a designated register and those left to chance. Upon analysis of the score, the randomising process becomes clearer. Using a traditional staff, a series of markers (shown as crosses, instead of dots) indicate a predetermined, melodic contour.

> These are markers that show, by their positions, the approximate register for each instrument.[19]

Compared to Feldman's use of high, middle and low pitch ranges in *Intersection I*, "Approximate" places greater control over the melodic shape. With the approximate shape of the melody given, the musicians simply follow its undulations. This provides a possible explanation why the listener can perceive sequences and repetitions; musicians often play melodic shapes on their instruments, and these can easily be transposed at random intervals. In larger ensembles, such features would be less obvious due to the increased timbral density. Interpretation of the score becomes interesting during moments where the melodic contour levels out. These flat sections give the impression that a random pitch ought to be repeated, and this is what happens in both *Stage* versions. However, there are no instructions in the score to suggest this is the case, leading one to conclude that in fact, it merely implies the same degree of randomness as elsewhere in the score.[20]

Quasi-Randomness, Conceptual Continuity & "Approximate"

The 'randomness' of conceptual continuity is a matter of perception. Strictly speaking, it is not random at all, but a type of quasi-randomness described in cryptography as 'obscure complexity'. The patterns are so complex and intricate that they appear random until one understands the processes involved in their creation. In the 1982 live version of "Approximate", members of the group replaced parts of the score with the following vocal lines:

(1) Heinz, Heinz ...
(2) Make food
(3) Ah-Oh-Eh-Ah ... (Ieee!)
(4) Dagmar, Din-din!
(5) Stayin' alive—Ah, ah, ah, ah
(6) There's a '39 Buick blocking the driveway

To the occasional listener of Zappa's music, this most likely reads as six lines of postmodern, deconstructed irrelevance, when in truth, each line is packed with cross-references and themes relevant elsewhere. Watson makes a valid argument for Zappa the modernist by raising this point:

> Conceptual continuity may well serve as a term for an underlying substratum of associations that anyone uses over the years in order to express themselves—the network of meanings revealed, say, in Samuel Taylor Coleridge's notebooks, which show irrational attachment to words that appear at key points in his poems—but what makes Zappa's use of it modernist is that he brings this substratum to consciousness.[21]

It is difficult to assess the spontaneity of the vocal lines without comparison to other performances from around the same time, none of which are currently available. Later versions of "Approximate" sound increasingly 'fixed', accelerating the performance tempo. It is tempting to assume that the same applies to these lyrics. This theory is backed up by a copy of the score provided by Barrow, showing in his own handwriting, the word 'cornhole' written in pencil, above the music. However, changing the words to songs was extremely common during live concerts.

But Zappa was not simply fixing the infinite; he was applying the principal of cryptography, aiming to disguise a message behind a screen of gibberish. Each line of lyric acts as a conceptual trigger. (1) Bottles of Heinz Tomato Ketchup conspicuously made their way onto the front of two albums in 1984, *Them or Us* and *The Perfect Stranger*, by way of Donald Roller Wilson's artwork. The word 'Ketchup' can be traced to "San Ber'dino"[22] and "When the Lie's So Big". (2) The theme of making/preparing food is common in Zappa, but unusual in popular music. Examples occur in *200 Motels* (1971) "Sealed Tuna Sandwich" ('This town we're in is just a/*Sealed Tuna Sandwich* with the wrapper glued'), *Joe's Garage* (1979) "Crew Slut" ('Add water, makes its own sauce') and *Broadway the Hard Way* (1988) "Why Don't You Like Me?" ('*Make me a sandwich*'). (4) 'Dagmar' appears for the first time in "Broken Hearts Are For Assholes" on *Sheik Yerbouti* as the drag queen at The Grape nightclub. (5) By 1982, "Stayin' Alive" by the Bee Gees was assimilated into "Approximate"; the inclusion of a line from such a rhythmically simple song, in such a rhythmically complicated one, emanates Zappa humour. (6) The final line recalls an uncharacteristically banal moment during a Mothers of Invention concert in 1969, when Zappa announced to the audience that a Chevrolet, parked outside, needing moving.

Then, suddenly...

Today, with new pop acts under pressure to enter the charts or be dropped, performances are carefully worked out in advance, effectively ruling out the possibility of unplanned events. But apart from computerised dance music, it is difficult to remove them all, since musicians are never 100% accurate. Wrong notes notwithstanding, musicians always make subtle tempo and dynamic variations. Since Zappa's death, other methods of randomising music have evolved in the form of sound manipulation software packages and plug-ins with randomisation facilities. But these are rarely used in popular music in ways that might challenge listeners.[23] This is not surprising, since popular music is designed to be 'catchy', a quality depending on repetition and structural conformity. A pop song, which changed each time it was performed, would soon be under pressure from the powers that be, the record executives and other dip-shits, to become fixed in the form of a definitive version. But somehow Frank Zappa managed to do things his way, and for that we should all eat our greens and things that look like meat.

1. The word 'aleatory' comes from the Latin for dice, *alea*. It simply implies that a process of random selection (*e.g.*, rolling dice, drawing playing cards) is used to make decisions usually made by the composer. Also counted as aleatory are those pieces where the order of execution of each section is left to the choice of performer.
2. Frank Zappa with Peter Occhiogrosso, *The Real Frank Zappa Book*, New York: Poseidon, 1989, p. 163; see also the interview with Spencer Chrislu where it becomes 'Anything, Any Place, Any Time, For No Reason At All', *Zappa! from the Publishers of Keyboard and Guitar Player*, ed Don Menn, 1992, p. 81.
3. Frank Zappa interview, *Los Angeles Times*, 1 October 1992: *<http://www.science.uva.nl/~robbert/zappa/interviews/LA_Times.html>*
4. See Kevin Courrier, *Dangerous Kitchen: The Subversive World of Zappa*, Toronto: EWC Press, 2002, p. 131. This piece of spoken word appeared on *Lumpy Gravy* (1968).
5. Frank Zappa, "Louie Louie", Uncle Meat, 1969.
6. Frank Zappa, "Cocaine Decisions", *You Can't Do That on Stage Anymore Vol.3*, 1988.
7. The musicians 'are given different rows of notes to use against each chord but they choose their own notes and play them in their own style', Charles Mingus cited by Diane Dorr-Dorynek in the liner notes to *Mingus Ah Um* (1959).
8. Hans Richter, *Dada: Art and Anti-Art*, Thames and Hudson, London, 1997, p. 51.
9. *Ibid*, p. 57.
10. Leigh Landy, 'Duchamp Dada Composer and his Vast Influence on Post-World War II Avant-garde Music', *Avant-Garde*, No. 2, p. 234. According to the CD booklet for *Marcel Duchamp: The Entire Musical Work* (Dog w/a Bone, 2000), the original dictionary definition read: *'Faire une empreinte, marquer des traits, une figure sur une surface, imprimer un sceau sur cire'* or 'To make an imprint, mark with lines, a figure on a surface, impress a seal on wax'.
11. Review from *Oor* magazine, 27 September 1972, edited by Charles Ulrich, translated from Dutch by Jillis Stada.
12. This comes from a bootleg recording of Zappa at the Hollywood Bowl, 10 September 1972.
13. Frank Zappa, *Dub Room Special*, Honker Home Video, 1982.
14. As opposed to 'heart-turning', Out To Lunch's description of tunes by Evil Dick and the Banned Members.
15. Arthur Barrow on "Approximate", correspondence with the author, 6 December 2002. Arthur kindly answered my questions and provided me with a scan of his "Approximate" score (for study purposes only!) upon which many of these new revelations are founded. Cheers Arty!
16. Dominique Chevalier, *Viva! Zappa*, London: Omnibus Press, 1986, p. 113 (citing The Grand Wazoo's tour programme, 1972).

17. The experiments of Lantz and Cuddy conclude that the duration, rather than the rate of recurrence of a pitch, plays the crucial role in establishing a tonal centre: M.E. Lantz and L.L. Cuddy, 'The Effects of Surface Cues in the Perception of Pitch Structure; Frequency of Occurrence and Duration', *ICMPC Proceedings* (1996), pp. 281-286.
18. Occurring from 18 seconds to 21 seconds in the *Stage Vol.2* version, and from 33 seconds to 37 seconds in the *Stage Vol.4* version (times measured from first notes of each piece).
19. Dominique Chevalier, *Op. Cit.*, p. 113.
20. The next section from my PhD, on conceptual continuity as a quasi-random process, was not presented at ICE-Z because it seemed slightly off-topic. But since it utilises "Approximate" to make its point, the decision was made to include it here as a kind of 'bonus track'.
21. Ben Watson, *Frank Zappa: The Negative Dialectics of Poodle Play*, London: Quartet Books, 1994, p. 229.
22. Johnny 'Guitar' Watson says 'ketchup' on the left speaker at the end of "San Ber'dino" on *One Size Fits All* (1975). Although missing from the official lyric sheet, it is pointed out by *<http://globalia.net/donlope/fz/lyrics/One_Size_Fits_All.html#Berdino>*.
23. Unless, of course, you're listening to *Rock'n'Random* (2002) or *Steak'n'Cheese* (2004) by Evil Dick and the Banned Members, available from *<www.polemicmusic.com>*. *Editors' Note:* Hemmings has been allowed this plug for his musical *alter ego* because we like these CDs so much. They constitute one of the few formal extensions of Zappa's methods to have come our way outside Simon H. Fell's xenochrony.

The Secret Meaning of 'Arf': Canine Continuity in the Output Macrostructure[1]

Dominique Jeunot

In the great Zappa menagerie a special role is assigned the dog, and in particular the poodle. Zappa said to *New Musical Express* in 1976:

> If they think I have a fetish about dogs, they are sadly mistaken. It's not profound—it's entertainment. Poodles serve as a convenient

> mechanism for conveying certain philosophical ideas that might otherwise be more difficult. (*NME*, 17 April 1976)

In 1988, Bob Marshall asked him 'why the dog image?'. Zappa replied:

> I don't even know how that got started. There are some absurd things about the poodle as a species unto itself. What especially women have decided to do to poodles is probably something that if there were a Big Guy on a cloud who meted out punishment at the time of our demise, there would be a lot of women that would be tortured forever in the Lake of Fire for things they have decided to inflict on poodles. So there's a pretty good metaphor there if you really think about it. In the beginning the poodle had hair evenly distributed all over its small, piquant, canine-type body. Figure it out. They don't start looking weird until some woman decides that she wants to shape all that stuff to make it look like a walking shrubbery. Now, that tells you two things: that the dog's co-operative and that the woman's got some problems.[2]

The tale of the poodle is above all a story of the vicissitudes of the life of a dog. You've got to let yourself be clipped and combed by a hysteric, for example. Or serve as a slipper-carrier for a master with Stink-Foot. The material history of the poodle is that of the transformation of a hunting dog, a retriever which swims in the water, and was first bred in Germany. Its name in English derives from the German for a stretch of water, *Pudel*. Its vile transformation into an ornamental monstrosity was something achieved by the French—hence the term 'the French poodle'. This mutation is the expression of an aesthetic which turns the poodle into a symbol of ultimate beauty at dog shows. The poodle is judged by its 'look'. The poodle, Zappa has taught us, is a divine creature, and therefore a mistake, an aberration, a catastrophe. This story is told in "The Poodle Lecture", which can be found on volume five of *You Can't Do That on Stage Anymore*. After His first two mistakes—the creation of Man, and that of the Wo-man—God wanted to create a regular dog, a Schnauzer, but he fucked up! The result of his error, the poodle, is a misbeggotten travesty, whose long hair displeased its mistress. She therefore decided to clip him, to make him more cute and pleasing—more 'mod'. As an accomplice in the aesthetic fantasies of his mistress, the poodle is therefore the aesthetic manifestation of animal subjection: 'Beauty knows no pain!'. A perfectly docile animal, the poodle allows itself to fulfill the apex of its figurative potential with the aid of a variety of accessories: scissors, clippers, and of course the ever-popular—hitherto unknown in Somers Town, but destined to become a favourite item for the denizens of this area—zircon-encrusted tweezers.

Of course, the poodle is also valued as a pet, and for the many little services it can supply. In *The Negative Dialectics of Poodle Play*, Ben Watson observed that 'Poodles seemed to arrive with *Overnite Sensation*, but they had been around in latent form before... on the sleeve of *Absolutely Free* a dog collar appears on an advertisement hoarding above the slogan 'BUY A FYDO fits swell', a phrase which later evolved into the album title *One Size Fits All*.' (p. 235). With its accoutrements advertised all over American cities, the dog has become a stake for vast and sinister commercial interests. Zappa exposed the society of consumerism in one of his most outrageously trivial pieces of dialogue. In "Eddie, Are You Kidding?" from *Just Another Band from LA*, Mark Volman asks 'Where can I get my poodle clipped in Burbank?'. Zappa said to Bob Marshall 'Everyone wants to save the whale, but who cares about poodles?'.[3] Actually, the manufacturers of scissors and other chic accessories for poodle-grooming are laughing all the way to the bank: the poodle's has *commercial potential*.

Brave companion and working animal reduced to a passive, uncomprehending vehicle for various industrial products aimed at pets, the dog is also the victim of uncontrolled experimentation. One example is "Evelyn, A Modified Dog", whom we meet in *One Size Fits All*. In *Them Or Us [The Book]* (pp. 155-8), we learn that Evelyn is a collie belonging to Jimmy, a seven-year-old boy. His father, Barney, did special effects on the last big Kiss tour, and claims to be 'the most important show business figure in the entire Southern Californian area'. His mother, Florence, used to sell cosmetic products to her neighbours (something Captain Beefheart's mother did at one time). All four characters—dog, Jimmy, Mom and Dad—have their heads and feet encased in canvas bags like the Elephant Man—they're so monstrous they need to be kept covered up. After using some fennel shampoo sold by Florence, they all became 'UGLY AS FUCK'.

The poodle is an object for laboratory experiment, like the ponies of *Them Or Us [The Book]* which a mad professor places inside a space capsule which will explode in flight. But the trials and tribulations of Evelyn don't stop there: having removed its face-bag, and using a cardboard tube, Barney makes the dog sniff an ounce-and-a-half of cocaine. The torture never stops for the dog-slave, victim of Man and his instinct for domination.

This experimentation leaves no domain of research untouched. It extends as well to sexual activities. Having exhausted her aesthetic fantasies, the Wo-man decides to transform her modified dog into a sexual partner, saying, in a lascivious manner, 'Give me your dirty love...'. The fabulous adventures of poodle aesthetics could not remain the privilege of the few. On the contrary, it had to encounter and penetrate mainstream culture. The zircon motif is Zappa saying to us 'Modern America is a fake'. 'Zircon-encrusted tweezers' become the ultimate horizon of the Work of Art. Art & Commerce, no foolin'... Frank exposes the far-out destiny of the poodle in his text 'Say Cheese'. This article was written at the request of *Newsweek*, but the editor rejected it as 'too idiosyncratic'. It ended up as 'decorative filler material' on the *You Are What You Is* album. Zappa asks us about the 'Quality of our Lives', measured according to 'How much of what we individually consider to be Beautiful are we able to experience every day?'. The answer is obvious: an insufficient quantity, since 'Works of Art... Taste and The Public Interest' are 'all tied like a tin can to the wagging tail of the sacred Prime Rate Poodle.' [on the 2LP original release the words 'Prime Rate Poodle' were printed, uniquely in the document, in red ink *Ed.*] The incessant wagging of the tail of the Prime Rate Poodle derives from the volatility of the rate of profit under capitalism, and explains the aesthetic, economic and political blunders of the United States today. Set up as a regulator of artistic activities and canon of good taste in the US, the poodle puts the arts to death and destroys public life and liberty.

This threat of death and destruction, which hangs over American society, does not spare the poodle himself. Whilst it displays gigantic adverts for pet products on the walls of its cities, American industry actually works towards their extinction. Zappa's text for "Food Gathering in Post-Industrial America" on *The Yellow Shark* album goes: 'When the last decrepit factory had dumped its final load of toxic waste into the water supply and shipped its last badly-manufactured, incompetently-designed, consumer 'thing', we gaze in astonishment as the denizens of New Perfect America dine on rats, poodles and styrofoam packing-pellets all floating in a broth of tritium-enriched sewage.'

Like a lot of the animals in Zappa's universe, dogs are also rebels. In "Nanook Rubs It", the death of the baby seal is avenged by the terrible 'defliction' visited on the beady little eyes of the fur-trapper by Nanook's application of the Extract of the Northern Dog—the famous sledge-dog urine or 'huskie wee-wee', which makes him blind. Frunobulax, the poodle monster of "Cheepnis" on *Roxy & Elsewhere* becomes Public Enemy Number One in a low-budget science-fiction film. 'DON'T LET THE POODLE BITE ME! WE CAN'T LET IT REPRODUCE!' expresses the dominant emotion: terror. A full-scale war is launched against the scourge, with soldiers from the National Guard and the deployment of napalm. The zappatistical dog knows how to bare its fangs, like the poodle of "Dirty Love" and "Stink-Foot": 'The poodle bites, the poodle chews it...'. Even the aimiable Patricia, the Schnauzer in the high chair on the cover of *The Perfect Stranger* (and the *Francesco Zappa* album), doesn't exactly appreciate the vacuum-cleaner salesman's licentious cavortment in front of her mistress, and pulls a face. In real life, Zappa's pet dogs demonstrated an astonishing ability to sniff out fishy characters, as shown by the behaviour of Fruney, the Zappas' family dog, one evening when Bob Dylan visited. Bob, recently a convert to Christianity, had called to play Zappa demos for his next album [*Infidels Ed.*]. Zappa explained the persistent growls coming from the dog: 'he doesn't like Christians!'.

Because of repeated visual and sonic representations, the poodle as such is a privileged object of observation in Zappa's work, but its most important aspect is that it gives us the key to the zappatistical aesthetic. On the most basic level, the message is 'cheap is beautiful'. As Zappa once said: 'if you can't be free, you can at least be cheap'. The song "Cheepnis", with its nostalgia for trash B-movies and their inexpensive virtues, echoes Zappa's own budgetary preoccupations. It also affirms his personal aesthetic: the beauty of a film does not derive from its budget. The beauty of the dog, if it exists, doesn't rely on the sophisticated treatments of the high-grade poodle parlour.

Zappa's aesthetic is revealed to us by the talking dog in "Stink-Foot" on *Apostrophe(')*. Asked to define his 'conceptual continuity', Fido replies 'the crux of the biscuit is the apostrophe (')'. In English punctuation—and in French, incidentally—the apostrophe indicates a missing letter, as in the phrase 'Rock'n'Roll'. *Apostrophe(')* is the name of Zappa's album where the title tune is the only track without words. The apostrophe points to something which is neither visible nor audible—to something hidden. This enigmatic manoeuvre transforms the poodle into a sphinx, expressed in the phrase: 'what really matters is kept from view'. This leads us on to the paradoxical blue-print for Zappa's life-work, the famous 'conceptual continuity of the group's output macrostructure', otherwise known as the 'project/object'.

Simultaneously a means of communicating Zappa's critical project and an object of mockery, the poodle is the perfect symbol for the zappatistical aesthetic. It gives us a clue to the hidden macrostructure, but it also allows us to appreciate its textural content. The macrostructure is the ensemble of heterogeneous elements in Zappa's *oeuvre* which are given context and overall shape by a 'continuity' which, more than in any other band's musical *oeuvre*, we're continually reminded of. It includes:

> Life on the road, which has furnished material for many lyrics or 'routines'. To take just one example, there is nothing in the annals of rock equivalent to *Playground Psychotics* in the way it plumbs the depth of confession and gossip.
>
> The audience—with whom Zappa had a special rapport on stage—was granted special explanations of songs, and also invited to participate. This duplex problematic was best expressed on *Roxy & Elsewhere*, with Zappa's 'preambles' to each of the four sides of vinyl and the 'audience participation' of "Bebop Tango (of the Old Jazzman's Church)".
>
> Technical procedures for recording and processing the music, with a particular emphasis on recording materials and editing:

> more than anyone else in rock, Zappa gives very precise technical data, with extremely detailed and pertinent sleevenotes. This logic reached its ultimate flowering in *Sheik Yerbouti*: the inner gatefold of the double album showed us a mixing desk, on which you can see a packet of cigarettes and a cup of coffee—which were also essential tools for Zappa's work practice.
>
> God (as energy).

There exists outside the limits of the visible and audible a cosmic connection which draws us beyond space and time, and which nevertheless brings us closer to actual history. In a bogus self-interview concocted for Warner Bros. sales executives in 1970—for the 12-disc *History & Collected Improvisations of the Mothers of Invention*, a project which was never released—Zappa explained:

> There is, and always has been, a conscious control of thematic and structural elements flowing through each album, live performance, and interview. What I'm trying to describe is the type of attention given to each lyric, melody, arrangement, improvisation, the sequence of these elements in an album, the cover art which is an extension of the musical material, the choice of what is recorded, released, and/or performed during a concert, the continuity or contrasts of material album to album, etc., etc., etc.... all of these detail aspects are part of the Big Structure or The Main Body of Work. The smaller details comprise not only the contents of The Main Body of Work, but, because of the chronology of execution, give it 'shape' in an abstract sense...

To conclude this analysis of the role of the dog in Frank Zappa's *oeuvre*: can we take it seriously if humour is one of its essential characteristics? Let me finish by observing that, read backwards, the dog's bark, transcribed as 'arf', gives us the first three letters of Zappa's first name: 'F R A'. Let's also note that the dogs Fydo (with a 'y'), Fido (with an 'i'), Frunobulax, Frenchie and Fruney all have the same initial: 'F'. Just like their master and creator.

Arf!

1. This paper was translated from Jeunot's original French by Ben Watson, with help from the author.
2. This is from a lengthy interview set up between Zappa and Bob Marshall by Gerry Fialka, who also joined in, as did Dr Carolyn Dean, on 21 and 22 October 1988. Loren Gagnon transcribed the tapes. This particular quote may be found on *<www.mcluhaninstitute.org/baedeker/bobs_articles/zappa_interview-02.html>*.
3. *Ibid.*

"The Torture Never Stops" Frank Zappa & the Mental Hygiene Dilemma

Simon Prentis

Not being an experienced public speaker, I have brought with me a small Japanese good-luck charm—complete with its own tiny pillow—to help steady my nerves (since this is being filmed perhaps we can insert a close-up later on for those of you not blessed with 20/20 vision). As some of you may already be able to see, this is in fact a miniature replica of a golden turd [Fig. 11]. You can buy these tasteful little doodads from the stalls that line the entrances to shrines and temples all over Japan, and they come in a variety of sizes and applications—I used to have another one that doubled as a device for scraping wax out of your ear—but the reason why they are so popular, the source of their magic charm, is that the Japanese pronunciation of the character for *luck* [幸運] resonates pleasingly with that of the slang word for *shit* [うんこ]. The Japanese take a special delight in the sympathetic magic of such fortuitous homonyms, but there is evidently a particular pleasure in the *luck/turd* interface due to the sheer absurdity of the pairing. In its own way, it is very Zen: an arresting image that simultaneously celebrates and subverts the tradition it is part of. I hope it will also serve as a useful symbol for what I have to say about Frank Zappa, a man whose own deft pairing of doody with duty is distinctively Zen—not to mention the happy retro-continuity with the concept behind the characters famously uttered by the barking pumpkin: [聖糞] 'Holy Shit!', or—more literally—sacred turd.

Fig. 11: Golden Turd

Zappa once said of "Who Are the Brain Police?" that it was a religious song[1], a comment that—as far as I am aware—has received very little critical attention. Given his views on organised religion, it is highly unlikely that he meant this in the conventional sense of the word, and yet it points to a serious intent. So who exactly are the brain police? The song often seems to be taken as some sort of reference to 1984-style state surveillance and/or as a comment on the pernicious influence of manufactured mass culture, but in fact the song is asking a very personal question: What would you do? What would you do if your familiar world broke down? If you saw through the plastic and chrome, and woke up one day to the realisation that everything about your life was fake? Or that the reason you were beat was because you had played the game? The answer of course, is that you would probably freak out—an eventuality for which the middle section of the song conveniently supplies the soundtrack, a cartoonishly scary evocation of the panic that would doubtless ensue in such a case.

But this was not the kind of freak-out that Zappa had in mind when he named the album. It is merely a prelude, a necessary preliminary to an act of self-liberation defined by the liner notes in what amounts to a manifesto: 'On a personal level, freaking out is a process whereby an individual casts off outmoded and restricting standards of thinking, dress and social etiquette in order to express CREATIVELY his relationship to his immediate environment and the social structure as a whole.'[2] As he remarked on several other occasions, people tend to police their own brains;[3] so the key is to recognise this tendency in yourself and reject it—to realise that the mind is the ugliest part of the body, and the only person who can clean it up is you.

Which brings me to mental hygiene—a favourite Zappa concept—and its relationship to the teachings of Zen. Many years ago I spent eight years in Japan, partly in pursuit of the golden turd at the end of the Zen rainbow, and it intrigued me that there appeared to be so many true Zen sayings embedded obliquely in Zappa's work. One day I finally got the opportunity to talk with him about it. He told me that reading about Zen had been the catalyst that changed his mind about Catholicism, of which he had been a devotee until the age of about 18—even to the point of wanting to become a monk (a factoid that I believe has never been revealed before). I asked him if he had ever tried any of the practices commonly associated with Zen: whether as pure meditation or through any of the other traditional disciplines. 'No,' he said, 'I got the picture straight away. And if you can see what it's all about, why bother with all the shit in between?'[4] Now that could be taken as an extremely arrogant thing to say. Perhaps it was. On the other hand, it might simply be an unvarnished statement of fact. For if the enlightenment that Zen offers is a state of being, not a state of mind, the following description of a Zen master does sound spookily familiar:

> The Master in the art of living makes little distinction between his work and his play, his labour and his leisure, his mind and his body, his education and his recreation, his love and his religion. He hardly knows which is which. He simply pursues his vision of excellence in whatever he does, leaving others to decide whether he is working or playing. To him he is always doing both.[5]

But whether or not Frank Zappa could or should be considered to have the mind of a Zen adept (and in this context one should never forget that other true Zen saying: 'If you meet the Buddha on the road, kill him!'[6]), his famous principle of 'Anything, Any Place, Any Time, For No Reason At All' is undoubtedly pure Zen in action. And the more you start to look for it, the more you find a distinctive philosophical sub-text running like a purple thread throughout his work, tirelessly working to crush the boxes of convention and conformity with which we voluntarily police ourselves into a state of unfreedom. This is the 'dirtiness' that Zappa is drawing our attention to, a somewhat different species of dirtiness to the one he often stands falsely accused of.

For there are people out there, even within the Zappa community, who apparently think "Ms. Pinky" is about how much fun it can be to have sex with an inflatable doll, or that "Dinah-Moe Humm" is an incitement to the chauvinist abuse of females of the species. I'm sorry, but it's time to get a life. Despite any number of irrational prejudices to the contrary, it is—and will doubtless continue to be—quite possible to describe an unsavoury attitude without being in favour of it. Furthermore, it is also possible to imaginatively locate oneself as the subject of the experience for the purposes of artistic expression and not thereby endorse it. And while we're at it, it is quite legitimate to exaggerate or distort the true nature of a circumstance in order to draw attention to its intrinsic absurdity. This does not mean that you necessarily like it. It is called satire.

It's really quite astonishing how pervasive the *knob gag* heresy is amongst those who claim to appreciate Zappa's music. Charles Shaar Murray's recent memorial barbecue series of broadcasts and articles[7] continued to peddle the hoary old platitude that 'Frank's music was fantastic, if only he'd just cut out that puerile humour'. Well let's just get this straight. The knob gag is the province of Benny Hill and the *Carry On* films; a tradition that lives on in such classics as the 12-inch pianist joke, the Bishop of Birmingham limerick, the Good Ship Venus and all the venerable variations on that theme. Jokes such as these rely on the snigger factor, the sad fact that the mere mention in a public place of the pleasures than can be had by the owner/operator of a male genital is apparently enough to induce irrepressible laughter in the minds of the socially retarded. Knob gags are all 'Nudge, nudge, know what I mean?' stuff—the sole agenda being to insinuate, not to mock. But the songs that excite such wrath amongst Zappa's detractors are specifically designed to undermine the behaviour being described, not to encourage or celebrate it. Bringing it out into the open, openly stating what others merely insinuate actually helps to achieve some closure, to allow us to acknowledge and thereby perhaps overcome some of our sicker urges. Suggesting that the members of a rock and roll band, whilst posing as heroes of our time, are often obsessed with casual sex of the most gross and demeaning kind is not about endorsement, or even about denigrating some wholesome image that the youth of today might otherwise aspire to: it is about recognising that this image is a lie that only helps foster the very perversities it denies. To anyone who has read accounts of what really went on behind the scenes on Beatles tours, the fact that Zappa was able to persuade Ringo Starr to appear in *200 Motels* is an even more delicious irony.

And yet the illusion persists. I remember being at UMRK once when some Japanese record company types showed up to discuss forthcoming projects. On the table in the basement was a copy of a specialist piercing magazine, the very same one that was later to feature in *Everything is Healing Nicely.* Someone had sent it to Zappa, thinking (correctly, as it turned out) that it would amuse him. Whilst we were waiting for Frank to arrive, we flipped through it together, marvelling at some of the bizarre extremities on display in the organ in question. His visitors were convinced that this was definitive proof that he really was a pervert with a sick and twisted mind. Much teeth-sucking and highly scrutable disappointment ensued when I explained that his interest was that of a disinterested observer of human foibles rather than an enthusiastic participant.

For if 'dirty' is sinful, it is only so because it is locked in, hidden away and fetishized. Copulation and defecation may be acts that humans generally prefer to perform in private, for reasons of feigned delicacy or otherwise, but to pretend that humans do not do them, or do not enjoy them even when they admit to doing them, is a recipe for a dirty mind. And what you hide away from yourself will eventually find you out and eat you like the worm in William Blake's rose. To complain that Zappa is dirty is like complaining that Hieronymous Bosch, Hogarth or the Chapman Brothers are obscene: it is to profoundly misunderstand their motives.

"The Torture Never Stops" seems to be one of those songs that most conspicuously gets people going. Opinions divide down the fault line of political correctness: it's either offending against feminist shibboleths or down & dirty with its bad self. Am I the only one who hears something else entirely? Let's take a look at the title of the album it appears in, *Zoot Allures*. Whilst Ben Watson has done his usual fine job in drawing attention to the deeper meanings lurking here[8], I beg to differ somewhat on the conclusion: Zoot, symbolising the flashy and trashy aspect of the world out there, is alluring: we are all suckered down the primrose path at some time or another, and whether your poison is sex, drugs or plain ol' rock & roll, you'll run into the brick wall at the back of the theatre in the end. But so long as we fall for the allure, the torture will go on; and the night of the iron sausage turns from pleasure to pain when you can't get off. The orgasmic squealing in the background, far from being the soundtrack to some dodgy S&M bondage fantasy, is a metaphor, symbolic of the agony on the flip side of the ecstasy, the torture chamber that lies just the other side of the disco.

All is suffering, said the Buddha, but the message of Zen (and Zappa) is that there is a way out. 'Some of you may not agree/But you probably likes a lot of misery'; Broken Hearts, whether resulting from cheap romance or an otherwise unsustainable view of reality, are indeed for assholes. The flies may be all green & buzzin' in the dungeon of despair, but—just like a sin—all that is needed to create a dungeon is the act of locking something in. And we hold the key. It's a voluntary thing. Let's not forget that we're talking about the dungeon of Despair, the last refuge of a miserable self still unwilling to accept that the deal we're dealin' in ultimately involves taking full personal responsibility, 'cos if you fall for the game not only will you get beat, you will probably end up working in a gas station, working out with

Ms. Pinky to blot out your disco sorrow. And in the harsh but true words of the sage: 'If you wind up with a boring, miserable life because you listened to your mother, your Dad, your priest, to some guy on television, to any of the people telling you how to do your shit, then you deserve it.'[9]

Here's the big picture: despite the myriad improvements to the world that might yet be effected by applying concepts hitherto unacted upon in our philosophy, we still have no idea of what we're ultimately involved in. We arrive in ignorance and depart little the wiser. It has never been explained, since at first it was created. We may be crazy, we may be sainted, we may be nothing more than pointless zeroes someone just painted. But sometimes you can be surprised to discover that the universe works whether or not you understand it. And since it just might be a one-shot deal, you'd better be digging it while it's happening...

'I have taken your time/I have sung you my song/Ain't no great revelation/But it wasn't too long'.

Jeder Mann sein eigener Pudel!!

1. Frank Zappa, interview with Frank Kofsky, *Jazz and Pop*, September-October 1967; edited Pauline Rivelli and Robert Levin, *The Rock Giants*, New York: Da Capo, 1970, p. 22.
2. Liner notes, *Freak Out* 1966
3. This is from a lengthy interview set up between Zappa and Bob Marshall by Gerry Fialka, who also joined in, as did Dr Carolyn Dean, on 21 and 22 October 1988. Loren Gagnon transcribed the tapes. This particular quote may be found on <*www.mcluhaninstitute.org/baedeker/bobs_articles/zappa_interview-10.html*>.
4. Interview with the author, October 1986.
5. Unattributed Zen Buddhist text.
6. Attributed to Rinzai (Lin-chi I-hsuan).
7. *Jazz File: Jazz From Hell*, BBC Radio 3, 23, 29 November and 6 December 2003; see also Charles Shaar Murray's contribution to *Mojo*, December 2003.
8. Ben Watson, *Frank Zappa: the Negative Dialectics of Poodle Play*, London: Quartet, 1994, pp. 209-302.
9. Frank Zappa with Peter Occhiogrosso, *The Real Frank Zappa Book*, p. 233.

Houston... Fort.. Marcuse: Sin versus Archetype in Zappa's *Oeuvre*

Ben Watson

When I first met Danny Houston, the Zappa freak from Glasgow, in 1976, both our brains exploded, and I'm not sure I've recovered yet. Danny had come down to London from Glasgow in the mid-70s to live on the dole and be a freak and explore everything the English capital had to offer. They gave him a fierce interview in the unemployment office, one of those ones where they ask if you've been looking for work, and where they threaten to cut off your payments if you can't prove you're trying. So he looked for work and got a job as a clerk in London Transport. One of the benefits of working for the underground—in the locomotive, rather than cultural sense—is that you obtain a pass allowing you to travel free all over London. Experiencing London accompanied by Danny was like a dream or a drug trip, because he knew how to get across the capital so fast. We'd usually get extremely drunk, and by the end of the night, it was hard to work out exactly where we'd been. London was transformed into a warren of pubs, stairwells, bedrooms and kitchens, all interconnected in unexpected ways, with different opportunities for partying at every moment—in halls, back passage-ways, tube carriages, deserted rooms, bus stairwells, strangers' kitchens. I remember distinctly dancing with Danny to Johnny 'Guitar' Watson's *Funk Beyond the Call of Duty* round a pink double bed in someone's bedroom. I've no idea where I was.

Danny lived in a bedsit in Ealing Broadway. The room's four walls were covered in counter-cultural trophies and detritus. Indeed, it was spookily like Gerry Fialka's end-of-the-garden shack in Venice Beach, Los Angeles. Gerry Fialka is the Zappa freak who wormed his way into the Zappa empire, so that at the point of Zappa's death in 1993, he was employed answering the telephone for the Barking Pumpkin hotline. That, he told me, was how he found girlfriends. Fialka also hosts a *Finnegans Wake* reading group in the Los Angeles Public Library (I think they've only got one). Gerry believes if you add Frank Zappa to Marshall McLuhan and *Finnegans Wake*, the world will suddenly wake up to the idiocy of its abuse of public communications for sterile profit rather than lived fun. In both their homes, it felt like the colour posters of Robert Wyatt and the photocopies of Captain Beefheart lyrics and the cassettes of Sun Ra and George Clinton and a polystyrene totem-pole decorated with a signed ticket to see Arthur Brown and signed photo of Jimmy Carl Black were all that held the ceiling up. I think this was quite literally the case with Fialka's 'funny farm', as he calls it, though I may be confusing his shack with the garage inhabited by the founder of 'Americans For A Darker America', who'd managed to extinguish all the street lights in his immediate neighbourhood. His garage home was reached through an extremely dark—and rather alarming—hole in a privet hedge. Charlie Parker was playing on his tiny transistor radio when Gerry and I visited on Halloween, and he was dancing and opening bottles of beer. He'd built a wall of books and records to replace the garage door which was stuck in the open position.

Danny's house, though, was a typical Victorian suburban building on an Ealing street. In the 70s Ealing hadn't been colonised by the Asian community, it was straight and colourless and boring—but Danny's room was a treasure trove, gleaming with counter-cultural rareties. I'd visit to tape his records—he listened to everything on a little mono box gramophone—and then we'd go to a pub called the Wheatsheaf, and get blasted out of our skulls on Fuller's ESB, which started to stand for Extra-Sensory Bitter. If I came down to visit for the weekend—hitchhiking down the A10 from Cambridge—we'd meet in a pub near his work on Saturday lunchtime. Danny's colleagues worked overtime, and didn't like it if he didn't do the same. He seemed to spend most of Saturday afternoon in the pub anyway. He'd pop in and out, there were always other friends of his there to talk to. He lived with a continual buzz of people around him. I was his eccentric student acquaintance from Cambridge University who was also nuts about Zappa.

Danny first got in touch with me when I had a letter published in *Street Life*, a short-lived attempt to create a British *Rolling Stone.* He wrote to me at the college address they'd printed. I remember holding up the note he'd sent to show my friends—not just signed but *singed* all round the edge—and everyone saying how weird it was to get a letter from a stranger, out of the blue. Now I write to people I haven't met at every opportunity. Life's too short for protocols. Like most Zappologists, our obsession upset and annoyed almost everyone else we knew in regular life. It was odd that we hung out together, considering his slogan at the time was 'all students are cunts' (this was long before the c-word began gracing the pages of *Time Out*). Danny's now doing a degree in Communications at Auckland University, I hear. Danny always had shitloads of friends and acquaintances, he was an organiser, a mischief maker, a leader. He'd buy ten tickets for an Iggy Pop concert and sell them to his friends to make sure we'd meet ahead and arrive sufficiently lubricated. I'd meet him at a pub in Earl's Court, and there'd be twenty-five Glaswegians and Antipodeans sitting round in a circle.

Why am I telling you about Danny? Because his *use* of Zappa seems to me to be absolutely right: the point for him was using culture rather than simply consuming it. He used Zappa's music as an opportunity for play, for pranks, for up-ending the passivity enforced by the star system, that gawping-at-the-famous which commercial interests (and the Idiot Bastard Son website) turn everything into. He knew Zappa's *oeuvre* was a battle over meaning, and exerted great efforts to insert himself into Conceptual Continuity. When I got to know Danny, I was starting to learn about revolutionary Marxism. I attended the Socialist Workers Party discussion week in London called 'Marxism', and Tony Cliff, the old Palestinian Jew who invented the whole thing, blew me away in his talks. Danny was completely suspicious of organised politics, and fiercely anti-intellectual. He'd tried attending college in Scotland, and the way he was failed condemned intellectual pursuits in his eyes. When I say Danny 'was failed', I'm referring to a Penguin paperback by the anarchist John Holt called *Why Children Fail*, which explains how our schooling system is actually designed to tell 75% of the population they're stupid. I think the percentages may be a little different today, but the same split still exists—especially among Zappa fans, who always seem to be over-educated super-intellectuals (25%) or proud-to-be-*lumpen* opponents of book culture (75%). Danny once made me burst into tears when I came back all excited from hearing Cliff explain the difference between Leninism and Stalinism, and he denounced me for using terms 'no working-class person had ever heard of' (he wasn't to know that these terms were *invented* by working-class militants!).

I also remember Danny ruining a holiday when a bunch of us got hold of a house on the fish-slope in Cromer on the Norfolk Coast—with a big bay window looking at a turbulent North Sea, and with a fantastic pub with Adnams and Abbot round the corner. We used to get the bar manager, Eric, to pump beer into a huge glass vase as a takeaway. We'd also ask for a 'half' fill-up in a pint glass and he'd give us three-quarters of a pint, which was great news as we were as poor as we were alcoholic. The house—it had five storeys—belonged to my girlfriend's mother, but she was away, so we occupied for a weekend, which is a fantastic treat when you've been living in flats and apartments too small to accommodate anyone more than a couple. Anyway, on Saturday night Danny went into a diatribe about 'middle-class student revolutionaries' and how we actually knew nothing, all because there was a toilet under the stairs, and everytime you put the light on, a fan started whirring, in case any of the odours emitted during pissing or defecation 'might offend anyone's prissy little bourgeois nostrils'. It was *years* later that I discovered that people installing toilets without windows are obliged *by law* to provide electric ventilation. Nowadays, every time I'm having a pee in a curry-shop toilet which has been built in some recess, some odd spare corner without windows, and the fan starts whirring, I reflect on the strange way young people persecute each other over their class backgrounds, and how the simple information that fans in closed toilets are *obligatory by law* might have made for a more pleasant evening in Cromer.

Except it probably wouldn't have helped. Martin Bennell, who recruited me to the SWP originally, and now works as a porter at St James's hospital in Leeds, was there too, and he and Danny—both older than me—were fighting for my soul and allegiance. On the one hand, an abstract, political concept of the working class, on the other hand, a really existing, but atomised, alienated and culturally-*outré* example of 'the real thing'. But now I think everything Danny did and does should be understood as a struggle waged against the alienation of capitalism. His activities—putting people in touch with each other, writing to magazines, putting slips of paper with his phone number into Zappa albums in record shops, swapping photocopies and tapes, perpetual pursuit of unreleased Zappa material and coincidences and connections, organising visits to pubs and gigs, practical jokes, freak-outs—were never about some paltry individual career or advantage, some tedious pursuit of fame and fortune. It was always about creating situations where something magical could happen, something not driven by the time-is-money are-you-a-celebrity crap of everyday life as conceived by the tabloids and TV. Magic moments where dead capitalist time was revealed as an illusion, where genuinely bizarre things happened. Like the Sex Pistols, Danny was a Situationist and didn't know it. His every thought was anti-capitalist. His eagerness for bootleg tape recordings and postal communication inoculated me against the cyber-boosterism and net-frenzy of the mid-90s: thanks to him and the Zappa circuit, I'd been listening to unofficial material from across the globe and making virtual friends for two decades.

But it was when listening to a bootleg tape Danny made of Zappa at the Hammersmith Odeon on 24 January 1978 that I realised quite how freak-fueled and futuro-fantastic his aesthetic was. During "Titties 'N Beer", at the line 'it looked to me/Like it was titty skin', the sound quality—already boomy and boxy because Danny's microphone couldn't really cope with the volume of the PA—worsens and becomes distant and faint. It was like that moment in "Kaiser Rolls" on *FZ:OZ* where the PA tape reel ran-out and Dweezil and Gail patched in some seconds from an audience recording, except on Danny's tape there was no sleevenote explanation. I listened with consternation. You hear a door slam. Someone mumbles: 'Got any dope to sell round here?'. Danny says: 'No, sorry mate... actually there's some people standing just there, the first line... [*unintelligible mumble, mmmf*]... I don't think they've got any to sell but they're smoking, they're American... [*more unintelligible mumble, mmmf*]...' Then there's Danny's inevitable question: 'You haven't got any tapes have you? Any tapes?'. The other guy in the toilet has no idea what he's talking about. Another Zappa maniac. (Why is it when I think about civilians trying to understand a Zappa maniac like Danny, I just feel like bursting out laughing?)

Danny was as addicted to live tapes of Zappa as the dope smoker was to his marijuana. Danny collected them, swapped them, duplicated them—but he never sold them or made money from them. He didn't have a portable tape-recorder, so it was my task to tape the Hammersmith gigs, which meant strapping a tape recorder to my back underneath my 'OUT TO LUNCH' raincoat and walking past the door-men with a backwards lean so the bulge wouldn't be noticed. Danny knew he was making a raid on Zappa's copyright and knew how much he hated bootleggers (we hadn't yet received the message—outlined in the American edition of *Society Pages*—that tape-swapping was okay, Zappa just hated the sleazy way bootleggers can charge high prices for inferior quality recordings just because they're 'rare'). For Danny, the fact that tapes could be duplicated was *Potlatch* all the way (and he'd never heard of Guy Debord). Then, during his tape recording of the Hammersmith gig from 1978, as the rest of the dialogue from "Titties 'n Beer" leaked through the toilet doors, there was a trickling sound, and you realise, through the magic of recording technology, we're in the gents and we're listening to the sound of Danny's urine splashing into a urinal. As usual, Danny had to get his cock in there, a case of inevitable insertionism. Then the sound is cut.

The tape resumes with Zappa asking for innocent volunteers to dance to "Black Page #2", so we haven't missed much—it was the next song in the show. In the same period, Danny also dangled his microphone into the band's dressing room from an outside window in order to catch moments of the Project/Object *even Zappa would not have on tape.* This idea of introducing your own recorded urine into what Gail Zappa calls The Loop—the international circuit of Zappa tape, CD and MP3 swappers—is for me the definition of the entire Zappological project: self-extension via grotesque invasions of privacy, a satirical attack on the discreet individual, a translation into absurd social fragments. It's as crucial a moment in Modern Art as *The Fountain* (1915) by Marcel Duchamp: genuine 'theater-piss'.

But what of the *oeuvre* itself? Zappa's work is exciting because his art is not the product of an ideology or theory, it wrinkles and overlaps and concentrates bits of the material world so that the whole universe may be viewed in it upside down, tiny, like the image inside the convex mirror in the parlour of your great aunt in Chingford. Hence theorists as different as Charles Fort and Herbert Marcuse might be used to apprise us of its multi-layered, multi-valent energies. Charles Fort published *The Book of the Damned* in 1919. It laid the foundations of an anti-authoritarian approach to knowledge which is now enshrined in the magazine *Fortean Times.* In 1976, *Fortean Times* wasn't in regular newsagents, and when Danny showed me a copy, seemed more like a dried muffin remnant of the counter-culture than the prototype of a popular 90s title. Danny believed my theories about Zappa would appeal to the Fortean crew, and encouraged me to report the bizarre discoveries I was making to the editor. Danny dropped by the editorial office, and was surprised to discover how earnest and 'not insane' they were. For a Bolshevik Punk like Out To Lunch, though, *Fortean Times* and its crop circles and flying saucers seemed off-puttingly hippie and mystical; I didn't quite understand how lacking in any belief—New Age or not—the Fortean method actually is. Out of loyalty to Danny, I bought *Book of the Damned* second-hand, a cheap paperback published by Sphere in 1979, but couldn't read much of it. Now when I look at Fort's book, it reads as a powerful statement of anti-positivist monism, a kind of plainspeaking man's Hegel. In fact, it reads like Josef Dietzgen, the leather worker whose book *The Nature of Human*

Brain-Work Presented by a Workingman: a Renewed Critique of Pure & Practical Reason was published in 1896 as part of *The Positive Outcome of Philosophy.*

Charles Fort pointed out

> If science could absolutely exclude all data but its own present data... it would be a real system [*The Book of the Damned*, p. 28]

and then went on to list all the facts and reports which science ignores in order to pretend that it's a seamless system. Fort didn't like intellectual systems. In this, Fort is like Karl Marx. The bourgeois misconception of Marxism as 'rigid dogma' is not borne out by reading anything Marx actually wrote—or anything by Marxists worth their salt like Herbert Marcuse, whose *One Dimensional Man* was another popular paperback issued by Sphere. According to the cover of the edition of 1964, *One Dimensional Man* sold more copies than Mao's *Little Red Book.* Since, unlike Mao Tse Tung's, Marcuse's work wasn't a collection of poetic platitudes and paradoxes which could apply to any political position under the sun, this fact is rather amazing. Frankfurt School radicalism—*contra* Andrew Greenaway's Thatcherite notion that it's all just stuff for academics and toffs—*can be popular*! But what concerns me here is Marcuse's analysis of Soviet Marxism, a system which had betrayed Marx's concept of a free society and individual self-development for all. Marcuse said:

> What is irrational if measured from without the system is rational within the system. [*Soviet Marxism*, p. 28]

This is the same thought as that of Charles Fort 39 years before! Here it is again:

> If science could absolutely exclude all data but its own present data... it would be a real system [*The Book of the Damned*, p. 28]

I want to argue that you can't understand Frank Zappa unless you take what Fort and Marcuse say on board. Zappa was the only historical materialist in rock, a genre which in essence was a bourgeois/idealist steal from the materialism, honesty and directness of the blues (okay, let's except Iggy Pop and Gary Glitter). So, in rejecting Danny's suggestion of approaching *Fortean Times*, I was blinded by generational identity tripe and failed to see how constructive and insightful he was being. What Zappa's father says about official history in *The Real Frank Zappa Book* has exactly Fort's skepticism about power's use of knowledge.

Zappa's albums present such an outlandish splice of complete madness and cutting sanity that he forces the listener to speculate about the relativity of madness and sanity, the dialectical involvement of opposites like order and chaos, rationality and irrationality. The oppressive *boredom* of the capitalist system is interrupted. The 'irrational' is the threat to an ordered system which only an undogmatic, flexible and living dialectic can deal with ('The man who was talkin' to the dog...'). This commitment to the irrational also explains why Frank Zappa's song "The World's Greatest Sinner" is the key to his work (something which, funnily enough, is true of *every* song he wrote).

In *The Myth of the Eternal Return: Archetypes and Repetition*, published in Paris in 1959, Mircea Eliade explains what 'sin' is. It's simply the *irrational* being excluded from a socially-recognised 'system'. That's why Charles Fort called his book *The Book of the Damned*. Fort's book lists in stunning succession all the observations and material evidence—showers of jelly, frogs and blood, thunderstones—which science has so far failed to explain. For his part, Eliade shows that, to the religious mind, 'personal events'—eccentric, individual, particular—are *intolerable*: they sin against the 'archetype', which in the Christian system is named 'virtue'.[1] Zappa's positive view of masturbation—almost unique in hippie rock (apart from Cream and Hendrix)—was thus a polemic against religious 'virtue' and all mythical thinking which crushes personal experience under archetypes. Zappa wanted to make an art consisting entirely of 'sin'—of unabstracted, specific, personal expressions unrepressed by any generalised archetypes. That's why the records he produced are so delightfully knotty, gnarly and pleasing, even when you can't understand a word—and once you've worked out all the ingredients of "Debra Kadabra", all the stuff about B movies, Mexican rubber masks and dental flossers, you're really no wiser. *Why* did he put all that junk in there? Because it resists the abstract concept!

A brief musicological parenthesis in case people think my potato has been baking too long. Of course, Punk Rock's realism meant it was replete with masturbation songs: "Orgasm Addict" by the Buzzcocks; "Phone-In Show" by the Members (the great, reforgotten troupe of white-reggae soulboys from Camberley who discovered their souls on the Seven Sisters Road, and whose phallic pun is honoured in the name of the band playing at the College Bar for our entertainment tonight[2]); "Turning Japanese" by some awful band whose name I can't remember, but which Steve Parry of Chocolate Sandwich told me was about wanking; and not to forget "Teenage Kicks" by the Undertones, which was apparently released with altered words to hide its real meaning (when I first heard the song on the John Peel show, I remember its image of blissful teen coupling rang false).

The materialist and dialectical view of the world is not that of abstract dead matter being shaped by unchanging, eternal laws: it is that of self-defining, irreversible and unique processes which create their own laws, and this applies to hydrogen atoms and dwarf nebulae as much as to human beings. Zappa's music is constructed according to these principles, which is why dialecticians unclouded by left identity-thinking love it so much.

That's my conclusion really, so I'm going to peter-green out with some random remarks and a coda about *King Kong*. In this I'm following the structure of "Handsome Cabin Boy", which Simon Fell once described as 'doing that Zappa thing where he fiddles with the possibility of some classic form, does something utterly original and unexpected with it, seems like he's going to resolve it nicely, then throws it all away as if it's all too finicky and buggers off and does something completely different...'.

It was a great day, or rather 4:00am alcohol binge moment, when Danny noticed that Ruth Underwood is wearing an enamel *Zoot Allures* badge on the seat of her jeans in the photograph in the inner gatefold of *Zappa In New York*. This explains the psychic tendency of the pungent aroma which surrounds the *Zoot Allures* album. Of course—and this is why we love conceptual continuity—this explanation was only vouchsafed to fans *after* the release of *Zoot Allures*. Time is not linear, it's a spherical constant: while you're at home *what's everyone else doing*? Linear time is a bourgeois-individualist illusion. Zappa's records never stay still (as long as you're not such an Idiot Bastard that you fail to open up to the non-Zappological world enough to get some chance, so-called 'random' or 'red herring', connections in there, that is). 'One whiff of it,' says Julia in *First Training*, the pornographic classic of the 1910s, referring to the allure of anal zoot, 'and men follow you around like dogs.' But, much as I'd like to explain how George Clinton and Swamp Dogg mainline, stressify and overdose on canine continuity, I'm leaving dogs to Dominique Jeunot, Président of Les Fils de l'Invention, the Parisian Frank Zappa chapter.

However, there is time to tell you that Didier Mervelet of Les Fils (who will be performing a *Tableau Vivant Qui Bouge* about Francesco later on) caused me a similar ganglion of the imagination as Danny did—perma-scar, war wound, benign trauma, permanent damage, psychic growth, what-you-will—when he showed me the cover of Peter Frampton's 7" single "I'm In You". The line from "Punky's Whips", 'He's little fond of chiffon in a wrist array' was finally explained, even though "Punky's Whips" was not about Peter Frampton, but about Punky Meadows (have you ever reflected on what a *ludicrous* name that is? Did we really used to discuss Angel and the lawsuit and Warner Bros. 'pulling the track' *seriously*??). It took me several years to find it, but the single with the pic sleeve—French issue—was finally tracked down in a second-hand record shop on a cold rainy day in November 2003 in Lille. For a mere 30 Euro cents. As Danny taught me, the way that conceptual continuity is undervalued by record dealers in the grim grey world of the Zappologically untouched, makes many of our purchases VERY GOOD BARGAINS! I've never been able to work out whether it was drunken wishful thinking which caused me to see this astonishing aspect of conceptual continuity, so I'm going to invite controversy and discussion by actually showing you the sleeve and what I saw in it.[3] (see Fig. 13)

This record sleeve contains another 'sleeve'—Frampton's chiffon-in-a-wrist-array sleeve—and so hints at *mise-en-abyme infinitus* ... Just like the strange 'Z' which popped up in Hermann Kretzschmar's name in the transition from Thomas Mann's *Doctor Faustus* to *Civilization: Phaze III*, something uncanny happens around the semiotic materials manipulated by Zappa. The gross material suddenly speaks new, unheard concepts, the sedimented content breaks the tight taut

membrane of the fact/value dichotomy, and monsters walk the soft earth of your mind. Because Peter Frampton isn't just wearing 'chiffon in a wrist array'—he's got letters sewn there! [see Frampton sleeve close-ups (Figs. 14-16)]

Here's an 'F'. Well, Frampton's name begins with an 'F', it's possible...

But look here, there's an 'R'! I admit this is far-fetched letter, but 'R' is always 'R'-fetched, since it stands for Rover the Dog (the retriever, the *Pudel*), or maybe 'raver', which is what I am now, probably ... unless everyone in the Theatro Technis auditorium agrees with my diabolical vision/projection, and my irrational 'sin' is subsumed under a virtuous archetype by the Internationale of ICE-Z delegates. I must inform you that this particular feature was revealed to me after seven bottles of beer at Didier's *maison de famille* in the *dixième arrondisse-*

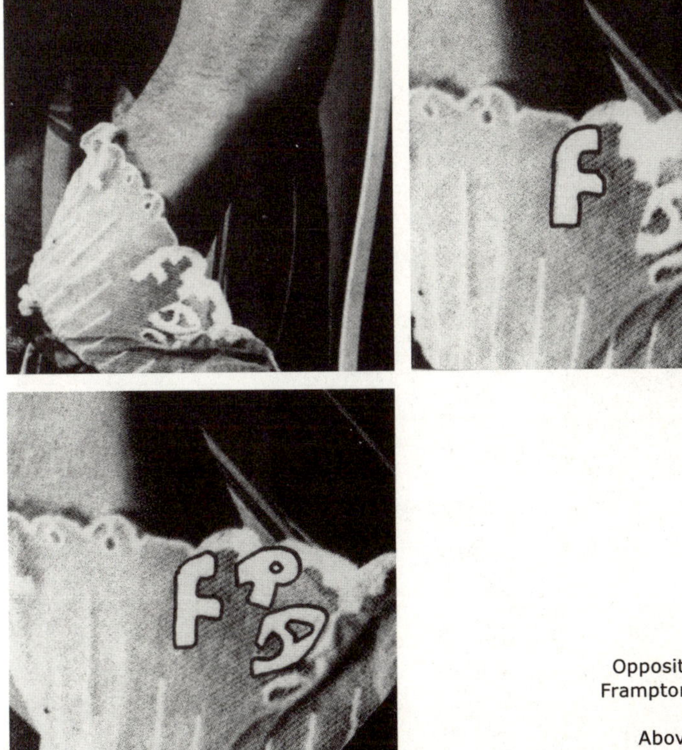

Opposite: Fig. 13:
Frampton 7" sleeve

Above and left:
Figs. 14-16: Frampton sleeve close-ups

ment of Paris in 1998, beneath the twinkling fairy lights on the Mervelet Christmas tree, and the flickering of Stan Brakhage wondermeat on the video. All of which was most conducive to poetical visioning. But wait, we've got an 'F' and an 'R'—what's this, an 'A'! Put them all together and you get ...

'F R A', or 'arf' backwards! Whether in the actually-existing (or 'alienated') world 'F R A' goes on to spell 'FRAMPTON' or 'FRANK ZAPPA' is a fact that's not yet been ascertained. We'd need to find Frampton's *costumier* and ask her.

With Zappa, the bizarre coincidences never stop. To finish, here's a recent one. This one was triggered by a record lent to me by a Somers Town neighbour called Ray Kane (well, actually, Ray lives on the *other* side of Crowndale Road, but let's not be pedantic). Hailing from Liv-

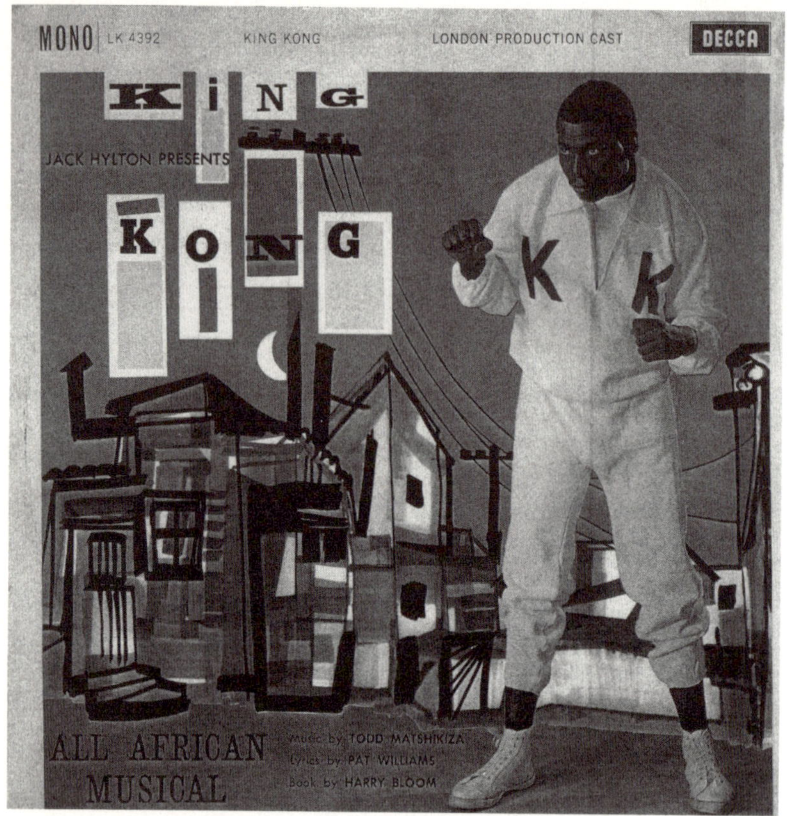

Fig. 17: Cover of *King Kong*

erpool and growing up contemporaneously with the Beatles, Ray has had brushes with the music business—tour managing for local bands in the mid-60s, working his way up to association with Robert Stigwood, and doing promotional work for Flo & Eddie in the early-70s. Ray was also involved in the pub rock/punk rock explosion of the late-70s, working for the Ace and Chiswick labels. I was interested in the way Ray's involvement with the music industry peaked when things were real and rocking and relatively uncapitalised, and troughed in the years of plastic stars and corporate hegemony. So I invited in Ray as a guest on my radio programme on Resonance 104.4FM, *Late Lunch With Out To Lunch.*[4] Ray brought in some records to play, including one whose cover caught my attention immediately.[5] [see Fig. 17]

King Kong was a musical which opened at the Princes Theatre, London, on 23 February 1961, after having taking South Africa by storm. The 'Jack Hylton presents' on the cover seems to have been added as some assurance of quality entertainment, as the music was by Todd Matshikiza and musical direction by Stanley Glaser. The sleeve carried this message on the back:

> No theatrical venture in South Africa has had the sensational success of King Kong. This musical, capturing the life, colour and effervescence—as well as the poignancy and sadness—of township life, has come as a revelation to many South Africans that art does not recognise racial barriers.

Most of the songs are actually dated sub-Sondheim, but "Gumboot Dance" allows in some pretty infectious rhythms, recognizable as authentic from the work of South African exiles in London like Chris McGregor, Dudu Pukwana and Louis Moholo, and brought into early-80s punk clubs by Neneh Cherry, Gareth Sagar, Mark Springer, Sean Oliver and Bruce Smith as Rip Rig & Panic.

Unlike Zappa's tune of that name, "King Kong" did not refer to Edgar Wallace's giant ape, but to Ezekiel Dhlamini, a Zulu boxer who became a folk hero for his disrespect of authority (though he apparently derived his name "King Kong" from a poster for the film based on Wallace's novel). Dhlamini's meteoric rise to the top of South African boxing dwindled into lost bouts, drunkenness, off-ring violence and murder. He knifed his girlfriend when she arrived in a club surrounded by rival gangsters. He asked for the death sentence, but got 14 years hard labour—and drowned himself in March 1957 at the age of 32. A perfect story for the first township musical.

King Kong's proto-hiphop tale of triumph and tragedy casts an intriguing light on the title of the tune "King Kong", Zappa's "Caravan" for spotlighting the soloistic virtues of his various bands. On stage, Zappa once explained the story of "King Kong" as 'there was a giant ape who lived in the jungle in Africa—some Americans decided they could make some money by bringing him to this country, then they killed him'.

Decor and costumes for the *King Kong* musical were by Arthur Goldreich, who also designed the LP cover. Goldreich was a leading architect and visual designer in Johannesburg, a Jewish Communist who was arrested by the apartheid regime in one of the clampdowns in the early-60s. It was Zappologist Jonathan Jones who pointed out that Frank Zappa's *oeuvre* creates a 'paranoid listener'. Goldreich's cover supplies one of those bizarre 'coincidences' which make Zappa's 'paranoid listeners' prick up their ears, take a deep breath and check their historical-materialist sanity.

In 1967, repelled by the mess Verve's design department had made of his text and photographs with *Freak Out!*, and applying the skills he'd learned doing graphic design for a greetings card manufacturer, Zappa constructed his own cover for *Absolutely Free*. The way he chose to depict a typical Los Angeles high street is uncannily like Goldreich's cover for *King Kong*: loose washes of banded bright colour pinned down by bold strokes of black ink, paying particular attention to the skyline of an insalubrious urban neighbourhood (tin chimneys with conical hats to keep out the rain, telegraph poles and telegraph lines, cramped, higgled-piggledy housing, barred windows). [see Fig. 18]

It's as if Zappa is bringing out all the political and social implications of Goldreich's design, a kind of Tourette's Syndrome avalanche of modern urban horrors. Where Goldreich had a barred door and window, Zappa has a 'Jenny Birch Police Center', implying incarceration and corporal punishment (note the black face peering out of one of the barred windows). Using Lettraset and a Rotring pen, Zappa names today's mechanisms of social control and humiliation: religion, TV, liquor, hard sell. A stream of helicopters on the right reference the key weapon used by the US establishment against both the Vietcong and protesting students. Just like on the record ("Uncle Bernie's Farm"), Zappa draws connections between commerce and militarism: 'War means work for all'; 'Buy America: move your goods with patriotic sell'. A high street choked with aggressive, bumping traffic illustrates the Sacred Cow of the post-war capitalist economy: the private car, with its pollution of the atmosphere, danger to low-income pedestrians, encouragement of Fast Food (the meal you can eat in a car: 'chicken delete'), and wars for oil.

The voice of reason might explain the 'coincidence' between these two designs as perhaps a common commercial style, derived from a handbook or even a box of inks-with-instructions. However, Gold-

Fig. 18: *Absolutely Free*

reich was a prestigious artist and designer: would he have adopted an off-the-peg style for the cover of a politically-momentous musical like *King Kong*? As usual with Zappa, we're left unassured that 'he knows what he doth' (to quote Rance Muhammitz in *200 Motels*).

However, to picture Los Angeles like apartheid Johannesburg—whether or not by design—makes a powerful political point (and one also made by Philip K. Dick): if you're black in America, it might not be so crazy to believe that you're actually living under apartheid. Like György Lukács, who admitted after being investigated and harassed by the KGB that Franz Kafka's writings were more 'realist' than he'd thought, maybe Zappa's 'paranoid listener' is just seeing things as they actually are. It hurts that Frank's not still alive, because whether or not he saw Arthur Goldreich's cover in the early 60s, I think he'd have found the correspondence fascinating.[6]

1. Mircea Eliade, *Le Mythe de l'éternel retour: archétypes et répétition*, Paris: Gallimard, 1949; translated Willard R. Trask as *The Myth of the Eternal Return or, Cosmos and History*, 1959; Princeton: PUP, 1991, p. 75.
2. A reference to Evil Dick & the Band Members, of course—see <*www.polemicmusic.com*>.
3. This is actually a fraudulently re-enacted situation created by with one of those little 'scan-it-yourself' devices ... the night before, the arrival of Marco Maurizi and Jürgen Gispert

and Les Fils from abroad had so twanged his tiny brain Lunch FORGOT to load the jay-pegs onto Esther's laptop ... but you get to see 'em here anyway ... *yummy yummy yum yum.*

4. Every Wednesday at 2.00pm on Resonance 104.4 FM—if you live in London, tune in, if not try <*www.resonancefm.com*> on Wednesdays 14.00 GMT.
5. A colour scan of this cover may be found on <*www.militantesthetix.co.uk*>.
6. Ben Watson's paper didn't actually have the treatment of *King Kong* (inevitable insertionism strikes again), but instead ended with the words: 'I've kept this short. As Jacques Derrida might put it, "I've already written too much about (*différ*)Rance Muhammitz". Since Zappa relentlessly emphasized the cusp between personal events or eccentricities—in short, socially unredeemable acts of sin—and public display in its most heated and blatant kind, I'm going to stop attempting to shovel Zappa into a system, and let other people have their say. Zappa's *oeuvre* is, after all, a tissue of oral, unbookish culture, and everyone should sneeze in it. May the Poodle bless you all! At about 12:30 or so, we should stop the discussion and form an International Esemplastic Zappological phalanx on the street outside—solemn and turgid, although slightly historically inaccurate—in order to bear the Data Projector back to the Working Men's College on Crowndale Road, where, if we can find the Mystery Door, Brazilian lunch awaits...'

"Watermelon In Easter Hay" The Function of the Reverb Unit & the Poverty of the Individual Spirit

T.H.F. Drenching

Disclaimer

Although "Watermelon In Easter Hay" is part of a narrative, and fulfils a program-music function within Joe's Garage*, I want to leave that largely to one side because it impedes us approaching the music concretely. That is, it diverts our attention from the actual effect of the music on the listener into vulgar Zappology; where the specifics of music are too easily abandoned in favour of mere concepts.*

Zappa's attempts to interrupt the smooth flow of musical illusion, his *Verfremdungstechnik*, has been dealt with at length elsewhere. What have been less discussed are the relatively rare moments when he enlists the forces of illusion, when he mobilises emotional rapture. The embattled emotional core of "Watermelon In Easter Hay" has done much to enshrine it as the revelation of 'Zappa the Man', pure and unspoiled by the astringent intellect of 'Zappa the iconoclast'. When *The Late Show* (BBC2) produced a special on Zappa, near the end of his life, the closing images of Zappa, heavily-drugged, struggling to navigate from a standing to a sitting position due to the advanced stage of prostate cancer, were overlaid with the opening measures of "Watermelon In Easter Hay". Already, to the hypocritical glee of the establishment, the 'cynicism' and 'crass smut' of Zappa's *oeuvre* were suffering a conversion. Heartless iconoclasm was reinterpreted, under the pressure of mortality, as one man's search for the expressive sublime.

As was to be expected, this trend reached its peak in the immediate aftermath of Zappa's death. The Zappa Family Trust, along with registering a trademark of his moustache, released a CD called *Frank Zappa Plays the Music of Frank Zappa*. The release compiled various renditions of Zappa's 'signature songs'. These tracks were "Zoot Allures", "Black Napkins", a hitherto unreleased blues and two versions of "Watermelon In Easter Hay". Dweezil Zappa stated in the sleeve notes that "Watermelon In Easter Hay" was 'the best solo Zappa ever played', adding that the quality of the tune results from Zappa's unique 'tone and personality'.[1]

An earlier report from Ben Watson that Dweezil had claimed these tunes as representative of Zappa's 'soul', proved to be exaggerated (as is so often the case), but the philosophical implications are the same.[2] In the place of the soul we find the secular bourgeois equivalent: the free-floating, self-contained personality. Like all hard business-people, the Zappa Family Trust is profoundly sentimental. As usual, the belief in private initiative runs in natural tandem with an isolated and heartfelt individualism.

In *The Jargon Of Authenticity*, Adorno spoke of Hegel's undialectical inheritors who

> cleanse inwardness of that element which contains its truth, by eliminating self-reflection, in which the ego becomes transparent as

> a piece of the world. Instead the ego posits itself as higher than the world and becomes subjected to the world precisely because of this.[3]

Dweezil's remarks present an identical paradox wherein the greatest piece of music Zappa ever recorded is the piece where he sounds least like himself. Dweezil's reading of "Watermelon In Easter Hay" is a classic piece of transcendent idealism. As the great personality is purified and concentrated through the magical prism of self-expression, the extraneous jokes and contradictions are burnt off like slag, leaving just the Man under the stars.

This transcendental schema is engraved into the musical language itself, as the opening guitar note sounds in a medium-high register and then soars like the soul from the body towards unfathomed heights. The opening phrase comes to rest and the concluding note is held in suspension, the mortal fingers straining to maintain the spirit's vibration. As the note fades the fingers allow the tightened string to relax back into silence. After the second repeat of the phrase, the guitar offers a parenthetical comment, of the kind at which David Gilmour excels, ending with two trembling *glissandi*.[4] The blissful mumble on the death-bed as the perishable body returns to eternity; this is the unbearable pathos which accompanies the extinction of the unique personality.

But what seems to have escaped Dweezil's notice, and the notice of many other Zappa experts, is that this 'soul-searching', far from concentrating the elements of which Zappa's music is made, does the reverse, it dissolves them. This is precisely because, stripped of its materialism, its 'transparency as part of the world', Zappa's music no longer possesses any power. The music 'becomes subjected to the world', that is, it becomes subjected to the conventions of heroic rock guitar-playing.

This is a dynamic peculiar to "Watermelon In Easter Hay". Whilst there are other equally emotional guitar outings in Zappa's catalogue, none has the stupefying aridity of "Watermelon". Consequently, no other tracks have been so effective at drawing the praise of those who desire to neuter Zappa's consistently embarrassing refusal to play by the rules of bourgeois art.

For the purposes of comparison it is instructive to consider "Stucco Homes" from *Return of the Son of Shut Up 'N Play Yer Guitar* (1981).

Although certainly emotive, spacious and 'progressive' in the '70s sense, "Stucco Homes" nevertheless manages to maintain a dialectic between the speculative harmonic shifts of the two guitars and Vinnie Colaiuta's drums. Colaiuta's playing is a tough negotiation between the discipline of the bar and the freedom of movement which implies its negation. As such the drum-part alone appears as an almost unsustainable balancing-act. Although superficially a 'free-floating' guitar showcase, the actual musical effect is one of tension, as the listener attempts to follow the divergences and correlations between the musicians' lines of thought.

It is in vain that we search for comparable engagement in "Watermelon In Easter Hay". It is precisely stupefaction which it engenders. It is a replica of emotional rapture which attempts to quarantine the intellect, and its characteristic negative role, in favour of dissolving the listener in sentimental solidarity with a perceived individual expressive subject.

But since it is nothing more than a replica, the promised dissolution of the listener's ego realises itself as the opposite: he is confronted by a formalised internality where his identification with this stupid and partial sublime merely confirms his isolation. As Adorno says:

> inwardness becomes a value and a possession behind which it entrenches itself; and it is surreptitiously overcome by reification.[5]

Speaking on Radio 1, Zappa revealed the 'real title' of the song as 'Trying to play a guitar solo in this band is like trying to grow a watermelon in Easter hay'.[6] Equally when freedom becomes the private property of the isolated individual, artistic production is like trying to grow authentic expression in a desert of freeze-dried abstractions.

The surrounding music itself forges a fully-furnished replica of eternity, cycling between two arpeggiated chords, the drums booming and dream-like under swathes of reverb and delay; a serviceable illusion of endless space. Colaiuta is reduced to Nick Mason by the oppressive pseudo-import of the production.[7] No speculative thought is allowed to disrupt the eternal cycle. It is a schema which tries to do away with time. In so doing it also attempts preclude the possibility of material analysis.

An early prototype of "Watermelon in Easter Hay", recorded live in 1978, was included on *Frank Zappa Plays the Music of Frank Zappa*.[8]

Shorn of reverb and the isolation of studio conditions the piece sounds, if anything, less immediate. The guitar stands in sharp relief to the rest of the music which rings with emaciated purity. Zappa seems to be struggling to plot a route through this juiceless setting. The effect is like that of a diner furiously peppering a slice of white bread. Zappa's blue-notes sound curiously misplaced, the band seem helpless to intervene in the stand-off. The whole experience, though it manages to retain its celebrated poignancy, is utterly different to the experience of the finished album track. Free of the domination of reverb, the fabric of the music comes apart. The cracks in the cardboard sublime are revealed, the façade of expression falls away from eternity and we see, as Zappa said elsewhere, 'the brick wall at the back of the theatre'.[9]

Faced with this document, it becomes clear to what extent "Watermelon" owes its powerful narcotic effect to studio production. Zappa always insisted on a professional approach to production and employed a whole barrage of effects to this end, even when, as on *You Are What You Is*, it results in a stifling flatness.[10] This professionalism draws fire from punks as well as original Mothers fans, but has the merit of eschewing the frequent fetishisation of the 'authenticity' attributed to poor audio quality.

However, "Watermelon" is unusual from the point of view of its production. Firstly because it refuses the rupture of Zappa's *musique concrète*, or the openly parodic polystyrene-gloss of *Sheik Yerbouti*, but more importantly because it uses unconventional amounts of reverb for very conventional ends.

The use of reverb in "Watermelon" corresponds illuminatingly with the history of the reverb unit itself. The company Sound Enhancements include, on their website, a blurb describing its invention:

> When Laurens Hammond introduced the first Hammond Organ in 1935, most people were only familiar with the traditional pipe organs they had heard at churches and theaters. So, when they purchased a Hammond for their homes, they expected the same room-filling sound they had come to know and love. Of course, in their thickly carpeted living rooms with low ceilings and drapery covered windows, they didn't get it.[11]

The reality of physical sound refused to underwrite the ideological

Fig. 20: Easter Grass

prejudices of the consumer. Searching for a solution to this abomination, Laurens Hammond then approached Bell Laboratories, who had stumbled across spring reverberation whilst developing long-distance telecommunications technology. From 1939 onward consumers were treated to the latest in artificial audio-grandeur.

There is a hint of mocking condescension in the anonymous blurb-writer's depiction of '30s American domesticity, which characterises the commercial expert's contempt for the craven consumer. Beneath the marketing gloss is a little satirical sketch: a picture of the petit bourgeois who revels in the sonic grandeur of the church organ or the opera-house and seeks to purchase his own little slice of the expansive sublime. Once outside of the power structure of the church or the spectacle of the theatre, in his dingy home, he finds he has been cheated out of his share of universal exultation and must make do with his impoverished replica-transcendence.

In "Watermelon" reverb is returned to its original function as an artificial means to disguise the domestic as the sublime. An analogous phenomena is included in the title itself: Easter hay, an American trade-name for the plastic mock-straw in which Easter eggs are packed, is itself another artificial means of replicating a romantic ideal[12] (although the example I'm illustrating this with, brought back from Baltimore by Dr Esther, is named Easter Grass). In this case the rustic homeliness by which the alienated consumer attempts to transport himself back to the craft era—by buying bags of shredded plastic.

In a 1999 interview, Steve Vai spoke of the track in hushed tones, employing some terminology which revealed that reverb and bourgeois individualism are close linguistic bedfellows:

> Frank textured that song with guitar tones and endless sustain ... On "Watermelon", there's such a beautiful, clean, bell-like tone. That song just invites you in. I don't think people understood the depth of Frank's experimentation with guitar tone. It's one of Frank's signature songs.

The interviewer comments:

> He ranks "Watermelon" alongside "Zoot Allures" and "Black Napkins" as prime examples of Zappa's depth as a guitarist.[13]

The extent to which Vai has internalised the Zappa Family Trust's party-line is a salutary lesson for anyone who believes that expert musicological knowledge alone is sufficient to understand Modern Art. The phrase 'signature song', which Vai borrows from Dweezil, appropriates the language of the legal contract. It is a telling turn of phrase as the signature compresses the individual's social power into a squiggle on a cheque, a Texan death warrant, or an autograph-hunter's pad. Vai's 'endless sustain' plays on the properties of the immortal soul, the unending movement only possible in a gravity-free zone. Most conspicuously of all, 'depth' is the premier compliment in bourgeois art criticism. The humanity that the ruling class so brutally deny to their subjects in the economic and political sphere is permanently quarantined in the aesthetic, where it is revived as a specious, privately-owned sublime insulated from the vulgar herd.

This individualism and its accompanying rapture is not without its more sinister precedents. Dweezil's sleevenotes again:

> Without words Frank was able to communicate his ideas, emotions and his personality to international audiences.

Wherever there is talk of the heroic, unitary individual, there is its counterpart: the hypnotised and adoring throng. In his book *The Mass Psychology of Fascism*, the Freudian-Marxist Wilhelm Reich spoke of the rise of Hitler and of the 'reactionary historians' who believe that:

> A great man makes history only inasmuch as he inflames the masses with 'his idea'.[14]

Reich goes on to unpick the irrationality of Nazi theory, explaining the way in which the energy held in stasis by sexual repression can be mobilized by reaction. He emphasises that the Nazis gained power, not by rational political argument, but by harnessing the irrational desires of the German people.

Likewise, in "Watermelon" the distinctive musical argument of Zappa's usual soloing unravels, the listener finds himself, in Vai's words, 'invited in', rather than smashed against Zappa's usual contradictions. However, once inside, the listener is caught in an hermetically-sealed environment, where communication is replaced by mystification. That even informed listeners frequently appear unable to recognise the

0 71765 05001 2
STEPS TO MAKE
BEAUTIFUL
EASTER BASKETS
1. GATHER BASKET, GRASS, EGGSVILLE® OR BARTHOLOMEW B'S® SNAP TOGETHER PLASTIC EASTER EGGS, CANDY, ROLL OF DECCOFILM AND TWIST TIE BOW.
EASTER GRASS
DECCOFILM
2. PLACE CANDIES INTO SNAP TOGETHER EGGS, AND/OR MAKE SMALL PACKAGES OF CANDY WITH DECCOFILM.
3. FLUFF UP EASTER GRA USE
DIFFERENT COLORS TO MAKE MORE
COLORFUL) AND PUT IN BASKET.

4. PLACE LARGE
CHOCOLATE OR (USUAL
CENTER AND SECU UNNY)
WITH TAPE HAN
5. PLACE SMALL PACKAGES OF CANDIES AND SNAP TOGETHER EASTER EGGS AROUND INSIDE EDGE OF BASKET.
6. OVERWRAP WHOLE BASKET IN DECCOFILM, AND WHILE GATHERED TOGETHER AT TOP, SECURE WITH A TWIST TIE BOW.
EASY & SIMPLE!
YOU HAVE A WONDERFUL
GIFT FOR SOMEONE'S
HAPPY EASTER

Figs. 21 and 22: Instructions #1 and #2

difference attests both to the totalitarian irrationality of commodity culture and the attendant sickness of consciousness under Capitalism.

Zappa once remarked to Dan Forte that the 'sabotage' which ruins his music for the casual listener is the 'real information'.[15] Amidst the consistent interruption, the splatter and outrage of Zappa's *oeuvre*, these rare moments of high-flown conventional beauty are the most pernicious sabotage of all.

1. Since I don't own a copy of this album, this information was given to me over the phone by Simon Prentis. Thanks to Simon for this telephonic service.
2. Watson's claim can be found on p. 103 of *The Complete Guide To The Music Of Frank Zappa*, London: Omnibus Press, 1998. Well below the high standard of academic scholarship we have come to expect from this meticulous author. [Yo! And fuck you too, Drenching!! *The Complete Guide* doesn't say the 'soul' quote emanated from Dweezil, but from the Zappa Family Trust. If I archived Trust material as scrupulously as I did FZ's, I'd be able to quote you chapter and verse on this one too. If anyone could track down this 'soul' reference, something I think Gail said in an interview or press release about the tunes on the CD, and sent it to me c/o SAF, I'd be most grateful. *BW*]
3. Theodor Adorno, *The Jargon Of Authenticity*, 1964; translated Knut Tarnowski and Frederic Will, London: Routledge, 2003, pp. 59-60.
4. See, for example, Gilmour's scene-setting doodles which preface the main body of "Shine On You Crazy Diamond" on Pink Floyd's *Wish You Were Here* (1975). The track was inspired by Syd Barratt's drug-induced isolation and so qualifies as another overwrought guitar show-case which duplicates the alienation it purports to mourn.
5. Theodor Adorno, *Op. Cit.*, p. 59.
6. Frank Zappa speaking on Radio 1 quoted at <*www.arf.ru*>.
7. Witness any number of Mason's appearances. Notably *Atom Heart Mother* where his extremely unimaginative fills are out of time, and the video *The Delicate Sound Of Thunder*, where a sweaty, dynamic percussionist is drafted in to handle the fast stuff, whilst our Nick plods away like Jabba the Hut. [Jesus! I had no idea you were so informed about The Floyd, Drenching ... *Ed.*].
8. See footnote 1. Likewise, Simon Prentis played me the live version of "Watermelon In Easter Hay" over the 'phone. Which, given that the album costs £27, was considerably cheaper.
9. Quoted in Ben Watson, *Frank Zappa: The Negative Dialectics of Poodle Play*, London: Quartet, 1994, p. 217.
10. The flatness of the production on *You Are What You Is* was pointed out to me by Nathan 'Nes.Co.' Blunt, who bemoaned the lack of sonic shocks in its evenly-mixed palette. He contrasted it to the exhilarating entry of Captain Beefheart's harmonica or musette (I haven't decided) on "Tarotplane" from the album *Mirror Man*.
11. Unattributed blurb-writer <*www.accutronicsreverb.com/history.htm*>.
12. Many thanks to Andrea Brady for this information.
13. Steve Vai quoted at <*www.cht.qc.ca/cht/zappa4.htm*>.
14. Wilhelm Reich, *The Mass Psychology Of Fascism*, 1933; translated Vincent R. Carfagno, London: Pelican, 1978, p. 68.
15. Quoted in Ben Watson, *Op. Cit.*, p. 387.

Bogus Pomp and Bourdieu's Paradox: Zappa and Resentment

Paul Sutton

In light of what I'll be saying later about Zappa's aggressive defensiveness concerning 'high art' status I should, perhaps, begin by warning that this cheesy little home-made paper was prepared for the amusement of people who already enjoy Zappa Music. It is not for intellectuals or other dead people.[1] Surprisingly, I seem to be the only speaker today to mention the 'p' word. For the purposes of this paper, I shall define postmodernism as that strand in contemporary thought which, in the name of subjectivities allegedly trampled upon by the grand narratives of art and politics, repudiates ambition and judgment in favour of an easygoing cultural relativism and a celebration and defence of hitherto beleaguered identities. Identity politics, which began as a salutary corrective to the blinkered workerism of the Old Left, had, by the 1980s, become a substitute for, rather than a supplement to, a genuinely radical politics. Indeed, it had become a political variant of, and adjunct to, market research. In the context of British Cultural Studies, it means an emphasis on consumption at the expense of production so that, while attention to artistic substance is often perfunctory, purchasing a pair of 'Mod A Go-Go stretch-elastic pants'[2] is celebrated as a creative act of resistance and self-formation, rather than deplored as a capitulation to market-induced self-loathing. Consumer choice is not to be impugned, except perhaps by egregious reactionaries such as Roger Scruton who pop up periodically as if to remind us of our good fortune in having Jonathan Ross. It is at this point that Zappa presents himself as a figure uniquely qualified not to negotiate between these two extremes, but to short-circuit the entire sterile debate. However, before discussing Zappa, I shall deal with the work of the French sociologist Pierre Bourdieu.

It might be wondered why I'm interested in Bourdieu when British intellectuals, particularly those affiliated with the Birmingham Centre for Contemporary Cultural Studies, deal more directly with popular culture and are more explicitly populist in their approach. However, while the latter evince the postmodernist disdain for the overarching and monumental, Bourdieu's thought is remarkable for its coherence, rigour and ambition. While this lays him open to the charge of scientism, we are at least spared the spectacle of the affluent, intellectual and middle-aged sentimentalising the lives and consumer choices of the poor, uneducated and young (Dick Hebdige, for example, is often no more than Pete Townshend with footnotes, as we shall see below). Moreover, while the story of the Birmingham School is one of a managed withdrawal from socialist positions, Bourdieu's commitment to social transformation was lifelong. I come, then, not to bury Bourdieu but to show how postmodernism and Zappa can be mutually illuminating. This is not an attempt to recuperate Zappa for postmodernism; I want, rather, to show how such pertinence as postmodernism possesses is both exemplified and transcended in his work.

For Bourdieu, culture is a field of struggle in which agents (producers, consumers and distributors) occupying varying socially determined positions seek to advantageously realise the cultural capital entailed by those positions in the form of symbolic capital. Bourdieu's depiction of this field is both subtle and dynamic and he is extremely attentive to the complex strategic problems faced by agents. His account of the evolution and character of the institutions of art is such as to commend it to any properly materialist criticism.[3] However, this cogent rendering of social praxis is bought at the expense of serious discussion of the artworks as artworks. As Adorno observed, 'for the truth content of art Cultural Studies substitutes its social function and its conditioning by interests, while refraining from a critique of that content itself'.[4] This elision of the aesthetic is also to be found in his account of cultural capital. This consists of educational or acquired capital and inherited capital. Without educational capital, which includes such aptitudes as literacy, score reading, instrumental technique *etc.*, cultural activity is scarcely possible. Nevertheless, Bourdieu regards inherited capital as prior, for it invariably entails the other. So what is inherited capital? It is *sprezzatura*, insouciance, taste, the ability to wear wealth and learning lightly, a concept of gentility which has remained remarkably constant since Castiglione formulated it in the sixteenth century. It is, in a word, class, or, rather, the veil worn by that vulgar social-scientific entity in polite society. It is Sergeant Wilson in *Dad's Army*, while an example of a bearer of acquired capital might be the kind of odious autodidact found in the novels of the Bloomsbury Group.

Such a character is a victim of Bourdieu's paradox.

If, in order to resist, I have no other resources than to lay claim to that in the name of which I am dominated, is this resistance? Second question: when, on the other hand, the dominated work at destroying what marks them out as 'vulgar' and at appropriating that in relation to which they appear as vulgar... is this submission? I think this is an insoluble contradiction. This contradiction, which is inscribed in the logic of symbolic domination, is something those who talk about 'popular culture' won't admit.[5]

Whether to feast upon and celebrate the paltry pabulum of pop, in the manner of British Cultural Studies, or to fall too gratefully upon the rich banquet of bourgeois art, that alibi and congealment of domination, is surely to endorse, rather than to question, the current distribution of resources. All cultural products, including even Elvis

Costello string quartets, bear the scars of domination (Bourdieu's preferred, non-Marxist, term for class struggle): the paradox admits only of a political solution. However, this is not to say that there is no advantage to be derived from a provocative, insightful and obsessive staging of this paradox.

Bourdieu began his career with an ethnographic study of Algerian peasants. Zappa was to turn a similarly scientific eye on rock musicians, roadies and groupies. While contemporaries such as the Beatles vouchsafed their fans a glimpse of the Wisdom of the East, Zappa preferred to document, in *audio verité* style, what his musicians were really interested in—paid gigs, beer and 'groupie action'. The existential drama of the Doors was eschewed in favour of songs which addressed, in overtly contrived manner, issues of genuine concern to adolescents—borrowing Pop's convertible, losing status at high school and the indignity of having a fat girlfriend. He was no more respectful of the world of classical music, which he regarded as accommodating the entertainment needs of deceased kings and popes.[6]

> Flute players look to me like they have a bad attitude because of all that *cloud and angel music* they have to play. French horn players are arrogant too—they have to play all the shit that sounds like graduation[7]

Saloon bar bigotry or a characteristically pungent account of the way in which sedimented traces of royal and ecclesiastical power leave their mark on performer psychology and adolescent rites of passage alike?

So far, I have discussed the way in which anthropology directly, and with full consciousness on the artist's part, impinges on Zappa's work. Set aside Zappa's habitual grotesqueries, and it is surprising how little translation is involved in this process. The mad scientist is a persistent trope in Zappa's work and, as *The Real Frank Zappa Book* shows, the composer had been an enthusiastic materialist and experimentalist since childhood.

> Just give some *stuff,* and I'll organize it for you. That's what I do.[8]

However, Zappa is no reductionist (although he may very well be a vulgar caricaturist), for his social scientific concepts are given sensuous embodiment. 'Information is not knowledge, knowledge is not wisdom, wisdom is not beauty', says the girl on the bus, thereby affirming Kant's cognitive trinity, if not its hierarchy. Bourdieu, on the other hand, signals in the very title of his *Distinction: A Social Critique of the Judgement of Taste* his intention to strip the subject of Kant's third critique of its cognitive status. It is tempting to surmise that, in order to secure maximum realisation of symbolic capital, Bourdieu has to depress the market value of aesthetics. Zappa sublates what is valuable in Bourdieu by means which I term Bogus Pomp and the Phenomenology of Zappaphilia.

What is Bogus Pomp? 'Arrogantly twisting the sterile canvas snoot of a fully-charged icing anointment utensil, he poots forth a quarter-ounce green rosette ...' evinces, with its mincing but menacing meticulousness, the subaltern grandiloquence which has been particularly noted of Black and Irish verbal culture.[9] Zappa seems to have believed that any claim to literary attention his work possessed resided in the 'snide political stuff', but it is in lines such as these that the essence of Zappa's poetry is to be found. Piquant connotations of power, tweezers, sexual dysfunction and religious unction are more than sufficient to goad the alert listener, but such language is remarkable, above all, for its congruence with Zappa's musical language, particularly in his 'serious' pieces. When drawing upon the classical tradition, Zappa is inordinately fond of such toadying forms as the march and fanfare, to which he characteristically gives preposterous and thrasonical twists. Melodies are, typically, extraordinarily long and elaborate, while his orchestrations favour parping brass, buffoonish bassoons and, even in the 'purer' orchestral and electronic pieces, that most lumpen of instruments, the drumkit. On the other hand, that most consecrated of the sections of the orchestra, and the principle bearer of musical logic for most of 'classical' music's history, the strings, does not particularly interest Zappa. Together, his choice of instrumentation and of forms bespeaks an attention to 'art' music's servile and martial origins rather than to its autonomous and 'profound' maturity.

Nevertheless, there is more to such Bogus Pomp than just cocking a snook at the bewigged and liveried provenance of posh pastimes. Zappa was fond of comparing his work with that of the sculptor, Alexander Calder. He describes a Calder mobile thus

> *A large mass of <u>any material</u> will 'balance' a smaller, denser mass of <u>any material</u>, according to the length of the gizmo it's dangling on, and the 'balance point' chosen to facilitate the danglement.*[10]

A geometer's conception of music worthy of Edgard Varèse, were it not for such characteristic Zappa-isms as 'gizmo' and 'danglement' (at a conference of Zappology it's scarcely necessary to commend 'danglement' to the listener's attention). However, construction is not Zappa's only metaphor for artistic creation. Much of his music, after all, was produced in the Utility Muffin Research Kitchen, where things are not so much constructed as pooted forth (rather like the canvasses which the situationist Giuseppe Pinot-Gallizio produced by the yard). The poodle implied by 'poot' and the poetic diction of 'forth' both exemplify Bogus Pomp, but pooting forth is yet more significant as a truly dialectical concept. In its suggestions of defecation, adornment and industrial extrusion it exemplifies the history of alienation. Humanity exchanges with nature, transforms itself and transforms nature.[11]

Having given an account of the Project/Object's prevalent aroma, I shall now consider its effect on the subject, or the Phenomenology of Zappaphilia. Who listens to Zappa and what does it do to them? The Mothers of Invention began as a bar band, and Zappa's music was to retain that spirit of working man's entertainment. Songs such as "Trouble Everyday" and "Cocaine Decisions" are typical in their expression of underclass resentment, while Zappa's conspicuous instrumental and compositional skills (there are lots of fiddly bits) resonate with the artisanal fantasies of the wage labourer. In practical terms, so entranced are male adolescent rock consumers with Zappa's toilet humour, such fantasies are financed by the pocket money of Beavis and Butthead. The implied listener, then, might be expected to feel the force of Bourdieu's paradox particularly acutely. However, what Bourdieu, in his zeal to honour the subject and demean the aesthetic object, fails to allow is that the subject might realise itself through the object.

Zappologist Jonathan Jones has written of Zappa's music creating a paranoid listener.[12] I want to talk about it creating an *annoyed listener.* Rock critics such as Greil Marcus and Lester Bangs dislike Zappa's cynical take on rock and suspect his treacherous classical aspirations; bourgeois moralists condemn his documentation of contemporary *mores* as sexist and racist; admirers of jazz and classical music are irked by the knob gags; and art purists resile at the ostentatious opulence of his production. These are not just issues for occasional listeners. Indeed, they structure the long term responses of the hardcore fan too. Even after such individuals have learned to thrill at the merest glimpse of a poodle, the initial resistance is, in Hegelian fashion, both cancelled and preserved as a moment of apprehension with each listening. Zappa's music is so irritating, yet so evidently accomplished and original, that the listener's aesthetic categories are called into question. This might best be clarified by way of a comparison of Zappa's work with that of Pete Townshend.

Both Zappa and Townshend document pop culture and both combine Afro-American music with European music (in Zappa's case, Varèse and Stravinsky, and in Townshend's, Gilbert and Sullivan). Townshend was famously a celebrant of the Mod lifestyle, a subject which cultural studies academics have also found particularly congenial. The elaborate consumer choices of inarticulate youth provide rich pickings for semiotically-minded sociologist and wouldbe rock statesman alike. That pop is, as Matt Worley writes, 'the last gasp before the day job grabs you [...], an inevitable failure, a second of brilliance and a lifetime of grey [...] disappointment in multiple'[13], is, for Townshend and Hebdige, an occasion, not for a rethink of their uncritical valorisation of popular pleasure, but for pathos. It is their very emphasis on culture as a social rather than a cognitive activity which blinds them to the only social effectivity their beloved pop might have.

With Zappa, pathos is precluded by his never having had any illusions in the first place, but also by his systematically denying the mystical closure sought by Townshend. The latter writes pithy, exciting and climactic songs celebrating, and speaking for, those who, inspired by pithy, exciting and climactic songs, seek, with often tragic consequences, to lead pithy, exciting and climactic lives. Zappa is not a purveyor of quanta of adolescent adrenaline. Modular construction, doo-wop derived polyphony, segues and estranging contexts militate against both identity affirmation and unreflective immediacy. To be sure, the music is frequently visceral, but rarely immediate. "My Guitar Wants to Kill Your Mama", for example, is destabilised as a rock song by its context, horn arrangement and the knowing dumbness of the lyrics. However, the listener with more in mind than cheap thrills fares no better. For many, Zappa is, apart from his intrinsic merits, a gateway to 'higher things'. However, the seeker of exquisite Webernian interludes is sure to find amplified snorks or chipmunk choruses as well. Zappa's music may be a sculpture, but it is a sculpture festooned with hairtrigger stinkbombs.

The legitimate concern with art as social praxis professed by the practitioners of sociology and cultural studies is bought at the expense of art as a distinctive cognitive activity. Zappa, in contrast, is able to give such concern sensuous embodiment. Nevertheless, Bourdieu's Paradox remains a salutary reminder of art's limits, so it is worth prospecting for the inevitable cracks in the monstrous edifice that is Zappa's *corpus*. *Joe's Garage* represents a convergence of artist and fanbase of which Pete Townshend can only dream, particularly in the extraordinary closing sections: 'I'll be sullen and withdrawn/I'll drift off into the twilight realm/Of my own secret thoughts/I'll lie on my back till dawn/In a semi-catatonic state/And dream of guitar notes/ That would irritate an executive kind of guy'.

The composer in the Utility Muffin Research Kitchen and the fan in his (*sic*) bedroom are united in a vision of impotence and futility, an effect heightened by the spacey and xenochronous music. The banality of "Watermelon in Easter Hay"[14] is not far off, to be redeemed only by the much greater banality of "A Little Green Rosetta".[15] Zappa's relationship with his fans ('people like you/Who smile & think you know/ What this is about') is usually more ambivalent, as can be seen in the *Baby Snakes* film. In the onstage sequences one can discern beneath the lineaments of the authoritarian ringmaster a touching, if on this occasion unjustified, faith in the capacity of his audience to be wild and creative. It is during this period that Zappa's claim to have got into rock solely because he couldn't afford a symphony orchestra began to seem less disingenuous. During the teen metal years of robbing Beavis to pay Boulez, the Dadaist anti-art gestures seem increasingly perfunctory and extraneous, confined as they are to sleevenotes (*The Perfect Stranger*) or certain tracks (*The Yellow Shark*). Classical respectability beckons, notwithstanding Zappa's oddly defensive asseverations about his insignificance as a composer.

Ultimately, the torn halves of Zappa's music, the circus and the concert hall, do not add up. Such resolution is strictly for idealists, so I'll conclude by adapting some remarks Adorno and Horkheimer[16] made about Beethoven and his business acumen in disposing of his late quartets, those dreams of dissonances which would irritate an absolute monarch kind-of-guy. Zappa is the most outstanding example of the unity of those opposites, market and independence, in modern culture. Those who succumb to the ideology are precisely those who cover up the contradiction instead of taking it into the consciousness of their own production as Zappa did.

1. See the foreword to Frank Zappa, *Them Or Us [The Book]*, North Hollywood: Barking Pumpkin Records, 1984, p. 1.
2. 'Take Your Clothes Off When You Dance', *We're Only In It for the Money*, 1968.
3. Bourdieu's account of French Impressionism has much in common with that of T.J. Clark. Unlike Bourdieu, however, Clark insists upon the specific cognitive value of art. For the sociologist, the stuff of art has all the specificity of chips at a gaming table and is entirely dependent for its value on the timing and positionality of its deployment.
4. Theodor Adorno, *Negative Dialektik*, 1966; *Negative Dialectics*, translated E.B. Ashton, London: Routledge and Kegan Paul, 1973, p. 197. *Editors' note:* Adorno actually said 'A sociology of knowledge fails before philosophy: for the truth content of philosophy it substitutes its social function and its conditioning by interests, while refraining from a critique of the content itself, remaining indifferent toward it.' However, in the cause of making Adornoism livid and rampant and obnoxious to academia as currently constituted, we applaud Sutton's substitution of 'art' for 'philosophy' and 'Cultural Studies' for 'sociology': it's the same deal, where the so-called objective view actually patronizes and misrecognizes the object.
5. Pierre Bourdieu, 'The uses of the "people"', *Other Words*, Cambridge: Polity, 1990, p. 155.
6. Frank Zappa with Peter Occhiogrosso, *The Real Frank Zappa Book*, London: Picador, 1989, pp. 186-7.
7. *Ibid*, p. 143.
8. *Ibid*, p. 139.
9. Asked to provide chapter and verse for this assertion, Sutton replied: You're right. Beware of such weaselly passive constructions as 'it has been noted that ...'. Shoddy research is invariably afoot. However, while I have not been able to sniff out an unambiguous *imprimatur* for my claim, I have got a couple of leads. I'll begin, though, with my understanding of the socio-linguistic set-up. In both cases, we have a situation in which one language/culture (English) is imposed upon another (a reasonable well-defined Gaelic in one case, a rather more diffuse and beleaguered African in the other). Linguistic struggle, therefore, takes place in two spheres, the endogenous and the exogenous. The former is the pub, street corner or the blues bar, and is (relatively) autonomous; the latter is the university and the metropolitan media, and is (relatively) heteronomous, in that its values are largely those of the elite. 'Subaltern grandiloquence' emerges at the point where mimesis turns into mimicry, when the aspirant emulation of the 'civilised' and 'cultured' other becomes joyous destruction. As far as the Irish are concerned, a mere list should suffice to illustrate my point: Swift, Sterne, Wilde, Joyce and Beckett. Note also the way in which 'blarney' is presented as a passive opting out of responsibility in the plays of Sean O'Casey.
   Another list: *King* Oliver, *Duke* Ellington, *Count* Basie, *Professor* Longhair, *Baron* Mingus, *King* Curtis, *Earl King*, *Major* Lance, Five *Royales*, Little Anthony and the *Imperials*, *Dr.*

Dre. But it's not just my favourite acts. In her 'Characteristics of Negro Expression' (*The Norton Anthology of African American Literature,* ed. Henry Louis Gates and Nellie Y. McKay), Zora Neale Hurston mentions 'angularity', 'assymetry', 'mimicry' and 'the will to adorn'.

10. Zappa, *Op. Cit.*, pp. 163.
11. See my forthcoming paper 'The Phenomenology of Spurt: Merleau-Ponty Plays the Music of Frank Zappa'.
12. See Ben Watson, *Frank Zappa: The Negative Dialectics of Poodle Play,* London: Quartet, 1994, p. 142.
13. Matt Worley in booklet, Suicide, *American Supreme* (Blast First, 2002).
14. See T.H.F. Drenching's '"Watermelon in Easter Hay": The Poverty of the Individual Spirit' in this volume.
15. Watson correctly points out that "Rosetta" is '*musically* more complex, singular and interesting than "Watermelon"'. However, according to the phenomenology of actually-existing Zappaphilia, the apprehension of "Rosetta"'s cynical throwaway cheesiness is anterior to the apprehension of its musical excellence. Most Zappa fans have the "heavy sounds" of Pink Floyd, or, even, Wishbone Ash, to purge from their systems e'er they can savour the noxious puerilities of Zappa. [*Editor's Note:* Not sure I'm happy with the righteous boogie of the Turner brothers being associated with the leaden spectacle of Stink Ployed ... but this would require another conference.]
16. Theodor Adorno & Max Horkheimer, *Dialectic of Enlightenment,* 1944, translated John Cumming, London: Verso, 1979, p. 157.

Trout Mask Replica: A Dagger in the Head of *Mojo* Man

Sean Bonney

I first heard *Trout Mask Replica* in a squat in the Forest Fields area of Nottingham, around 1990. The album's mythology had preceded it; it was the most insane album ever made, the band was playing different songs at the same time, *etc etc etc.* Certainly, the person who owned the album seemed to believe these myths. When I asked him to play it he grumbled that it was rubbish, unlistenable and so on and so on. To shut me up, he agreed to play a bit of it, believing that I would be begging for it to be removed from the turntable within thirty seconds.

He eventually cut it off halfway through "Moonlight on Vermont", and gave it to me as a present. But not kindly, he was angered, and thought that I was just pretending to like it to be "cool". I've heard the same argument since, with reference to most of my favourite things. Nobody can like *Finnegans Wake*, or Sun Ra, or the recent poetry of J.H Prynne, and those who say they do are elitist scum trying to buy a bit of mystique through their choice of notoriously "difficult" cultural products. Poets and revolutionaries have a duty to mercilessly mock persons with such opinions as saddoes who like to project their own cultural and political misery on everyone else. *Trout Mask Replica* is, quite obviously, one of the greatest seventy minutes of fuck-music available on the sexless plains of Oxford St. It is also great for dancing.

In Iain Sinclair's recent novel *Landor's Tower*, when the narrator is arrested at a service station on suspicion of murder, the cops who drive him away are listening to Bob Dylan.[1] It is a bitter observation on the recuperation of once rebellious rock'n'roll, and the failure of the sixties counterculture. It is unlikely that cops would be found listening to Captain Beefheart. *Trout Mask Replica* has been granted the status of classic, of course. But in its case, as with *Finnegans Wake* being described as "unreadable" on the back of its Penguin Modern Classics cover, its classic status is implemented to save classic rock fans the trouble of listening to it. I associate the concept of classic rock with the magazine *Mojo*, which emerged in the 1990s around the same time that Tony Blair was being photographed strumming his Fender Stratocaster, and terminal dullard Noel Gallagher was mumbling away about 'proper songs' and authenticity. Rock'n'roll was always improper. *Mojo* magazine and classic rock in general is a celebration of music being nailed up in the lair of the accountant, only to be listened to through expensive systems, with all the fizzes and pops and memories of what its energy could actually mean digitally erased.

The conservatism of rock'n'roll classicism was not, however, a phenomena new to the 1990s. Detractors of *Trout Mask Replica* miss the point: it is one of the best blues albums of the 1960s. The blues was a music under attack. Eric Clapton and his pub rock imitators reinterpreted the blues as a rhythmically fixed and largely formulaic shuffle, to the extent that it is actually incredibly surprising to go and listen to the records of Howling Wolf or Muddy Waters. Moreover, the recordings that Blind Lemon Jefferson made in the 1920s have the same rhythmic fluidity—and the same viciously ringing guitar lines running counterclockwise to the vocal patterns—as the best of Beefheart's work. The problem with Eric Clapton is that, like Wynton Marsalis in jazz, he saw the music as a fixed and possibly sacred form, with any attempts to develop it as tantamount to heresy. He also forgot that the music was not there as an expression of empty virtuosity, but as a violent expression of hatred for the oppressor. Robert Johnson didn't spread the rumour that he had sold his soul to the devil out of superstition or ignorance, but because he knew that it would terrify the godfearing bourgeoisie.

In Europe, at roughly the same time as the first blues players were reinventing popular and traditional musics as an expression of hatred and alienation, Tristan Tzara and Richard Huelsenbeck, among others, were attempting a similar thing with poetic form. Writing in 1919, Tzara pointed out that poetic rhythm had become 'the beating of a dried up heart, a little tinkle in putrid, padded wood.' He insisted instead that the poet must

> know how to recognise and pick up the signs of the power we are awaiting, which are everywhere; in the fundamental language of cryptograms, engraved on crystals, on shells, on rails, in clouds, or in glass; inside snow, or light, or coal; on the hand, in the beams grouped round the magnetic poles, on wings.[2]

The romantic staples of the cliched idea of what a poet is—'clouds', 'snow, 'light'—are negated by their proximity to 'cryptograms', 'rails', 'glass' and especially 'magnetic poles'. Light, the mystical image par excellence through the history of poetry, is suggestively transformed into electric light. And the poetry of Tristan Tzara, in the years immediately following both the horrors of the first world war and the hopes of the Russian Revolution, were the sounds of poetry injected with a few thousand cryptographic volts:

> here the drum major and the castanets step in
> for there are zigzags on his soul and lots of rrrrrrrrrrrr here the
>   reader starts to scream

he starts to scream starts to scream then in his scream there are
flutes which multiply corals
the reader wants to die perhaps or dance and starts to scream
he's skinny dirty stupid he doesn't understand my verses he
screams
he's cock-eyed
there are zigzags on his soul and lots of rrrrrr
nbaze baze baze look at the undersea tiara which comes undone in
golden seaweed
hozondrac trac
nfoonda nbababa nfoonda tata
nbababa[3]

Bob Dylan[4] is usually credited with introducing literacy to rock music. Although this is news to anyone who's listened to the lyrics (or even the titles) to things like "Fence Breakin' Yellin' Blues"—recorded in 1929 by Blind Lemon Jefferson—there is truth in it, Dylan being one of the first to combine blues forms with the poetic innovations of the European avant-garde. But Dylan's mix of Rimbaud, Woody Guthrie and the Memphis Jug Band never advanced beyond basic stanzaic poetic forms, thus highlighting an implicit conservatism in the hippy counterculture.

Beefheart was the first to take on the full implications of Dadaist poetics. "Neon Meate Dream of a Octafish", track 10 on *Trout Mask Replica*, unleashes a torrent of improvised word mutation to challenge anything performed in the Dada *soirées* at the Cabaret Voltaire. Powered by Beefheart's musette playing—a miniature bagpipe that sounds here like the offspring of a half-asphyxiated Hammond organ with a North African pan pipe—this is a song that should be studied by any aspirant pornographer. 'It's all about the birds and the bees', as Beefheart kindly pointed out in "Lick My Decals Off, Baby": 'neon meate dream of a octafish/artifactal rose petals/in flesh petals and pots/in fact in feast/in tubes/tubs/bulbs/in jest incest injest injust in feast incest/in specks/in spreckled spreckled/speckled/speculation'[5].

This is like free association of the best kind, echoing the fecund imagery of the words themselves. Words are experienced as material entities that themselves change into one another, just as plants grow from their bulbs in the song, and transform into fists and flesh and body fluids. Thus 'octafish' becomes 'artifact', 'in flesh', 'in fact', 'in feast'. And as that alliterative run exhausts itself, another direction comes in from behind, as the 't' at the end of 'feast' brings up 'tubes', 'tubs', 'bulbs'. As the words proliferate, so what they signify flickers and changes in the way of all good poetry; 'bulbs' and 'tubes' are from one direction plant material—from 'petals and pots'—but they're also lightbulbs and plastic tubes. A sexual mesh of meaning, which intensifies as Beefheart stutters, looking for the next direction in his word-flow, and the 'in', which had been used as a rhythmic anchor, starts growing new associations out of itself: 'injest', 'injust', 'incest'. The caution that this is merely wordplay—in jest—is internalised, ingested, and spat out again as 'incest', as the plant-fuck imagery intensifies, and the 'rancid buds burst': 'limp damp rose/peeled in felt fields in belts/ impaled on in daemon/mucus mules/twat trot/tra la/tra la'.

A compost heap of dead plant life and an exhausted sexuality, a 'limp damp rose', spirals up into new, weirder formulations. The same free association playing off 'in'—as if we were drilling further and further into the possibilities of a single word—is now throwing up specific imagery: peeled felt, field belts. And then, after a slight pause, a sudden certainty in the declaration 'impaled on in daemon'. An observation of the sexual centre of poetic action, as Beefheart's voice is fucked from behind by the spirit of inspiration spoken of by Socrates. 'Mucus mules' acknowledges the cross pollination of body fluids, the alliteration and repeated long vowels emphasising two entities becoming one, confirmed in the 'twat trot', which actually forces all meaning out of Beefheart syllables, who is left intoning 'tra la tra la'.

At the end of the song, just in case we've missed what he's really going on about, he makes it as obvious as he can with a jizz spattered string of final alliterative associations: 'squirmin serum in semen in syrup in semen in syrup/stirruped in syrup'.

And then the final ecstatic declaration to punctuate the whole thing, 'neon meate dream of a octafish', before Beefheart blows into his simran horn, and the whole thing shudders off in the direction of "China Pig".

The phrase 'neon meate dream of a octafish' appears elsewhere on the album, in one of the field recordings that pop up intermittently and go a long way to making the album a whole. Just before "Moonlight on Vermont", there's a faint recording of what sounds like Beefheart talking to two neighbourhood kids he's found loitering in the garden, eavesdropping on the music. 'Whaddya think?', he asks, to which the kids, shyly, but trying to sound cool, reply in unison, 'sounds good.' 'It's a bush recording, recorded in bush', Beefheart informs them, with an example of characteristic wordshift emphasising the connections between the human and the natural environment as extensions of one another. 'Bush' refers to a field recording, to the name of the manufacturer of the equipment they're using, and to the pubic hair around the female genital organ. Its unlikely he's referring to *faux*-Texan mass murderers of the future, but you never know. Beefheart then, as if it's the most usual thing to be chatting to your neighbour's kids about, says 'the name of the composition is "Neon Meate Dream of a Octafish"', before correcting himself with 'No, it's "Hair Pie"', thus underlining the sexual materialism of the former song.

Neon, classified as one of the noble, or inert gases on the Periodic Table of the Elements—the classification emphasising chemistry's implicit understanding of the uselessness of the nobility—was first discovered in 1898. It exists in the atmosphere as 1 part in 65,000, and has no biological use. It is so inert that it does not react with air—even under extreme conditions—or water, halogens, or acids. It is separated by first liquefying and separating the air itself, and the only thing that anyone ever does with it is place it in glass tubes before exposing it to high voltages, which causes it to change colour, thus producing the neon lights of American cliché.

"Neon Meate Dream" is a key to understanding the central purpose of Beefheart's poetics. As well as being a further example of associative word mutation, with its emphasis on N and M, the two letters at the physical centre of the alphabet, it is also suggestive of an eroticised, materialist poetics as attentive to the tiniest trace elements of the atmosphere as it is to its dominant forces of sexuality and noisy, discordant rock music. As opposed to the spiritualist pieties of much poetry, Beefheart insists on the fact that the dream has a physical function, and as such is made out of the same *meat* that all human activity springs from. Neon, as a trace element in the atmosphere, is an analogous with the trace elements in the human meat that flicker in imagination to create the strange characters that people Beefheart's songs, some human—like the tragic Big Joan whose hands are too small—some less so, like the Octafish, or Ant Man Bee. These characters are the element that make Beefheart's imaginary world come alive, and the not-quite-human figures emphasise just how deep into consciousness and subconsciousness he goes to retrieve them. This, from an article by Peter Morgane, 'The Anatomical Basis of Intelligence', quoted by the Olsonian poet John Clarke, goes some way to illuminating the depths of consciousness that Beefheart enters:

> The present moment of the brain always embraces the past's whole achievement. The embryo repeats, in rough summary, the events of hundreds of millions of years in nine short months, and the brain maintains them all simultaneously. In our own brain our past life, from worms through fishes and amphibians towards mammals, is summed up in what we sometimes term the old brain (paleo-cortex or archi-cortex), while advance toward humanity is expressed in the elaboration of the new brain (neocortex), whose overgrowth conceals its primitive antecedents . . . A great deal is known about it, but not enough to give really satisfactory accounts of how it works during a mental process.[6]

But Beefheart is not merely some diver in the murky signals of the archi-cortex; what gives his lyrics their quickness and humour, which separates them from the portentous and treacherous Jungianism of Charles Olson or his imitators, is a Dadaist sense of play emerging from the materiality of the words themselves. Thus 'Octafish'—whose spelling with an 'a' separates it from 'octopus'—is a play on Octave, as if musical terminology could come alive as a weird little animal.

Beefheart is often dismissed, by those not in the know, as one of rock's more far-out eccentrics, a novelty act at best. When he fell out with Zappa he accused the latter of marketing him as one of his stable of freaks. But *Trout Mask Replica* is also an alarmingly powerful social commentary. "Ant Man Bee" is built around a quasi-*lettriste* formulation, which contains within itself a critique of the category 'man'. 'Man' is interrupting the species sequence 'Ant' 'Bee', which is a recognition of the alienated human's position as a destroyer of the environment. Furthermore, 'man' is also interrupting the alphabetical sequence 'a' and 'b' which 'ant' and 'bee' are, in kiddies' picture-book terms. Thus, not only is the human the interrupter of the natural environment, but also the interrupter and destroyer of its own inventions. And as if that wasn't enough, the critique is made explicit by the possible reading "Ant Man Be"—or that human society makes ants of us all.

Most of the song is in straightforward protest mode, with its catchy chorus call of 'why do you have to do-o this, you got to let us be.' What saves it is the amazing word bending in 'war still running on, one lump of sugar', where 'one' is sung with such force that it bends and breaks into a repeat of 'war'. This builds an anti-war protest more subtle than a rabblerousing cry of 'what is it good for?', in that it equates the individualist 'one' scrabbling after its sugar lump with the cause of war. Word bending is an essential tactic. On "Frownland", right at the beginning of the album, he yells out an understanding of unity with the cosmos. The lyric booklet in the CD issue tries to tell us that this says 'my spirit's made up of the ocean and the sky and the sun and the moon and all I can see'. But ever since I've been listening to the album I've heard it as: 'My spit's made up/Of the ocean/And the sky/And the sun/And the moon/And all I can see'.

This in any case is a more accurate account of unity, in that spit—and the rest of the body—is made of the same basic matter that everything else, including sun and moon, is made of. If he was merely claiming that his 'spirit' was made up of these things, then he would be separating himself, and suggesting that a mystical abstraction was more real than his own being. A strange position for someone who famously said, 'stars are matter, we are matter, but it doesn't matter.' The cosmos described in *Trout Mask Replica* includes rare gases, electric tubes that turn into meat plants, strange antennae, voodoo, and amazing Ayleresque saxophone playing that can still terrify the *Mojo*-reading rock connoisseur. Most of all, it includes body fluids. More far-out than any psychedelic vision, it is closer to Trotsky's materialist vision at the end of the 1933 notebook on Hegel:

> Our concept of the earth, the 'most durable' of our conceptions, the 'most durable' of the objects of our everyday milieu, is based upon a total rupture with the revolutionary formation of the solar system. The concept is conservative. Its conservatism issues: a)

> from its utilitarian purpose, b) from the fact that the memory of a person, like that of humankind, is short.[7]

The official music industry, and its press that serves generally as an advertising outlet, is a key conservative force in the contemporary war economy. The unfamiliar and strange is increasingly denounced as too difficult for the 'way we live today'.[8] As Adorno said in 1945, in words chillingly applicable to our era, 'shoddiness that drifts with the flow of contemporary speech is taken as a sign as relevance and contact: people know what they want because they know what other people want'.[9] The culture industry's problem with difficult or weird art is not that it's elitist, but because there is a chance—however tiny—that it might jar people out of their shopping trance. It is the culture industry itself, and not the people it so cynically administers, about whom it is true to say that 'only what they do not need first to understand, they consider understandable; only the word coined by commerce, and really alienated, touches them as familiar'.[10]

Mojo magazine, and other publications which see their demographic as the alienated middle-aged yearning for the excitement of their youth, is particularly pernicious as it tries to reach into the past and absorb everything that's there. Everything pink and weird—like the cover of *Trout Mask Replica*—is to be normalised.[11] Come on, says the retro branch of the culture industry, wouldn't you rather listen to Rod Stewart? There's something they don't want us to know.

1. Iain Sinclair, *Landor's Tower*, London: Granta, 2002, p. 163.
2. Tristan Tzara, 'Note on Poetry', *Seven Dada Manifestos and Lampisteries*, 1919; translated Barbara Wright, London: Calder, 1977, p. 75.
3. Tristan Tzara, 'The white leprous giant in the countryside', *Chanson Dada*, 1918; translated Lee Harwood, Toronto: Coach House, 1987.
4. At this moment of bathos (Bonney left a brief pause after 'Bob Dylan'), the ICE-Z audience—in Tony Cliff's immortal phrase—'burst laughing'. Bonney is actually a Dylan fan, and was appreciative when I played him *Shot of Love*, a 'Christian' album he'd previously avoided. *Ed.*
5. This is Bonney's own transcription; it conflicts with the 'official' lyric sheet included with the CD twenty years afterwards, a transcription Bonney criticises later on in his polemic. *Ed.*
6. Peter Morgane, 'The Whale Brain—The Anatomical Basis of Intelligence', cited in John Clarke, *From Feathers to Iron*, San Francisco: Tombouctou, 1987, p. 86.
7. Leon Trotsky, *Notebooks 1933-1935: Writings on Lenin, Dialectics and Evolutionism*, translated Philip Pomper, New York: Columbia University Press, 1986, p. 78.
8. This is in part a reference to Nick Hornby, who reviewed a recent Radiohead album—Radiohead, for fuck's sake—in *The New Yorker*, and slagged it off because people today are too

busy to listen to such complex music (*sic*). Thanks to Burhan Tufail for telling me about this.

9. Theodor Adorno, *Minima Moralia: Reflections from a Damaged Life*, 1951, translated E. F. N. Jephcott, London: Verso, 1978, p. 101.
10. *Ibid.*
11. It's closer to red, really, but I like the words 'pink and weird' too much to stop now.

What's The Ugliest Part of Your Market-Researched Anaclitic-Affect Repertoire?

Keston Sutherland

In 1964, four years prior to the appearance of *We're Only In It for the Money* by Frank Zappa and the Mothers of Invention, the British Labour Party set up a Commission chaired by Lord Reith of Stonehaven, the first Director General of the BBC, to 'consider the role of commercial advertising in present day society and to recommend whether reforms are required'. Reith was an outspoken paternalist who regarded American TV economics as a kind of moral-weaponised dirty bomb in the hands of fanatics ready to terrorise the British plebs (whom he himself had betrayed during the General Strike of 1926).[1] Reacting to the advent of commercial television in 1956, Reith evacuated a stubborn warning from history into the House of Lords:

> Somebody introduced Christianity into England and somebody introduced smallpox, bubonic plague, and the Black Death. Somebody is minded now to introduce sponsored broadcasting ... Need we be ashamed of moral values, or of intellectual and ethical objectives? It is these that are here and now at stake.[2]

Reith might also have mentioned that somebody likewise introduced the House of Lords, moral values, and even himself; but at least two of these things had probably been introduced to England from the inside rather than from the outside, and it is introduction from the outside that tends to reawaken the chivalric attitude in a person of Reith's class.[3] His fatherliness was of a common sort, both true and false. True, because moral and intellectual values were in fact undeniably at stake, and would undergo extreme mutation as a result of the American influx he sought to prevent. False, because he failed to admit that it was the inevitable tendency of oligopolistic capitalist economies trying to remain competitive in the mid-twentieth century to substitute advertising for price competition as the principal weapon of profitability;[4] and false also, because the moral and intellectual values he so passionately mentioned were assuredly unknown to him from any perspective other than that of a career-propagandist. In any case, moral outrage at the tip of the superstructure was never likely to defeat capitalism on its own basic turf, and despite Lord Reith's fiery imprecations, Britain was soon to be overrun by a horde of image-makers and their made-up images, with its ears, minds and off-shore bank accounts kept thereafter permanently agape for all the fantasies of good living they could squeeze into their splitting apertures. By 1968 this invasion of compulsory commodity-life was, even in the United States, still in its infancy, most likely somewhere around the anal stage; which makes *We're Only In It for the Money* a first-rate example of what Georg Lukács called genuinely avantgarde art, that is, art which expresses from within the superstructure an accurate anticipation of forthcoming economic reality. The album's anticipatory power is expressed not in a straightforward critique of commodity-life and its human billboards, but more radically, in a sickening string of jokes at the expense of hippies and the whole dopey counterculture that imagined itself to be the enemy of the state, whereas in fact that counterculture turned out, as Zappa predicted, to be an object lesson in how to be recuperated by capitalism. The album, like much of Zappa's music, is a critique not of commodity-life itself but of the countercultural stupefaction that guarantees the continual success of the capitalist recuperation industry.

The first issue of *Internationale Situationniste*, published in June 1958, featured an unsigned article called 'The Struggle for the Control of the New Techniques of Conditioning'. Like much of the Situationist material that would appear in the journal itself, the article is pretty thin on the ground when it comes to outright proposals for practical action; but it does include a declaration of intent that plainly distinguishes it from anything that Theodor Adorno or other humanists[5] might have said:

> it must be understood that we are going to assist, to participate in, *the race between free artists and the police to experiment with and to develop uses for the new techniques of conditioning.* In this race the police already have a considerable advantage. The outcome of the race will depend on the appearance of passionate and liberating environments, or the reinforcement—under smooth scientific control—of the environment of the old world of oppression and horror.[6]

The article mentions the conditioning of an incarcerated Hungarian revolutionary, Lajos Ruff, by soviet police agents and psychologists in a specially designed, psychotropic jail cell, which sounds a bit like Patrick McGhee's experience in the cheerful 1960s TV show *The Prisoner.* The emphasis is on highly specialised, sinister, labour-intensive and secretive methods of conditioning practised by the state and its modernised inquisition; to which the Situationist response, at least in this early article, is to imagine a highly theorised, provocative, play-intensive and elusive method of artistic experiment.

Yet the most powerful form of conditioning was never secretive, in the sense at least that its purpose was to be as well known and pleasantly ingested as possible. This is of course advertising, and the shift in Situationist programmes for revolutionary aesthetics (from highly technical experimentation to quick and easy vandalism) can perhaps be understood as their way of keeping up with capitalism at large, not just the police, in the race for control of the means of conditioning. A stupid advert requires only a quick bit of damage to be turned against its owners, and this is one aspect of advertising—the fickleness inherent in its obvious stupidity—that made it nice and convenient as a half-baked if not raw material for Situationist art. To go a step further, revolutionary artists needed to understand not just the transparent principle behind advertising as a substitute for price competition, but also the research industry responsible for its particular strategies and aesthetics. That research industry has been unashamedly psychological from its beginnings. It has subordinated psychology to its own ends so effectively that some of the most cutting edge experimentation in the field is now in what is called 'neuromarketing,' a procedure for observing the physical and chemical behaviour of the brain of a volunteer consumer as he sits in a laboratory and gapes at a slideshow of prospective advert-types. This is all well enough known, though hardly well enough hated.

Of more interest from an intellectual point of view is the relation between Freudian psychoanalytic theory and market research. What is the value and utility of the basic Freudian tropes for market research; and what is their value to the enemies of capitalism, not as a means of describing why this or that individual may or may not feel dispirited that the position formerly occupied in his mental apparatus by his mother is now occupied by a Dyson hoover, but more radically, as a means of diagnosing the ontogenetic origins of *homo consumer* in general? Is Freudian theory up to the job of providing a critique of commodity-life under the dance-steps of universal marketing, or is Freud's total failure to produce such a critique of his own evidence enough that psychoanalytic thinking is essentially irreconcilable with revolutionary thinking? Put in Situationist terms: can Freudian theory be detourned? Can we pull off a detournement not just of the images of advertising, but of the psychoanalytic research methods used to come up with them? The history of the British and American pop song is a good testing ground for this problem.

In 1964, the same year that Lord Reith was commissioned by an anxious government to look into the effects of TV advertising, an American psychoanalyst called Frances Hannett published the most detailed and elaborate psychoanalytic paper on American pop music to date.[7] Hannett noticed that her patients would often arrive for their therapy sessions humming or whistling a tune, or would tell her that a certain tune was stuck in their heads, or they would find that certain tunes burst into their memory at important moments of self-recognition in the course of their treatment. After analysing the sudden appearances of these tunes and what Freud would call their manifest content, *i.e.* the narrative or sentiment in their lyrics, Hannett concluded that they are 'a 'voice of the preconscious' and must be understood in the same way as 'a dream fragment, a fantasy, or a repetitive act'.[8] This agrees with both Freud's and Theodor Reik's view, that, as Reik puts it, 'the incidental music accompanying our conscious thinking is never accidental'.[9] Hannett set out to examine the entire body of chorus lyrics from American hit songs published between 1900 and 1949. She explains her decision not to include contemporary hits as follows:

> This period [i.e. 1900-1949] was chosen because it covers the half-century during which popular music had its heyday and because the end of World War II ushered in various artificial influences which made it difficult or impossible to determine the intrinsic popular appeal of more recent so-called 'hits'.[10]

These 'various influences' Hannett lists as 'commercial rivalries among music producers, radio networks, disc jockeys *etc*'. Her definition of a hit song is one which has gained top ranking or appreciable acceptance by the public. Before radio, the popularity of a tune was determined by the sales of sheet music and Victrola recordings. Later, with the advent of radio and television, the success of a song depended on the amount of exposure it received through these media as well as on the sales of recordings and sheet music.[11]

Hannett's methodology excludes as a distortion of the real data the entire edifice of the culture industry in its post-war form. The underlying assumption is that permeation of the unconscious by music is more meaningful from a psychoanalytic point of view the less it can

ROMANTIC LOVE SONGS
Lyrics classified according to content
(Figures and percentages indicate absolute incidence of each content in the total number of songs. A song may have several contents.)

	1900-1949 (1470 Songs)		1800-1899 (153 Songs)	
	No.	%	No.	%
1. Love	850	57	77	44
2. Heart	475	32	39	24
3. Anaclitic Affects				
a. Possessive Dependence	462	31	16	11
b. Depressive and Hostile Affects	390	27	25	18
c. Separation Anxiety	356	24	46	30
d. Dreams of Wish Fulfilment	338	22	16	11
4. Duration of Love	276	18	45	28
a. Faithfulness	(192)		(36)	
b. Faithlessness	(84)		(9)	
5. Sexuality	245	16	6	3
a. Inferred Contact	(208)			
b. Explicit Contact	(37)		(6)	
c. Prostitution	(6)			
6. Affirmative Affects	176	12		
a. Bliss, Divine, Paradise, Rapture, etc.	(94)			
b. Power of Love	(80)			
c. Self-confidence	(2)			
7. Nostalgia	8			
Memory	104	7	7	5
Déjà Vu	9		1	
8. Romance	106	7		
a. Overvaluation	(22)			
b. Desire, Passion	(47)			
c. Romance	(51)			
9. Marriage	67	4.5	13	8
10. Mother, Father, Baby	54	3.6	10	6
11. Dance	47	3.2		
12. Sentiment	28	1.9	4	2
13. Mature Love	16	1	2	1
14. Fate	17	1		
15. Exhortation	9	0.6		
16. Death	3	0.2	17	11
17. Symbols	588	40	53	34
a. Moon	(185)		(10)	
b. Flowers	(161)		(24)	
c. Stars	(149)		(9)	
d. Spring	(111)		(15)	
e. Islands, South	(92)		(3)	
f. Magic, Music, Bluebird, Gypsy	(81)		(1)	
g. Sun	(80)		(13)	

Fig. 26: Hannett Data
First published in © *The Psychoanalytic Quaterly*, 1964, Volume 33, pages 226-269.

be chalked up to marketing, which Hannett calls 'exposure'. This is an obvious theoretical convenience, analogous in some ways to Wilhelm Reich's preposterous idea that 'there is no use in individual therapy ... from the standpoint of the social problem' except money-making, and that analysis conducted on socialist principles has to 'go back to the unspoiled protoplasm' of the strictly infantile psyche.[12] Both Reich and Hannett advocate an approach to analysis of the unconscious founded on the idea that the spoliation of an individual's psychic operations by capitalist culture makes psychoanalytic research either gratuitous or methodologically compromised. Both attitudes are plainly romantic and undialectical. Notwithstanding that criticism, Hannett uncovered some useful data on the manifest content of hits songs according to her limited definition of them, which I've reproduced in your handouts. [see Fig. 26]

The significant result of Hannett's observations is first of all that the great majority of all hit songs are love songs or 'romantic' songs; and secondly that the manifest content of their lyrics is limited to a pretty small and unvarying range of reference-terms, symbols and affects. She concludes that 'the popular lyric expresses unconscious infantile attitudes' and that 'unresolved whole or partial attachments to the image of the pre-oedipal mother provide the latent matrix for American popular songs'.[13] From this she extrapolates a judgement about human valuation of freedom in general: 'although man values his freedom, there remains in him the paradoxical tendency to feel it as a rejection when it means separation from the mother'.[14]

Amongst the most popular themes that crop up in the hits she examined is a category defined in Freudian terms as 'anaclitic affects': possessive dependence, depressive and hostile affects, separation anxiety and dreams of wish fulfillment. The frequency of these affects as themes in hit songs is shown to have increased significantly since the late 19th century, when hit songs were more often undisguisedly about death and sex (a trend that was powerfully restored to life in the last quarter of the 20th century by the mass popularisation of rap and hip hop).

So what is an 'anaclitic affect'? The term *Anlehnungstypus* or 'anaclitic type' was invented by Freud in his 1914 paper 'On Narcissism'. Translated literally, it means 'leaning-on type,' according to the

OED gloss 'a person whose choice of a "love-object" is governed by the dependence of the libido on another instinct, *e.g.* hunger'. Freud wrote:

A person may love: ---

(1) According to the narcissistic type:
  a) what he himself is (i.e. himself),
  b) what he himself was,
  c) what he himself would like to be,
  d) someone who was once part of himself.

(2) According to the anaclitic (attachment) type:
  a) the woman who feeds him,
  b) the man who protects him,

  and the succession of substitutes who take their place.[15]

Freud designates the two lists above as 'the paths leading to the choice of an object [*i.e.* a love-object]'. The translator James Strachey added a footnote:

> It should be noted that the 'attachment' (or '*Anlehnung*') indicated by the term is that of the sexual instincts to the ego-instincts, not of the child to its mother'.[16]

Freud said:

> The sexual instincts are at the outset attached to the satisfaction of the ego-instincts [*e.g.* the instinct for self-preservation, for the satisfaction of hunger, for warmth and protection; and later for less strictly physical forms of defence, *etc*]'.[17]

The English word derives from the Greek verb meaning 'to lean back, recline'. Strachey chose the derivation 'anaclitic' because of the grammatical analogy of this neologism to the English 'enclitic.' The OED gloss for *Anlehnungstypus* is 'leaning-on type', 'a person whose choice of a "love-object" is governed by the dependence of the libido on another instinct, *e.g.* hunger'. A more up-to-date definition might be 'laid-back type'.

The anaclitic type of person experiences the full potency of erotic longing for somebody only when he feels that this somebody will satisfy what Freud called his 'ego-instincts'. That is, he is driven by his libido to find a 'succession of substitutes' for the nourishment and protection that his mother and father provided for him in his infancy. He leans on these substitutes, driven by a sense that he will otherwise be exposed helplessly to the elements of a hostile environment that he couldn't possibly survive on his own. What Hannett lists as 'anaclitic affects' are the ravages of the world's hostility against him.

The great prominence of these pathogenic affects among the tired old themes of pop music both in the early 20th century and in our own eternally recurrent and samey chart music is, logically enough, evidence that a great part of the psychic life of their mass audience is anaclitic; or at least, that this mass audience is taught by lyrical rote to think of itself as anaclitic and thus actually to become so. As Adorno and Max Horkheimer insisted, the defence of the marketing men that they are 'just giving the people what they want' is undoubtedly true, but only because the condition of wanting has itself been downgraded in advance by these same innocent marketing men into a stupefying adjunct of the culture industry.

Hannett's data is essentially market-research. What it tells us about the drives and needs of *homo sapiens* finds its ultimate consequence in the life of *homo consumer.* What could be more useful to the marketing operations that decide the content of pop music than a complete breakdown of the sales figures for every symbol and affect, published under the disinterested imprimatur of *The Psychoanalytic Quarterly*? Yet her research is also conveniently incomplete. What Hannett's research excludes from vision by the ruse of ignoring the popularity of post-war hit songs is the one dominant category of which all the other themes in her list are sub-categories. This is the category of what I will call commodity-love. The heart, sexuality, nostalgia and all the other themes of pop music are not the unmediated symbols and drives of the lyrical psyche that Hannett implicitly proposes they are; each of them is transmuted by its appearance in a pop song into something quite alien to the human protoplasm. They become the symbols and drives of commodity-love, by which I mean both the love of commodities and love itself in commodified form. This is not to say that nothing can ever be wrung out of these hits songs except the experience of commodification; rather, it is by a process of transition in the mind of the adolescent listening to pop music that real love fresh from the bubbling libido is imperceptibly rehabilitated into commodity-love. Pop lyrics with their saccharine buffet of anaclitic affects are possibly the most powerful machinery discovered by capitalism to effect this transition. They are an inducement to choose one reality principle over another in the market-place of competing reality principles. The tears that sometimes reappear in our eyes when we're knocked about by an old love song are not 100% pure commodity; they have enough of our own infancy blent into them to keep the eyes from which they tip out firmly shut to the true business of their social and economic production and the problem of who owns the means of it.

In his essay on narcissism, Freud lists six possible 'paths leading to the choice of an object'. Anyone condemned only to one list or the other, or to an imperfect combination made up of both, cannot in Freud's reckoning ever be really happy. Freud writes: 'a real happy love corresponds to the primal condition in which object-libido and ego-libido cannot be distinguished'.[18] That is, we are only truly happy when we enter a love relationship that gives us the illusion of being once more primally unable to discriminate between love for ourselves and love for our partner. In more technical terms: love for a 'love-object' and love for the ego itself. Now, this 'real happy love' is exactly consonant with the commodity-love experienced by teenagers listening to pop songs; this psychological triumph of the culture industry meets its most ruthless criticism only in art which, like Frank Zappa's *We're Only In It for the Money*, conducts a full-blown assault not just on the bourgeois sensibilities of its audience, but on the deep psychical stupefaction that fuels capitalism's recuperating machines.

Picture a naked teenage boy prancing around in front of the mirror in his bedroom, with a hairbrush in his fist, singing "The Power of Love" by Huey Lewis and The News. Exactly what kind of narcissism is this? It is none of Freud's four types of narcissistic love, not even the third, since the boy would not like to be Huey Lewis so much as to believe that "The Power of Love" was actually his own creation. In

Totem and Taboo, Freud discusses what he calls the 'animistic' thinking of archaic societies and its residue in contemporary psychical processes. Animism is a structure of thought in which 'things become less important than the ideas of things,' such that 'relations which hold between the ideas of things are assumed to hold equally between the things themselves'.[19] Animistic thinking originates in the belief that thoughts themselves are 'omnipotent'. Freud remarks that 'in the animistic epoch the reflection of the internal world is bound to blot out the other picture of the world—the one which we seem to perceive'. The result, he says, is 'a general over-valuation...of all mental processes'.[20] The world turns into a spectacle of our own creation, its events and appearances governed by our own essentially infantile thinking. The contemporary American psychoanalyst Leo Balter describes how this kind of thinking is an important part of what he calls the 'aesthetic illusion', a kind of best-possible experience of art 'accompanied by narcissistically enhanced elation'.[21]

When we as teenagers listen to music that we love, we sign up for the illusion that it somehow makes us more loveable; but why, and how? As with much of Freud's writing, this moment in *Totem and Taboo* needs only a quick Marxist detournement to hit its peak truth-content. Freud writes of 'a general overvaluation' of mental processes in animistic thinking. But in the case of the 'aesthetic illusion' triggered by pop music in the heads of teenagers on the slide from real love into commodity-love, the 'overvaluation' is literal and economic: it is surplus value; and the 'mental processes' are no longer those of a primitive animistic community which constructs a meaning for its own life and death through ritual expressions of wishing; instead, the 'mental processes' are the data of market-research. Our teenage participation in the new ritual of pop music consumption is still animistic: we consume music-commodities as if they were our own mental processes. Think again of that nude 13 year-old. He writes out the lyrics of a song, and by writing them out in his own handwriting he gets this feeling that the song is being pulled into his life and his heart, and even that by writing it out it has become a song about him or to him, thus repressing in his mind as totally irrelevant the memory that he bought it in Woolworth's: it has become his own creation. And how does he love this part of himself? At once in a narcissistic and an anaclitic fashion:

a commodified mirror image of Freud's 'real happy love' in which 'object-libido and ego-libido cannot be distinguished'. We lean on the commodity we are.

The similarity of this adolescent good behaviour to the claims made by post-structuralist theoreticians of reading as a kind of production on the part of the reader herself are pretty obvious. I might even speculate that this theoretical attitude can be explained ontogenetically as a late resistance to the reality principle, mounted by adult litterateurs who never really stopped believing that the pop songs they bought when they were first learning how to masturbate were essentially their own creations. Roland Barthes made something interesting out of this fantasy, but he grew up playing Schumann sonatas on the piano; whether anything interesting will be made out of it by a generation fucked daily in the oval window by Girls Aloud and Justin Timberlake is open to some sort of debate.

The animistic thinking brought to life by the narcissism of this 'aesthetic illusion', says Balter, 'conceives the external world as having properties corresponding to the contents and forms of infantile mental life'. But the external world does have these properties, not just in the image of it projected by adolescent narcissism but in its real, material image. This is the triumph of the culture industry: it turns what Freud called the 'overvaluation of mental processes' into real overvaluation in the form of surplus value realised into capital. It will continue to do this for as long as it manages to deceive its flock of consumers into the conscious or unconscious belief that the 'mental processes' given to them as pop songs are out there only to be fused back into the consumer's own spontaneous feelings and needs. That is to say, for as long as adolescents on the slide into adulteration go on believing narcissistically that these cynical pieces of shit are in some magical sense their own creations, only to buy-in ten years or so later to a reality principle engineered by the culture industry that tells them to be forever nostalgic for that delusion. Narcissism is both the psychic end-point of the capitalist finishing school and its mass ontogenetic breeding ground; and if the self we fall in love with can be sold to us at a decent profit margin, so much the better.

So what would an irrecuperable art look or sound like? And why do I think that *We're Only In It for the Money* is one such work of art? One of the first conditions is that it should totally and violently frustrate the impulse of its consumer to fantasise that it is his own production. Art that matches the description broadcast by Roland Barthes is by definition recuperable. The 'reader as producer' is merely a lone practitioner of recuperation acting out in solitude her variations on the main act of social recuperation to follow. She is a one-woman test audience. How can art be so violent that it resists this kind of individualistic recuperation? At a very basic level, it needs to have within it somewhere or other an unadulterated FUCK YOU in the form of some ethical or political or sexual exhibition that the one-man test audience could never imagine to be his own production, because its confrontation against him is too powerful and total to be subsumed under the product-heading of his own immediate cognition. And it needs to be a FUCK YOU that has the final word, not one of those substitutes in capitalism's endless succession of substitutes that ends up sounding more like, fuck you because after all you sort of want to be fucked and anyhow we both know that neither of us is really the target of any of this so we can keep these sapient grins plastered across our half-sapient faces. That is, the work of art must have something in it, some moment, that is not capable of being subordinated to the free play of abstract interpretive fantasy that is then declared to be the work of art itself.

Art must get a stranglehold on the imagination of its audience until they are made to gasp out in panic for some real air, rather than the steady drift of ether through the consumption snorkel. It needs to be irresistibly mediated by the suffering that consumer narcissism causes and relies on for its continued dominance. It needs at some level to be something that we can't agree with or don't want, even if later, with the benefit of dialectical reflection, we decide that we agree with it on account of its disagreeableness and want it on account of its unwantableness. In fact, irrecuperable art is conceivable as a source of pleasure only with this dialectic up and running. It is a condition of our enjoying the irrecuperable art work that what we most sweetly enjoy is how it offends and needles against the institution of enjoyment itself as the latter exists in and for capitalist culture. At its best, Zappa's music is a jump cable clamped on to the dialectical motor of the brain and sexual body, using its unadulterated FUCK YOU to rouse that motor back into action after a life spent rusting cheerfully in the pop music garage.

We're Only In It for the Money grabs the market-research data out of the hands of its owners and reproduces every affect on Hannett's list in a gloating duplication of all the average love songs it can muster, thus decisively reducing their stupefaction-potential to zero. If I love it, it's because it also grabs hold of the commodified mirror of Freud's 'real happy love' and gets it out of my face, pushing it back in to the faces of those whose stupefaction amounts finally to job security for the market-researchers for whom stupidity is bread, butter, milk and honey all rolled into a revolting luxury *éclair.*

1. See the propaganda article against commercial-free broadcasting by Ian Murray, dated 11 August 2003, at the Competitive Enterprise Institute website, *<http://www.cei.org/gencon/019,03597.cfm>*: Reith 'believed strongly that the BBC should become a single broadcaster for the nation, bringing news and culture to those who had never experienced either before'. Reith felt the BBC needed 'the brute force of monopoly' in its mission to 'inform, education [*sic*] and entertain ... [and] bring the best of everything to the greatest number of homes'. Reith was very much an establishment man. During the 1926 general strike, he argued that the BBC ought to support the government absolutely, 'because the BBC was the people's service and the government the people's government'.
2. *Ibid.*
3. Compare Freud: 'a particular way is adopted of dealing with any internal excitations which produce too great an increase of pleasure: there is a tendency to treat them as though they were acting, not from the inside, but from the outside, so that it may be possible to bring the shield against stimuli into operation as a means of defence against them. This is the origin of projection.', 'Beyond the Pleasure Principle', 1920; *The Standard Edition of the Complete Works of Sigmund Freud*, London: Vintage, 2001, Vol.18, p. 29. Freud's analysis is something of an allegory for the social and economic manifestations of patriotism and xenophobia.
4. See Paul A. Baran, 'Theses on Advertising', 1964; *The Longer View*, New York: Monthly Review Press, 1969, p. 224: 'Under oligopolistic conditions, price competition is avoided as a response to the insufficiency of demand and other forms of sales effort are substituted'. I will return to this word 'substituted'.
5. *Editors' Note:* We weren't happy with this characterisation of Adorno, and so wrote to Keston asking: Is 'humanism' the right term for academic complacency and middleclass gentility? Isn't Debord proposing revolutionary activism as against academic careerism? The Situationists *hated* the structuralists, and had no time for Althusser's 'epistemological break' with the humanism of the young Marx. Given a choice between the 'humanism' of Marx (and Dunayevskaya and Cliff) and the 'anti-humanism' of the academy, we're humanists ourselves! We think—like authenticity/inauthenticity—humanism/anti-humanism is a bit of a red herring. Besides, calling Adorno a humanist isn't strictly accurate. In his paper, Marco stresses Adorno's 'anti-subjectivism', and there's lots in *Negative Dialectics* to back him up (Ashton's translation, p. 190). We object to the *faux* radicalism of academics saying they hate people. Of course, if you want to be in that camp, it's your article, but we'd prefer: 'Debord's practical view of class struggle distinguishes the Situationists from anything Theodor Adorno or other wait-and-see theorists might have said'. Theory/Practice seems to us the real debate within Marxism, although maybe an academic/activist distinction would work here too. Señor Sutherland replied: I think I'll stick with the humanism remark. I don't disagree with anything you said, but neither do I think that my comment about

Adorno and humanism was so obviously pejorative; it was simply a comparison. Maybe a hint of a scowl, but nothing solid. And in any case it's a rhetorical moment intended rather to provoke readers than to hand them a signpost.

6. My translation. In the original French: 'Mais il faut comprendre que nous allons assister, participer à une *course de vitesse entre les artistes libres et la police pour expérimenter et développer l'emploi des nouvelles techniques de conditionnement.* Dans cette course la police a déjà un avantage considérable. De son issue dépend pourtant l'apparition d'environnements passionnants et libérateurs, ou le renforcement—scientifiquement contrôlable, sans brèche—de l'environnement du vieux monde d'oppression et d'horreur.' *Internationale Situationniste* No 1, edited Guy Debord, June 1958, p. 8.
7. Frances Hannett, 'The Haunting Lyric. The Personal and Social Significance of American Popular Songs', *The Psychoanalytic Quarterly* Vol.33, 1964, pp. 226-269.
8. *Ibid*, p. 237.
9. Theodore Reik, *The Haunting Melody*, New York: Farrar, Straus and Young, 1953.
10. Hannett, 'The Haunting Lyric', p. 237.
11. *Ibid.*
12. Interview with Kurt R. Eissler, 18 October 1952, *Reich Speaks of Freud*, edited Mary Higgins and Chester M. Raphael, translated Therese Pol, Harmondsworth: Penguin, 1975, p. 52. [*Editors' Note:* Hmmm, Reich's argument sounds perfectly reasonable to us ...]
13. Hannett, 'The Haunting Lyric', p. 255.
14. *Op. Cit.*, p. 257.
15. Freud, 'On Narcissism: An Introduction', 1914; translated James Strachey, *The Standard Edition of the Complete Works of Sigmund Freud* Vol.14, p. 90.
16. *Op. Cit.*, p. 87.
17. *Ibid.*
18. *Op. Cit.*, p. 90.
19. Freud, *Totem and Taboo*, 1913; translated James Strachey, *The Standard Edition of the Complete Works of Sigmund Freud* Vol.13, p. 85.
20. *Ibid.*
21. Leo Balter, 'Magic and the Aesthetic Illusion', *Journal of the American Psychoanalytic Association* 50/4, 2002, p. 1165.

Xenoarrangements
or
Insane Grafts Day-Dreamed by a Zappa Hard-Core Fanatic Not Inclined to Come Out of His Own Monomaniacal World

Francesco Gentile[1]

"Drowning Witch" is one of those pieces in which guitar improvisations constitute actual 'movements' with their own role in the composition, and with a musical meaning dictated by the soloist. To take a contrasting example, the guitar solo of "Cosmik Debris" is conceived (though of course *à la* Zappa) more according to blues and rock standards. Zappa has worked very hard for accurate versions of "Drowning

Witch", both in live performance and in the studio post-production phase. The first released version was constructed using fifteen 1981 live edits.[2] Some years later, thanks to *You Can't Do That on Stage Anymore Vol.3*, we could hear a second version built upon at least 6 live edits from both 1982 and 1984 performances. In the liner notes Zappa wrote:

> This is a hard song to play. How hard? The 1984 band never played it correctly during its 6-month tour, and the 1982 band only managed to get close on one occasion. This edit collates the best efforts of both groups.

Hence, how to deal with "Drowning Witch" if you lead a rock band with enough *virtuosi* to play the thing, or (still better) an orchestra like the Ensemble Modern? In the first case, you may be tempted to programme two improvised solos in the sections where Zappa improvised so many times. The new soloist would need to understand his or her role: the first solo builds tension, the second relaxes the listener and prepares for the finale. Thinking about an orchestra arrangement, the idea of writing special passages arises, however the question of an adequate rendering remains.

Prior to facing this issue, let's see what happened in the case of "Revised Music for Guitar and Low Budget Orchestra". Here we can listen to a solo with a role similar to those of "Drowning Witch", as far as how that musical event contributes to the overall conception of the piece. Ali N. Askin wrote an arrangement of "Revised Music", solving the problem by transcribing the guitar solo for other instruments, just as FZ did himself by asking Mike Keneally and Paul Carman to arrange Jimmy Page's guitar solo on "Stairway to Heaven" for horns (see *The Best Band You Never Heard in Your Life*).

Deriving a composition from a transcription of a guitar solos is a Zappa custom. The second movement of "Sad Jane" is one example. As he put it:

> The last movement of "Sad Jane", kind of a marching thing, is actually a transcription of a guitar solo from the Shrine Auditorium, 1968, that Ian Underwood wrote out back then, and I came

> across one day in a pile of papers. I played it on the piano and liked the tune, and proceeded to orchestrate it.[3]

"Revised Music for Low Budget Orchestra" with a transcription of the guitar solo is now in the repertoire which the Ensemble Modern performed in 2000, in a show entitled 'Greggery Peccary and Other Persuasions' in 2003. The same programme appears on the RCA Red Seal CD with the same title. This is a very important album because it includes a lot of arrangements written by Askin after Zappa's death in 1993. Many groups and orchestras have performed music from the catalogue which Zappa's death closed 11 years ago. The Ensemble Modern is probably the only one which has played music that has *developed* since 1993, and developed in the right direction, as the Askin choices for "Revised Music" prove. Unfortunately Askin has (temporarily?) ceased working with this music. We hope that other arrangers will follow his example.

Anyway, let's go back to our original question. Are there convincing alternatives to either the transcription of Zappa's guitar solos or to supplying new guitar improvisations?

We answer in the affirmative!

I have emphasised how the solos we are dealing with play a very precise role in certain pieces. Therefore, if the arranger of "Drowning Witch" were to replace the two solos with two other Zappa compositions derived from guitar solo transcriptions, such transcriptions should be expressively akin to the music. We do not have a vast catalogue of candidates. The "Big Swifty" theme should be one of them, but as for the others, the hunt can now start. It's a risky business. If the arranger of this new hypothetical "Drowning Witch" doesn't want to use new guitar improvisations in place of the two 'movements' constituted by the two original Zappa solos, he could try to *graft* in two Zappa compositions that could play equivalent roles as far as statistical density and conceptual continuity are concerned. We anticipate that such a project would bring ferocious criticism down on the arranger from hardcore Zappa fans, no matter how good the outcome sounded. However, we do think that the idea is not so far-fetched. Zappa often resorted to patchworks, sometimes constructed using the music of other composers (a remark that suggests an even more risky project!). Recently, we have insanely day-dreamed of such grafts applied to

Burnt Weeny Sandwich, an album that probably features one of the best A-sides in the Zappa *opus*. We were wondering 'How could *Burnt Weeny*'s first side be performed by orchestra, vocalists and rock rhythm section'? Of course, the immediate answer tends to be: 'Without those guitar solos ("Theme from Burnt Weeny Sandwich" and "Holiday in Berlin, Full Blown") or that guitarist ... No Way!'. The more considered answer consists of the following programme (grafted music underlined):

1. "WPLJ" 2:53
2. "Igor's Boogie, Phase One" 0:36
3. "Overture to a Holiday in Berlin" 1:27
4. "The Clap" 1:23
5. "Igor's Boogie, Phase Two" 0:34
6. "Bogus Pomp Overture" 1:01
7. "Would You Like a Snack?" 1:22
8. "Holiday in Berlin" 2:41
9. "Janet's Big Dance Number" 1:18
10. "Aybe Sea" 2:46

1, 2, 3, 5 and 10 derive from *Burnt Weeny*, 4 comes from *Chunga's Revenge*, 6 is the first minute of "Bogus Pomp" as played on *London Symphony Orchestra Vol.II*, 7 (0:00 to 1:22) and 9 come from *200 Motels*, and 8 from the bootleg *Tengo na' Minchia Tanta* included in the second *Beat the Boots* box set issued by Rhino Records in 1992 (track 12, 1:55 to 4:36).

The sequence 6, 7, 8 replaces the first part of "Holiday in Berlin, Full Blown", but it's the same music. This hypothetical arrangement also includes the 1971 vocal version of "Holiday In Berlin", never released officially by Zappa (apart from being included in the *Beat the Boots* series). We have to admit that "The Clap" is not very satisfying as a replacement for "Theme from Burnt Weeny Sandwich", however "Janet's Big Dance Number" seems sort-of-suitable (considering that this whole exercise is a day-dream) as a follow-up for the "Holiday in Berlin, Full Blown" guitar solo.

Interpret the above as a crude experiment, just to illustrate my idea of Zappological 'grafting'. We are prepared for the quarrels and insults which are the inevitable reward for hatching new ideas in the realm of Zappology. We dream of risky projects involving musicians and orchestras—and hopefully inspired and generous institutions—who are willing to give their commitment to such musical work over a decade after the death of Frank Zappa. 'So it goes', as people say on Tralfamadore.

1. Francesco Gentile wishes it to be stated that he is a member of Debra Kadabra, the Italian Frank Zappa Appreciation Consortium. His monomaniacal self is contactable at <*effeg@tiscali.it*>.
2. Tom Mulhern, 'I'm Different, or Not Exactly Duane Allman', *Guitar Player*, February 1983.
3. Frank Zappa, 'Non-Foods', *Guitar Player*, November 1983.

The Conservatism of Easy Rider: Zappa's Critique of Dumb Concepts of Freedom

Jürgen Gispert

One day during my decade in Armenia, I went to see my professor. I saw he had a little video-tape library. It contained the original version of *Easy Rider*. This was interesting, because the year was 1999, thirty years after its release. It was shortly before Dennis Hopper announced that he was still of the opinion that *Easy Rider* was a revolutionary film. This struck me. I was wondering, how he could have said this. Up to this time I'd seen the film twice: in 1977, and in 1984 or 1985. So I borrowed this original version to see what would happen now; and to try and understand Dennis Hopper's statement.

Any text might have to be interpreted all over again every five years or so. This is an interesting idea, because it takes into consideration the fact that human beings are able to grow and develop during their life-times. Indeed, a Barbie doll might change its face over the years, although for a lot of people in the Western world, recognition of this fact is not possible. Thus it may make sense to take another look at *Easy Rider*. Now you perhaps may wonder, 'How has he got time to do this?'. In Bad Doberan at Zappanale #14, when I met Ben Watson for the first time, I told him about my experience in Armenia, seeing and writing about *Easy Rider*. Afterwards he wrote a letter to me, saying 'since you spoke to me, I've noticed how everyone really STUPID thinks the film is a definition of freedom!!'. He encouraged me to report on this film at ICE-Z. At first I was a little bit anxious. Taking a film which is already 35 years old only to demolish it? Cheepnis! Maybe a better intervention at ICE-Z would be to talk about something more recent, more relevant. I could have tackled Arnold Schwarzenegger and his films, or Donald Duck, that other Austrian.

But I think *Easy Rider* is still of great significance. It may seem to be only of historical value, yet its message reached a global audience. It swept the ocean, just like the Mud Shark did. It has been integrated into a so-called alternative world, and become legendary. I think it also tells us something about the US-American world of today, and so it should be subject to a special investigation. In contradiction to the beliefs of many concerned minds today—including Mr Hopper's—this film *ain't* revolutionary. It is in fact an advertisement for 're-evolution', which means making a repetition of the same or similar. The film is part of the machinery of the culture industry which it pretends to subvert. It's a new version of the same old stale thing. Let's look at the film.

The two main actors of this film are called Billy (*alias* Captain America *alias* Peter Fonda) and Wyatt (*alias* Dennis Hopper). The names recall those of the outlaws Billy the Kid and Wyatt Earp. In doing so one has to take into consideration that Kid and Earp are ambivalent figures in American perception history. In this respect, Billy may both be an outlaw and a national hero. This idea is emphasized by the jacket Billy is wearing. On the back, the stars and stripes can be seen. He also wears a helmet decorated with the US flag. As we know, the two protagonists make a drug deal to get their ride financed.

From the start, a polarization is evident. Billy and Wyatt are refused hotel rooms. American country people are hostile to them. This opposition accompanies us throughout the film. This main opposition could be called 'living alternative' against 'rigid conservatism'. But that is a superficial interpretation. Let us look at the first long sequence after the big drug deal. One of the bikes has a flat. Bill and Wyatt have to mend the tyre. They arrive at a farm. The farmer is working. He allows them to mend the tyre by saying: 'Go into the stable'. One hears the sound of a hammer, a horse is being shoed. Just beside this, the bikers are fixing the Harley Davidson's tyre. Shoeing the horse is equivalent to fixing the tyre. Already here we have a premonition of what happens in the rest of the film. An alternative is suggested, which however proves to be part of the mainstream it claims to be opposing.

In the next scene, the farmer's family and Billy and Wyatt are sitting at a big table. The family, a couple with many children, is praying before eating. They thank God for the food they've managed to grow. Billy is astonished:

> You're living from the earth. You harvest what you sow. You are your own master. Who from us can do *that*?

So these two hip guys from Los Angeles, the pinnacle of US consumerism and luxury, are impressed by people living close to the land—in a rough backwater where everyone dreams of visiting Los Angeles once in their lifetime.

On the road again, they pick up a hitch-hiker, who leads them to his commune in a camp in the desert. In a long shot, we see hills and mountains between the bikers. And this sequence somehow recalls Marlboro Country, as shown in the famous advertisement series. The cowboys smoke cigarettes on their horses, by that token enjoying the fresh air of 'free America'; the bikers smoke joints on their Harleys.

Meanwhile, the three have arrived at the hitch-hiker's home in the desert. There we witness several couples with many children. We do not know who's attached to whom. The hitch-hiker kisses several women one after another. These unconventional sexual relations make them Hippie-Mormons. They have a difficult life in the desert. In one scene, we see the hitch-hiker together with Billy and Wyatt in a field. Behind them we see other communards sowing something. The sun is burning down. It's hot. Billy asks 'Does it rain here at all?'. The hippie answers 'For this we have to dance'. Wyatt says 'They never will make it!'. Billy shouts 'They're gonna make it. They gonna make it!'.

In one of the next scenes, we see the commune praying before eating.

> We have sowed. We ask to be rewarded for our efforts. Thank you for the power to withstand. Amen!

We have here the construction of another opposition. At the start of the film, Billy and Wyatt visit a conventional family on a farm. They are a large family, and highly religious. In contrast, the Hippie-Mormons are 'other people'. The respectable family at the well-ordered farm pray for what will grow anyway, while the Hippie-Mormons are praying that anything grows at all. But listen to what Billy is saying: 'They're gonna make it!'. Sylvester Stallone is watching you: from winding up working in a gas station directly to the heart of Wall Street.

The seeming primitiveness of the Hippie-Mormons connects to the sacred aspect of their lives. Primitiveness here means origin, it means beginning. Here we have what I mentioned above as 're-evolution'. Origin is the condition and beginning of any evolution. The commune in the desert is a description of the growth of a new social cell, which—of course—has religion as its basis. This sect begins its existence in dust. In dust it begins, in dust everyone of them will end.

The rain-dancing by the Hippie-Mormons recalls the anti-rain chant sung by the crowd at Woodstock. But whereas the former is fictive, the latter actually happened. Standing and sitting in mud and rain, they chanted: 'No rain!'. Both recall archaic actions. The difference is that the man responsible for making rain in archaic society does it when he knows that rain is likely. If he fails, he endangers his social position. In Woodstock, everyone is there in the mud chanting 'No rain!'. This is weird, because it's illogical to roll in mud whilst praying against rain. But this, too, carries the same message: 'They're gonna make it!'. Thus, structurally, the respectable family and the

Hippie-Mormons are on the same horizontal level. The so-called alternative, the unconventional, is actually the convention itself.

In another scene, Billy and Wyatt are challenged by country bigots. Jack Nicholson acts the lawyer who gets them out of jail. He decides to go along with them for a while. He tells them a lot about the people living around in the countryside. We have one scene in a town bar, where people, among them the Sheriff, are looking suspiciously at the strangers. The latter aren't served. Nicholson explains the hostile remarks from the people sitting around as 'rural humour'. Some girls from the town are eager to be taken with them on their bikes. But they ride away—it would be too dangerous.

The same evening, they are discussing the past day round a camp fire. Nicholson says to Wyatt: 'They are afraid of what you represent'. This representation refers to freedom. Nicholson interprets rural life for the urban dissidents. The latter seem to be situated in an asymmetrical periphery, where the rural dweller is on top and the urban citizen is below. But the most striking point is the word 'freedom', by which the bikers are negatively ascribed. In entering the rural space, the bikers are demonstrating another life, which shows rural people the limited nature of the life they lead. But by ascribing 'freedom' to the way the bikers are living, 'freedom' in itself is negated, because already negatively defined. Nothing else than hate may arise out of this: Nicholson is killed in one of the next scenes. One could theorize that this violent way of producing negativity and projecting it on an imagined outer sphere is a fundamental principle for every sect, especially in the USA. This supports the above mentioned general opposition 'alternative/conventional', but on a vertical scale.

In the next important scene, we see Billy and Wyatt going along with two prostitutes. They are visiting New Orleans. They try some special drug, which the Hippie-Mormons gave them as a present. They are in a somewhat lonely place, a cemetery, or a park with a small lake. The drugs are working. Mumblings and incomprehensible words can be heard, and bible verses. We are confronted with spiritual music. The film image twists about, showing us the effect of the drugs. This experience is connected to the religious sphere by the music.

Later that day Wyatt says to Billy: 'We are rich. Money... Florida...'. Billy responds: 'We're duds!'

The last scene is the death of both of them on the road. Two men, having changed their horses for an old lorry, kill them.

Inner correspondences are working, which refer to the semantic connections between the chromium of the Harley and the plasticity of the horse in rural life. Direct transferences equate the farm family with the Hippie-Mormons. The latter already have all elements out of which a good farm-life is made: 'They're gonna make it!', or 'In God we trust'. Among them we have the new rising sect: the two bikers. They are seeking an alternative. But any alternative in the marketplace, if it wants to survive, has to find an economic niche, or create one. Thus, in the USA, they have got no other way forward than to start a new sect.

For us, the consumers of the film, a counter-culture is being proposed by the two bikers. But in fact it's an integral part of the old world. The opposition 'alternative/conventional' actually encodes the whole system of warring sects which characterises the American market economy. Any action versus this contradiction only reproduces the contradiction. There is no real action in the film against the contradiction anyway. Thus the simple question is: why do we need the freedom represented by Billy and Wyatt, if we already have a quiet convenient life on the other side of the borderline? Thus violence against outsiders is the ideological logic of the film, which therefore reproduces the American drama. The death of both our stars is not violence in the strict sense of the term. This death is a necessary condition; it is simply a positive action. As we know, Woodstock was start of a myth which swept the ocean. The 'spirit' of Woodstock died, while those who ruined and exploited its 'idealism' where the ones who thrived and prospered. But in fact there was no difference between the idealists and the exploiters. They were all the same class of people.

During his time in the USA, anthropologist Günter Anders had the following experience. He and two American friends walked up Mount Washington. For hours they heard music resounding up from the valley hotel. The song, which insisted on the message 'Love is only possible in Honolulu', pained Anders, but the other two liked it. Their mental state did not change until an 'acoustic borderline' was reached and the music was obscured. Then one of the Americans said: 'Sort of weird ...'. Anders answered: 'Weird? Aren't we in the open?'. They said they looked forward to returning within hearing range of the music. When they did, it dawned on Anders what they meant by their wish: 'Suddenly we heard music again; no, not only music, but the same monopolistic claim that love is only love in Honolulu'. And this happened on top of Mount Washington, which had been equipped with loudspeakers which 'covered the mountain like light from an acoustic lighthouse', as Anders writes. When the acoustic darkness, the Nothing, was behind them one of the Americans said: 'Wasn't it like crossing a river?'. The other answered: 'Isn't it nice to be there again?'. Anders interprets the 'there' as 'I am present (in the sense of being with it), thus I'm there, thus I am'. Anders transfers this phenomenon onto some kind of an acoustic map, where for the Americans not hearing the song signifies unfreedom. Americans crave the space of the commercial mass media like a poodle wanting to be put on a lead: the space of silence as freedom of the self lies fallow. For Anders, this is now a global problem.[1]

We may transfer this event to *Easy Rider*: the public as members of the counter-culture are present and absent at the same time. The consumer is serving the product, not the other way round. And the product is delivered into a cinema or sitting-room in an alienated state. By communicating in the space, the subject would be interrupting it. Things are circulating by themselves. If man intervenes, the movement of things is arrested. Billy's jacket shows us that only the stars and stripes can underline their bid for freedom. Thus no real moment of opposition becomes evident. They are bikers—but they're biking round a roundabout.

Collective praying and solidarity in an obviously infertile desert seem to represent another way of life, but in fact it's just another competitive strategy, sustained by the slogan 'They're gonna make it!'. They see their future in the sand of the desert, although it well might be a waste of time doing this. Individualism is saved by membership of a community, which encompasses and penetrates the members of the same community. Billy and Wyatt are looking for an alternative, but on so doing they only show us the recurrence of the same. The end of the outsiders is the end of an arising sect, which gets exterminated.

'The instrument is its own employer': in our context, this means that in the very moment we have an instrument in our hand, we are not served by this instrument, but became its servants. Thus the hippie movement in the USA was a simple reproduction of systemic complexity. It is presented as something 'new', a proposed super-system. Let's have a look at the science-fiction films which are supposedly leading us into a future world. But this future world is the present world transferred into the future. Those science-fiction films where you can see an amazing futuristic space vehicle, but it's still emblazoned with the stars and stripes on its wings, are very funny. In this respect Neil Armstrong is the real American freak. He's riding an 'alternative' vehicle. He may have more fans among the bourgeoisie than our sectarians on their Harleys, but all of them are bourgeois anyway.

Reality in itself can't be experienced, it is part of that reality which is constructing it.

> The real—the alleged model—has to be adequate to its possible pictures, has to be changed according to the picture of its reproductions.[2]

According to Anders reality itself becomes phantom, that means it is a fiction, thus no more subject to experience.

> All reality becomes phantomic, everything fictitious real.[3]

Referring to the perception of reality (*Wirklichkeit*), we have become inexperienced. The actual strange or unknown, which normally has to be experienced, enters our sitting-room as alienated reality. Thus we become actively *in*experienced. The German word for 'inexperienced' is 'unerfahren'. Anders uses '*un*-erfahren' meaning 'not having travelled the world'. Another German word for 'erfahren' is 'bewandert'. In former times, those people who wandered around the world were acknowledged as 'experienced'. Thus in the word 'Erfahrung', the wanderer's function is encompassed: he who only experiences reality by travelling away from home. Thus the famous slogan 'home is where the heart is' is not only ridiculous, it is antiquated. Heart is *lack* of experience, because the strange and the known are getting more and more inaccessible. In this respect, it is also ridiculous, when, after Silvio Berlusconi accused the Germans of being Nazis, the German Chancellor declared he didn't want to go for a holiday in Italy, but would stay at home in Hanover. But the strange or foreign isn't 'foreign' any more, it consists of all the things you already have at home, for example, Mr. Schröder. The home is the alienated foreign, and vice versa. And to recur to the slogan above: Any *body* is heartless. There is no individual heart, because an individual heart is itself the alienated strange.

Films like *Easy Rider* deny real protest against the American way of life, we're silenced. This was worked out by the young German writer Peter Handke in one of his poems from the 60s, where he is asked about the news from Vietnam and what he thinks about it. He gets angry and shouts: What should his opinion be? He is only given news which capitalism allows him! Thus the hearer can learn about the world, but he can not be heard by the latter.[4] Thus the transmitted events are present and absent in the same moment, real and apparent in the same moment, there and not there the same moment. In short, they are phantoms.[5]

TV, music and film are giving something without giving it in reality, because they're keeping it—they are keeping, while giving. Beyond that: in the same moment when keeping the given, it is already extinguished. Mass-produced consumer items are born to die[6]—not born to be wild. By the way, here we have the identity of what I mentioned above: the so-called 'wild' had to be killed in the end to give way to its successors.

Present-day virtuality of communication corresponds to the matrix state of communication itself. Let us take the worldwide newspaper forums, where people, who never have seen each other before, are discussing themes, which are provided by the newspaper. Thus the communication is already channeled by the newspaper itself, but passed off as 'free discourse'. In this respect the individual mind is not individual, but depends on a theme provided for him or her by something else.

You may wonder about the similarity of the word 'Matrix', used by Anders and those three little eternities of cinema named *Matrix*. The latter films are examples of the present-day situation described by Anders' term.

Easy Rider was a big shooting star, which however was very fertile. But in any case, it was a shooting star. There is a tendency of the rate of the shooting star to fall. It seems—I emphasize the 'seems'—that the constructing of shooting stars as children of the culture industry is today's main programme. Obviously, the European reception of *Easy Rider* followed a big PR-push. This is not a new story, as we know. But it is funny, how the decontextualization worked. In 1968, when the Mothers of Invention played some concerts in Germany, Zappa was confronted with the demand to connect with the left scene, which he refused. After that angry activists in Germany renamed his band 'The Mothers of Reaction'.

As kind of an officially sanctioned contradiction to this, the same activists probably welcomed the *Easy Rider* film with its message of peace and freedom. I can't work out here exactly the reason for this blind activism. Jürgen Habermas said about the revolutionaries.

> They confuse symbolization with reality, which, in medical terms is called a hallucination.[7]

Easy Rider, like all American cultural product, was integrated in an already existing sphere of reception and perception. Zappa's music was assumed to fit in the same way, and the left scene was puzzled when he didn't fit their myth.

But Zappa goes beyond this. What Anders calls 'matrix', Zappa calls 'plastic'. This means: *Easy Rider* is not progressive and the Mothers were not reactionary.

Let us take a few examples from the early records by the Mothers. This also gives us a chance to have a look at the period which produced *Easy Rider.* On *Freak Out!* we have the song "Who Are the Brain Police?", whose 1st and 3rd verse I want to cite: 'What will you do/If we let you go home/And the plastic's all melted/And so is the chrome/WHO ARE THE BRAIN POLICE?... What will you do if the/People you knew/Were the plastic that melted/And the chromium too?'[8]

The first part outlines the effects of manipulation by the industry, which protects its consumers from real acoustical freedom, the autonomy of the self, which has melted plastic as its condition. The second part focuses on the client himself, who is confronted with a new state, in which he must recognize that all he admired before was made of plastic. The line "Who are the brain police?" connotes the relationship among people in today's times, as described above.

"The Chrome Plated Megaphone of Destiny" on *We're Only In It for the Money* is similar. Here also the monopolization of the individual by the system is the theme. It is an instrumental, as we know, but the text given by Zappa on the sleeve is the core. He tells listeners to read Kafka's story "In the Penal Colony".[9] For our purpose, it is sufficient to notice that in the story the prisoner who is to be killed by the machine does not know the reason for his punishment. He is inside the process and outside it in the same moment. In Anders' terms, the client is 'present and absent' at the same moment. There is no personal relationship between him and the punishment he should suffer. Even between him and the machine, which will kill him, there is no relationship. In Kafka's text the traveller asks the commander if the convict knows the reason for his punishment. The commander responds:

> It would be senseless to say it to him. He will experience it on his body.[10]

The punishment isn't understood. This is the striking point. On the one hand, Zappa integrates the hippie movement into the process by warning the listener about Camp Reagan, about 'the FINAL SOLUTION of the NONCONFORMIST (hippie?) PROBLEM'. But on the other hand, and this refers to the sixth point in Zappa's text, where he repeats Kafka's conclusion: 'At the end of the piece, the name of YOUR CRIME will be carved on your back'. Thus, as the potential member of the Hippie movement, the listener is being assaulted in a way he or she cannot understand.

How is this apparent contradiction between Kafka's and Zappa's text is to be resolved? There is a similar paradigm at work in the song "Absolutely Free" on *Money.* In an interview, Zappa was asked about the meaning of 'discorporate'. He answered: '"Discorporate" is talking about not being part of the corporation. 'Discorporate' normally means to leave your body, but in the sense of that song, remember it also says "Unbind your mind, escape from the weight of your *corporate logo*".'[11]

Looking at the Militant Esthetix website, I read the article by Marco Maurizi, where he mentions the 'hippie discorporate ideal'.[12] This supports my idea that it is not a mistake to make an addition to the author's own interpretation of his song. One must keep in mind the normal definition of 'discorporate'. It means to leave one's body.

In the song, Zappa plays with this double meaning. If you imagine the music of this very nice song, in the first case it is a parallel situation: the flower power feeling in the music is reflected by the text and vice versa. It seems that discorporation as 'leaving one's body' promises discorporation from society. But if you take the second case, the music is attacked as rubbish ('flower power sucks!'). There is a hard irony taking place, whose result is that hippie discorporation and flower power itself are just another sectarian development.

Discorporate means 'leaving the corporation' means 'leaving the community'. This emphasizes the role of the individual as autonomous. In our context this also means autonomy against the sect and finally also autonomy against the culture industry. Being a hippie means becoming a candidate for Reagan's concentration camp. By the way, 'Camp Reagan' also could be called 'Guantanamo Bay'. The bad is constructed by the self-constructed good to an excess. And the real discorporation here is to be used metaphorically: not to be servile to any collectivizing movement. Kafka is trying to unmask the possible totalitarian state. Zappa is trying to encourage the listener to avoid the trap of the already-existing totalitarianism of the culture industry.

Refering back to *Easy Rider*, this means that the rustic character of the dirty horseshoe is still reflected in the glittering chrome of the Harley Davidsons.

> When man is in the sphere of art, he isn't in life and vice versa. Between the both of them there is no unit and no reciprocal penetrating of the inner in the unit of personality.[13]

I call this relation 'art is out of life'. This means that art is part of life, yet outside at the same time. It seeks to encompass life in an expressive way, but in fact it's apart too. And the artist must recognize this.

So making art in itself is a deeply individual action, which leads one into another sphere, which enables one to transcend borders.

In this respect one can analyze Zappa's texts and music as multivocal, because they encode different perspectives on a given situation. That's the reason why in Zappa's music we find the treatment of a given univocal situation as only one theme among others. The well-known words on "Packard Goose" from *Joe's Garage* may be used in connection with the prolonged shooting star Michael Jackson. 'Truth is not beauty' means that Jacko is sold as beauty and as truth, but in reality there is only a culture industrial motivation to construct, exploit and extinguish a matrix, a phantom.

The next sentence in *Joe's Garage* is 'beauty is not love'. Beauty and love in themselves are totally ambivalent. The pop industry sells love in the double sense of the word. By acoustical wrapping-up, love itself is sold, betrayed.

In one sequence, Zappa describes this relationship in a very funny manner. During a concert he unmasks Peter Frampton's "I'm In You". He describes a fictitious, but all too real scene, in which a teenage girl is luring the dream of her life, the pop star, into her bed. Zappa gives us a very plausible narrative: she's undressing herself, he's climbing on top of her, and then his little voice is screaming 'I'm in you!'. One has to take into consideration that this puritanical American culture industry does not just manufacture such pieces of music: it creates the conditions which the song describes. It required Zappa's independence from corporate record-industry affiliations to issue this song.

Michael Jackson is the very example for matrix and phantom in personal union. He is not just the music he arranged. Physically, he has become what Anders wrote about 60 years ago. Jackson underwent plastic surgery. This gives his music a physical touch. Thus Jackson followed the plan to become both a phantom and a matrix. As phantom he reproduced certain given images—to be white, for example, which had the new face of Jackson as its consequence. In the same moment he is his own matrix, a copy, which has got its own time, but will be thrown away.

And this is the process we witness now. It is a normal king's death which gives way to another Jacko. The culture industry creates, conducts and exploits racism. Interesting enough to remark that in responding to white man's myth by disfiguring his own face, Jacko himself is reproducing racism by his own action, personally. Thus he is subject to what he himself is reproducing.

From time to time, catharsis is demanded. There are the lawsuits. The leading state lawyer of Jacko's case pleaded for people to report on possible other cases of sexual abuse in connection with the accused.

There were thousands of calls. One gets to wonder, if Jacko had any time at all to make his music. It would be no surprise if real Jackson fans were among those thousands who called to allege sexual intercourse with Jackson. They really love him. It would be no surprise, too, if there were any fans, preferably not above the age of 15, who put their red candles at the window to light the way for the matrix, the zombie. Jacko is for peace, too. Jackson is plasticity in person, a fully-styled thing, the prisoner in front of the killing machine. He doesn't understand what is going on with him either.

Conclusion

As you might have guessed, my story isn't quite finished yet. The thoughts I wrote down may be understood as the first steps for discussing cultural elements such as music or film. Thus a fully informed story about these elements referring to the USA would have to include much deeper thoughts about the sect system in the USA. For me, it was a striking moment when I realised that *Easy Rider* could be analyzed by using the sect structure. To understand present American culture one has to undertake further study into sects.

Referring to Zappa's music, I would rather like to put it—in analogy to what I said above—in just such a framework of US culture, of which it is a part. By the way, this also plays a role in those misguided interpretations in Germany, for example, where they integrated the Mothers of Invention into an already existing anti-American image. He is American, and it is questionable, whether in Germany, we have a comparable example. Thus it would be interesting to look for the conditions, the platform, on which such music is made. For example, in Germany with the "Jewish Princess" song on *Sheik Yerbouti* (1978), the question was whether there was any anti-semitism in Zappa's lyrics and music. In the second songbook, which was released in Germany after Zappa's death, there is a small footnote, which states that in this song Zappa refers to middle-class Jewish women, who appear to be nasty enough to make a beautiful song about. It must have been a theme in the USA, too, because, as we know, hereafter Zappa made a song about "Catholic Girls", who do not seem to lead any better a life. Thus he has nothing to do with anti-semitism.

The next point is the polyphonic aspect of the work, which is worth investigating. I tried this in a few examples, but these need to be completed by more musicological analysis, which I have as yet been unable to do.

I think it is possible to describe the contemporary situation in the USA. I started by analysing an old film, which one could, of course, relate to some texts by Zappa. The possibility of translating philosophical categories into these texts means it is possible to work scientifically with this material. But this does not imply that the work itself is scientific, for that would be to reduce art to science and science to art. So I would interpret the term 'Zappology' as a seriously worked out ironic stance *vis-à-vis* science, amongst other themes. I have a striking example for possible misunderstandings in this relationship. At the University of Mainz, there is a professor at the Department for German Language who claims to be the chief interpreter of the work of German writer Heinrich Böll. Thus he may have worked out an ultimative pattern of interpretation, how to read, how to interpret the work of Böll. It is significant that at no point in his life did Böll take any notice of it—because he was an artist. On the other hand, one may ask, whether the German Professor does indeed do any sort of scientific work in obsessing over Böll's work using such strict categories. He reduces the possible welter of interpretations that the artist's work offers. This does not mean that one can't understand art by using scientific instruments. But in the case of art one has to take into account the difference between art and truth. By the way, this is also part of a possible interpretation of the sentence 'music is the best', because the complexity of music serves as a transmitter, as a vehicle, as the expression itself of given thoughts, but it transcends the latter in the same moment in order to give way to other thoughts, which are in themselves restricted by what Charles Sanders Peirce called 'infinite semiosis'. This infinite semiosis describes both scientific work and the work of an artist, but neither of them are compatible with each other.

Nietzsche's 'We possess *art* lest we *perish of the truth*'[14] can be taken as a possible—I think a necessary—sign on the road of interpretation.

1. Günther Anders, *Die Antiquiertheit des Menschen: über die Seele im Zeitalter der zweiten industriellen Revolution Vol.2*, München: Beck, 1992.
2. 'Das Wirkliche—das angebliche Vorbild—muß also seinen eventuellen Abbildungen angemessen, nach dem Bilde seiner Reproduktionen umgeschaffen werden.' *ibid*, p. 190.
3. *Ibid*, p. 143.
4. *Ibid*, p. 130.
5. *Ibid*, p. 131.
6. Günther Anders, *Die Antiquiertheit des Menschen: über die Seele im Zeitalter der zweiten industriellen Revolution Vol.1*, München: Beck, 1988, p. 38.
7. Jürgen Habermas, 'Die Scheinrevolution und ihre Kinder', *Die Linke antwortet Jürgen Habermas*, Frankfurt am Main: Europäische Verlagsanstalt, 1968, pp. 12-3.
8. Frank Zappa, *Plastic People Songbook*, edited Deutsch von Carl Weissner, Frankfurt am Main: Zweitausendeins, 1977, p. 16.
9. *Ibid*, pp. 130-1.
10. Franz Kafka, 'In the Penal Settlement', 1919; translated Willa and Edwin Muir, London: Penguin, 1963, p. 174.
11. This is from a lengthy interview set up between Zappa and Bob Marshall by Gerry Fialka, who also joined in, as did Dr Carolyn Dean, on 21 and 22 October 1988. Loren Gagnon transcribed the tapes. It can be found on *<www.mcluhaninstitute.org/baedeker/bobs_articles/zappa_interview-04.html>*.
12. Marco Maurizi, 'Theses on "Bis Er Spritzt" Feuerbach, Or, Why Zappa Fans and Rock Academics are Two Halves of an Integral Whole which, under Current Social Conditions of Exploitation and Injustice, Cannot Add Up ...', *<www.militantesthetix.co.uk/zappo/marco.html>*.
13. Mikhail Bakhtin, 'Art and Responsibility', 1919; translated Rainer Grübel and Sabine Reese, *Die Ästhetik des Wortes*, Frankfurt am Main: Suhrkamp, 1979, p. 93; *Art and Answerability: Early Philosophical Essays*, translated Vadim Liapunov, Austin: University of Texas Press, 1990.
14. Friedrich Nietzsche, *The Will To Power*, §822, 1888; translated Walter Kaufmann and RJ Hollingdale, *The Will To Power*, New York: Vintage, 1968, p. 435; *Kritische Studienausgabe* 13, München: Deutscher Taschenbuchverlag, 1988, p. 500;

Acknowledgement: Thanks to Mathias Schardt (Graz, Austria) for financial support and Norbert Brunner (Mains, Germany) for technical support.

Compliment Any Burger You Put On (Center Hinge Sliced); on "Kaiser Rolls"

Esther Leslie

Poodle Preliminaries

Des Pudels Kern—the core of the poodle. This is a German phrase meaning to get to the truth of the matter, to really penetrate to the core of something. It does not surprise any of us who know Zappa's *oeuvre* that the poodle, and indeed the poodle's core, should be where truthfulness resides. Zappologists have long recognised the crucial status of the poodle. The poodle is indeed the crux of the matter, or indeed a primal element of the known universe, as known from Zappa's "The Poodle Lecture"; 'the poodle bites/the poodle chews it" is the chorus which ends both "Dirty Love" and "Stink-Foot". The German phrase *Des Pudels Kern* was initiated in part 1 of Goethe's play *Faust,* (1808). *'Das also war des Pudels Kern!'*, Faust exclaims, 'So this, then, was the kernel of the poodle!'.

Faust says this once Mephistopheles, who had first revealed himself as a black poodle, bursts forth in his true form. The kernel of the poodle is an immense force. It appears as something intent on wreaking havoc. Faust asks who is this thing before him, and Mephistopheles replies

Ein Teil von jener Kraft,
Die stets das Böse will und stets das Gute schafft.

A part of that force,
That always wants evil but instead always creates goodness.

Faust asks Mephistopheles what this cryptic line means. Mephistopheles responds, *'Ich bin der Geist, der stets verneint!'*; 'I am the Spirit that always negates!'. Zappologists will recognise the poodle's line of argument from "Stink-Foot".

Mephistopheles' rhyme continues—

Und das mit Recht: denn alles, was entsteht,
Ist wert, daß es zugrunde geht;
Drum besser wär's, daß nichts entstünde.
So ist denn alles, was ihr Sünde,
Zerstörung, kurz das Böse nennt,
Mein eigentliches Element.

And quite right too, for everything that exists
Is only of value inasmuch as it is destroyed;
That's why it would be better if nothing ever came into being.
And everything that you call sin
Or destruction or evil
Is my own personal element.

Fig. 30: Poodles

Mephistopheles claims that he is part of the darkness from which light first emerged. Before light appeared, and all that we associate with goodness, brightness, whiteness, cleanliness, there was darkness. The darkness was chaos, nothingness, obscure, formless and associated with evil. Mephistopheles makes the point that originally all was a black nothingness. As this is so, then the black nothingness is prior to the light. It was here first and out of it emerged all else. It is itself the productive beginning of everything, the crux of it all. Darkness pre-exists the light, says Mephistopheles, and for that reason it is truth, the origin, the starting point. Light might try to claim its superiority, says the ex-poodle, but it will never succeed. He explains that while light is hindered by bodies, by materiality, darkness, a more primitive force and the very principle of evil, is not so hindered. It does not encounter resistance. Darkness moves on its destructive course unseen and unseeing. It knows it was once the whole, out of which emerged all the partialities we call life, bodies, humans, culture. These things—life, bodies, culture—it will destroy in time. Mephistopheles is darkness and evil as a productive force, and this is the secret at his heart. This evil is a force that constantly negates, says no, refuses, and in so doing invents anew,

Fig. 31: Kaiser Rolls #1

produces something out of its nothingness. But how can Mephistopheles set to work in the world? Faust spots his trick. Unable to achieve the wholesale destruction of the universe at one blow, he attempts to buy up souls on a small scale, one by one, in little deals. He has come to make Faust an offer that he cannot refuse—his soul in exchange for all worldly pleasures and immense power. Faust mocks him:

> Now I perceive your worthy occupation!
> You can't achieve wholesale annihilation
> So you go around trying to set up deals

From *The World's Greatest Sinner* to *200 Motels* and "Titties 'N Beer", selling your soul is a continual theme in Zappa's Project/Object. Goethe's *Faust* has the poodle preside over this transaction.

Des Pudels Kern: Zappa's songs and output set the very difficult task of trying to get to the core of the poodle. Zappa's lyrics are allusive and twisted. The record covers are complex and layered. Like the black obscurity of Mephistopheles the poodle, Zappa's meanings are elusive and suggestive. Negativity, nihilism and bile are always around the corner ready to burst out. The original records—the vinyl, the plastic, the closely encoded matter—and the packaging—cardboard and print—layer, contradict, compress, condense meanings and reference. In the end it is so dizzying, that a black hole of interpretation appears to open up to the faint-hearted. All meaning becomes its opposite. The

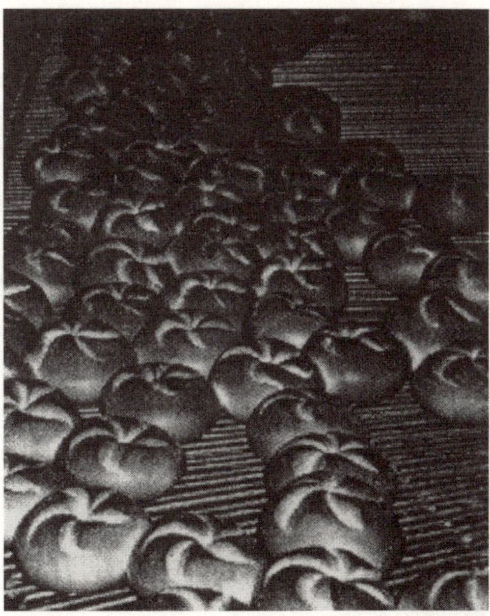

Fig. 32: Kaiser Rolls #2

nastiest chords ripping up the scales might become the height of musical correctitude and beauty.

The original darkness that exists prior to the light of the glitz of performance, the shiny blackness of the vinyl and the glint of the CD, can be tarnished by the dullness of fans' hero-worship when it refuses to engage with the universe evoked and mangled into its true face by Zappa's *oeuvre.* Truth is hard-won, and sometimes entirely elusive. When it is found, it too can be dark and nasty—the core of the poodle, some poodle doo-doo—what's inside lacks good taste and measure. That sounds like Zappa. What exists as the totality of the output macrostructure is chaotic. His 'spirit that negates' makes him unpopular among normal pop listeners, but it's also what makes him so inventive. Inside Zappa's poodles and on other *bric-à-brac* of the mad world around us, lie immense forces waiting to be discovered. [Fig. 30]

Zappa and Zank

There is no poodle in "Kaiser Rolls", the song that was played on the 1975 and 1976 tours, was rehearsed in 1981 and appears on the post-

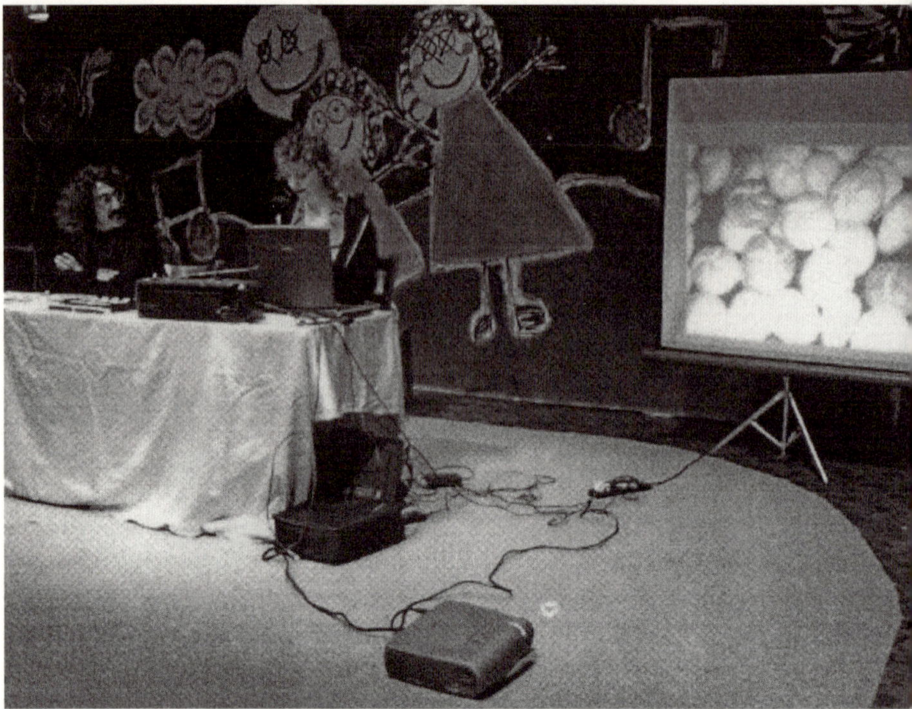

Fig. 33: Esther on Kaiser Rolls

humous release *FZ:OZ* from the performance in Sydney on 20 January 1976. There is no poodle, but there is a grotesque man, the stumblin' man, who seems to be a very principle of malevolence, perhaps much like Mephistopheles: 'A week ago, I met a stumbler man ...'. He is not making his first appearance. The stumbling man is referenced in "Village of the Sun" and leaves a trace on "200 Years Old". Zappa tells of a man he met who stumbled and flailed in front of the juke box in a local bar. He was known as '*The Stumbler*'. He danced in front of the jukebox in the bar as if it were *The Shrine of Music.* Other 'assistant stumblers' would jiggle along with him. One day, the stumbler man took Zappa back to a self-built house on a small turkey ranch. Inside there was a Magnavox stereo and Zappa found that Stravinsky's *Firebird Suite* was on the turntable.[1] The stumbler man is not quite what he seems. Appearance is deceptive. The truth comes only after closer examination and the shedding of preconceptions.

However, the stumbler man in "Kaiser Rolls" doesn't have a pleasant living room and new furniture. He is vile. He has 'stuff stuck up his nose' that 'crawled all over his clothes'. He pukes in a garbage can. The narrator gives him the finger and tries to evade him, but he blocks his path. In contrast to the tight frame of the music, he slobbers and pukes. This stumbling man is at the centre of a song that expresses a poetry of the everyday, the street-level, where all true creativity resides, in the abject and the sleazy. If poetry is sought then it will be found in the garbage cans and arbitrary street encounters, with all their dangers and unpredictability. As a poetry of the mis-communications that occur between people, this stumbling man speaks in riddles. The words he uses are unstable and impenetrable, apart from the one perennial question: 'How's about a dollar for some cigarettes?'. This request is fully comprehensible in any capitalist industrial society, for it echoes the basic law of capitalist society. Money buys commodities that satisfy desires, for a while. The stumbling man wants what is known colloquially as 'bread'.

At the end of the song, it seems that the stumbler man is pursuing the Kaiser Rolls: 'Kaiser Rolls, rolls and rolls, surprise to me they ain't catched him yet'. So what is he after? What does he desire? There is a very literal and immediate meaning. A Kaiser Roll is bread roll of a particular type, a white bread, with poppy seeds or sesame seeds often on top. It is crusty on the outside and inside it is rather soft, even aerated or hollow. It has a distinctive shape and design, with either five or four slits, perhaps to make it look like an emperor's crown, since Kaiser is German for emperor. Or maybe the name stems from the fact that the German Kaiser enjoyed this product so much he offered it his name, as he did to many other products. The roll is rich in eggs, oil and sugar. People seem to like it, especially Americans. It is widely available across the United States.

The Kaiser Roll was invented, some say, by August Zank, an Austrian who also brought the *brioche* to Vienna, and who was the publisher of the newspaper *Die Presse.* Incidentally, the innovation of *Die Presse* was to make the first part of the newspaper contain lots of adverts, which reduced the cover price and added to its commercial success. Zank, our possible Kaiser Roll inventor, said 'I sell advertising space like a haberdashers', and in this way he became a multi-millionaire in

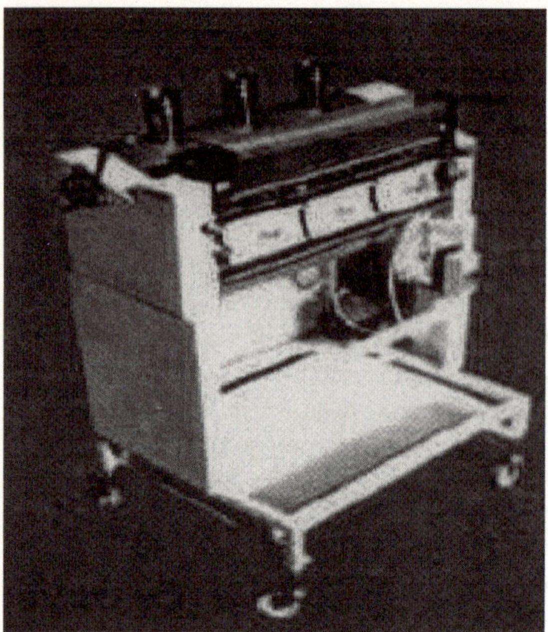

Fig. 34: Kaiser Roll Making Machine

nineteenth century Austria. Others say the Kaiser Roll debuted at the Vienna World's Fair of 1873 when Hungarian roller-milled flour was leavened with 'secret' yeast to produce the first famous Blue Ribbon Kaiser Rolls. In any case, the Kaiser Roll emancipated itself from this imperial situation, and made its way to the USA along with Austrian and German immigrants. Kaiser Rolls were made in the US from about 1898, by ethnic Germans and Austrians. The breadrolls caught on, becoming one of the principal homemade hamburger rolls. New Yorkers took them particularly to heart, and they were assimilated into Irish, Jewish and Italian cuisine. There is a very rich literature on the web pertaining to the use of Kaiser Rolls in recipes, and even modes of baking them. Kaiser Roll pictures, recipes and advertisements can be readily found. One anxious surfer posted a problem in 1999 that still lurks in the myriad by-roads of the information superhighway: Miles Cherkasky remarked, presumably in a bid for advice from someone, anyone, on 2 November 1999 at 11:27:02: 'I am experiencing a intermitant [*sic*] problem with the formation of internal air pockets at the cuts or creases of our Kaiser Rolls. They come and go for no apparent reason'. He received no answer.

There appears to be something irrational about the Kaiser Roll, so irrational the highest levels of the academy attempt to fathom its meaning. For example, there is a university course in the United States that examines the contribution of German-Americans to mainstream culture. It sets the following exercise:

> Visit your local grocery store, try to find the following: *knackwurst* (or *knockwurst*), *bratwurst* (or brats), *wiener* (often misspelled *weiner*!), *wiener schnitzel*, *frankfurter* (or franks), *hamburger*, *liverwurst*, *braunschweiger*, Thüringer sausage, *sauerkraut*, German potato salad, *kuchen*, *streusel* cake (or topping), apple *strudel*, *torte*, kaiser rolls, *pumpernickel* bread, *pretzel*, marzipan, noodle, *zwieback*. Look for Entenmann pastries and baked goods and check out the names on their selections. *Wunderbar* cheese, *Muenster* cheese, *Limburger*. Ask your grandparents about *Liederkranz* cheese; unfortunately it is no longer available.

According to this university-level course, the major contribution of German-Americans to mainstream culture in the US exists in edible form. The Kaiser Roll is at its heart. But this is a Kaiser Roll for a new age, made industrially and assimilated into the fast food nation's one-size-fits-all, quick-as-you-like-with-extra-fries culture. As one of the online advertisements for Kaiser Rolls says: 'Compliment [*sic*] Any Burger You Put On', and in case the effort of cutting is too much, it comes pre-cut as 'Center Hinge Sliced'. It is even possible to purchase simulacra Kaiser Rolls, for shop or home decoration. Some simulacra available to buy online advertise themselves with the following copy:

> We have 'bakery fresh' life sized bread and baked goods that are completely fake! Fun fake food that's great for display! Made of plastic, resin coated foam, paper & other materials. These baked goods are molded and hand-painted. Handmade items may vary in size and weight.

Nowadays Kaiser Rolls are made industrially in machines that can produce nine thousand every hour. Ironically the – handmade – simulacra may be more varied than the real thing, industrially made and identical in form, as they sit awaiting purchase in their see-thru plastic sacks. Still the names of the US companies that specialise in this bread are Germanic, recalling the immigrants who made good and made it big: Vosen, Wenner, Gutenplann, Bethel, Franz and Loeb.

Is our stumbler man one of these immigrants, someone who comes from elsewhere, an alien? But if he is, then he must be one of the ones who failed, who failed to realise the American dream. He longs for the Kaiser Roll—he is on its trail, but it seems to elude him. Is this the familiar outlining of nostalgia, the bewailing of the loss of home and its accoutrements, the melancholic lament over the idealised and lost past? 'The Kaiser *hratche* rolls since time began'... implies the immigrant's longing for the ancient homeland and its customs.

The stumbling man's grasp of the English language is shaky. He uses a linguistically logical but grammatically incorrect phrase, in pursuit of Kaiser Rolls, 'surprise to me they ain't catched him yet'. The ends of lines are swallowed up in the song—'a dollar for some cigarette', 'might raise some san''. These words refuse to be rounded off and communicative according to the logic of written language. On the other hand, they are expressive and owe much more to the actual words spoken by people, with all their indeterminacy, incoherence and grammatical anarchy. There is also an untranscribable mouth noise rendered here[2] in the traditional Zapparian manner as *hratche-plche*—signalling a further breakdown in communication and a return to the pure language of the body, such as is possessed by babies and the very old, and now voiced by this inscrutable tramp, who stumbles and pukes. It might also be a cleaned up substitute for the word 'fucking'—again a one-size-fits-all word indicating the impossibility of finding a word that expresses anything specific. The stumbling of the stumbler man might be both physical and also something akin to a stumbling over words, a stammer. Certainly the song's lyrics testify to this, as we get repetitions and indistinct phrases. Words slide around: 'rolls' could be a noun or a verb. On the second version of "Kaiser Rolls" on *FZ:OZ* the phrase 'How far the Kaiser Rolls' seems to be replaced by the words 'How far the skies are rolled'. This conjures up a Biblical image of the celestial skies rolled up like a scroll of parchment. Does our stumbler man have some sort of contact with the heavens, and so far from being a friend of Mephistopheles, perhaps he is a divine manifestation, yet in the shape of ugliness? Whether his calling is from above or below, the stumbler man is certainly part of myth. 'The Kaiser *hratche* rolls since time began', he says.

The stumbler man recognises an endlessness of time, but he also hopes for some sort of conclusion. 'All I wanna know, How far the *hratche-plche* Kaiser Rolls'. 'This is a story' says the opening line, that is to say, this is myth. Walter Benjamin has drawn connections between the tramp and myth.[3] The mythical figure of the tramp is perhaps underlined by his curious relationship to exchange, which is the fundament of bourgeois rationality. The stumbling man cannot speak for himself—he has not reached Kant's condition of exit from '*Unmündigkeit*', and so is unable to speak for himself, until the closing line when Terry Bozzio's voice as stumbler bursts in, guttural and phlegmy, with 'How's about a dollar for some cigarette?'. Here is the tramp who refuses exchange, except by proxy. He will not enter into wage labour, rewarded by measly wages for paltry pleasures. He will take the dollar from another, and exchange it for cigarettes, bypassing the rigours, exploitation and alienation of work.

There is some discussion on the web of the fact that Kaiser Rolls might refer to a type of car called a Henry J, manufactured by Kaiser, because Zappa's father bought one. It was named after one of the most prominent industrialists of the time and was a car for the masses. The Kaiser *rolls*, that is to say, the car moves, though in this line there is an echo of the car that is antithesis to the Henry J., the Rolls Royce.

From these researches, I might conclude that "Kaiser Rolls" refers to both hamburger rolls and a car. Of course, these are the two emblematic symbols of the postwar American economy. In fact the two depend on each other, for the hamburger was invented as a meal that could be eaten with one hand, that is while driving on the great American freeway. The phrase goes to the heart of America's mythology of itself—we are the land of cars and hamburgers, and everyone will not only know that but also become just like us, in our image: 'Cruising for burgers/In daddy's new car/My phony freedom card/Brings to me/Instantly/ECSTASY'.[4] On the cover of *Just Another Band from L.A.* (1971), the cartoon car the Mothers are driving is superimposed on a burger, a motif which reappears superimposed on a 'real' burger in the innerfold of *For Real* (1973) by Ruben and the Jets. Food and

Fig. 35: Henry J.

transport as commodity 'objects': the sinister surrealism of capitalist economics.

And yet "Kaiser Rolls" ironically challenges the car/burger equation (one made also incidentally by *American Graffiti*'s air-brushed vision of a 50s adolescence). It disrupts transparent communicability, transfer and exchange with its puke vomiting back up great American foodstuffs and its stumbling man, who is, precisely, a man who travels not by car but by foot. We witness the American Nightmare, which opens a space for something other than the American dream. The tramp's denial of current relations is as old as Diogenes, and will exist as long as hierarchical society does.

Fig. 36: Kaiser Rolls #3

But there is another echo... and is this song not about echoes, insinuations, mishearings, imprecisions? In mishearings, deliberate or otherwise, language is distorted, words elided, which imbues them with extra layers of meaning that makes language not only magical, but also communicative, for how can communication happen without flexibility, a tear and tug at verbal meanings? 'Roll and roll', as the song puts it in its closing lines, cannot but make us think of Rock'n'Roll. A moment of self-reflexivity flashes. What is roll without rock? Is this a comment on the aerated sweetened pop that moves without swinging, as puffy and unsatisfying as a Kaiser Roll, which has been de-ethnicized and assimilated into the US industrial bakery system?

Moustache Management

In 'The Philosophy of Furniture' (1840) Edgar Allen Poe says people who hold lengthy discussions about which carpets to buy have the air of sheep who are dreaming. Presumably Poe had a low opinion of the fantasy life of sheep, desire for grass and the fear of the dog its narrow parameters. He quips that these are the kind of folk who could not and should not be entrusted with *the management of their own moustaches.*

I am reminded of this line when I survey the current state of Zappological research. "Kaiser Rolls" is a case in point. One can find transcriptions of the lyrics. One can even find the revelation that Kaiser Rolls is a bread roll and a car on one website, but upon ferreting out this riveting information, the discussion abruptly stops. It has to be led back to Zappa the Man—did Zappa speak of such a car, did he ride in one, did his father own one, did he eat Kaiser Rolls? There is no sense in which his lyrics could be understood as social phenomena, as a social unconscious, the product of immersion in a social world of signs and customs. There is a dull empiricism at work in such analyses, and a fixation on the individual which denies both fantasy—our own subjective response to the work—and resonance, the objective social meanings that exist independently of Zappa's control. I hope in this short exposition I have opened up "Kaiser Rolls" to an imaginative and yet socially responsible practice.

But have we found the 'Pudels Kern', the kernel of the poodle? No, I am sure. But it is the investigation and speculation itself that is the point, the truth of the thing, the true form of the *oeuvre.* Critical thought finds itself always *in medias res* (as Walter Benjamin would say), with a world that's already going on. The stumbler man in the highways and by-ways, rooting through garbage cans, shows us the always convoluted way. Let Zappa tend his own moustache and the empiricist Zappologists learn to cultivate theirs—we Esemplastic Zappologists shall proceed as speculative hairdressers of the imagination and critical clippers of the objective world!

1. Frank Zappa with Peter Occhiogrosso, *The Real Frank Zappa Book,* Poseidon Press, New York, 1989, p. 49.
2. Or rather on the webpages <*www.lyricscafe.com/z/zappa_frank/kaiser_rolls.html*> and <*http://globalia.net/donlope/fz/lyrics/FZ_OZ.html*>. The lyrics on this webpage <*http://globalia.net/donlope/fz/songs/Kaiser_Rolls.html*>, transcribed by Jon Naurin, put 'motherfuckin' instead. There is also discussion here of the meaning of the term Kaiser Rolls and some fine 1950s advertisements for the Kaiser car.
3. Walter Benjamin, *The Arcades Project,* translated Howard Eiland and Kevin McLaughlin, Cambridge MA: Harvard University Press, 1999, p.400.
4. See Eric Schlosser, *Fast Food Nation: What the All-American Meal is Doing to the World,* Harmondsworth: Allen Lane, 2001.

Zappa's "Cheepnis" & the Poverty of Philosophy

Marco Maurizi

In 1968, Zappa released the doo-wop phantasmagoria of *Cruising with Ruben & the Jets.* While the Parisian barricades were still on fire, he chose to commemorate the 'cretin simplicity' of the 50s. Doo-wop was not the only feature to appeal to Zappa about this decade. There was also the sub-genre of monster movies, celebrated with an explicit song on *Roxy & Elsewhere* in 1974, "Cheepnis". In his introduction to the song, Zappa explained: 'Cheapness in the case of a monster movie has nothing to do with the budget of the film, although it helps, but true Cheapness is exemplified by visible nylon strings attached to the jaw of a giant spider.'[1] The importance of these lines can hardly be over-

The whole
'equivalent
earth' shall
be mine!

Fig. 38: Monster

estimated. The song itself is a tribute to the cheap aroma of B-movies: 'Can y'all see?/The little strings on the Giant Spider?/The Zipper From The Black Lagoon?'[2] It is as if Zappa was only interested in moviegoers who can spot technical mistakes and make fun of them: *active* observers. Zappa goes so far to declare 'that's all he really wants to know' about those films. He is attracted by their innocent fraudulence, the way technical limitations have an estranging, Brechtian effect on the audience. Seeing the zipper on the monster from the Black Lagoon produces an unexpected fault in the crystalline sphere of aesthetic representation, making it suddenly collapse. *Sleep Dirt* includes songs from the sci-fi musical *Hunchentoot*, a mutant blend of *Ruben & the Jets'* attack on love-song stupidity and Zappa's weakness for Cheapness. "Flambay" develops *Uncle Meat*'s love affair between female and monster (although here the female character ends up manipulating the monster). It contains the lines: 'Here I stand, all alone, a spider's fool!... And we'll have ecstasy for all eternity!'[3]

Although the song's finale is a summary of love-song clichés, the satire of these lines works by connecting rhetorical hyperbole to an imaginary cosmic relationship. The same critical attitude towards fraudulent notions of transcendental meaning is shown in the very title "Spider of Destiny". As a matter of fact, boastful words like 'ecstasy' and 'eternity' have an involuntary mocking effect even in so-called 'serious' love songs. Exaggeration is the indicator of falsity, the smokescreen of a merchant's persuasion. Similarly, the 'strings attached to the jaw of a giant spider' are nothing but the cheesy visual version of the phony cascade of strings that smother songs like "Smoke Gets in Your Eyes". The first exposes the fraud of the latter. Alban Berg was correct to say 'beauty is when you can't see the glue and the nails', but Zappa was even more correct to point out that therefore 'beauty is a lie'.[4] The whole culture industry is manufactured from such nylon strings. Thus, if you can see them, you lose beauty, but you're perhaps approaching the truth behind the lie.

In 1961, writing in defence of anti-subjectivism in modern music, Theodor Adorno pointed out that the first task of critical art is to destroy 'fake' subjectivity.[5] Zappa composed music in which a modernist assault on cliché seeks to re-establish a modicum of authenticity within mass culture. Unlike either the elitism of high modernism or post-modernist populism, though, Zappa was able to discern the double, dialectical nature of culture-industry products. Therefore his approach to mass music can hardly be reduced to 'satire' or 'intelligent use' of degenerated cultural forms. Zappa went far beyond such predictable exercises in smug critical vigilance. Satire as 'intelligent' self-defence against the 'boring' indoctrination of the culture industry falls short of any *liberating* effect. Zappa does not 'use' humour, so much as persistently detonate explosions of raucous laughter. This may not be such a difficult task after all, since (as he put it) stupidity is a basic element of the universe, like hydrogen. Zappa's real intent, however, was to discover laughter where it's not supposed to be. In this respect, even the originals which Zappa undertook to criticise cannot really be taken seriously. Seen this way, they become parodies of themselves. Zappa described this experience in *Ruben & the Jets*, and made it the crux of "Cheepnis".

The poodle dog is 'snappin' off the trees like they was bonsai'd ornaments on a dry-wobble landscape'.[6] This is a precise image for what happens in the making of a monster movie, save that a low budget makes it difficult to tell the difference between the 'making' and the final result. As a matter of fact, a miniaturised landscape is the only way you can make a 15-foot-tall witch appear on the freeway.[7] Characters in monster movies won't point this out, because it would reveal the trick and spoil the cheap thrill of the audience. Yet, it is precisely this interplay between fiction and reality which excites Zappa's phantasy. Of course, they are not 'real' trees, and you can tell the monster has only just put its mask on before shooting the 'scary' scene. That only goes to show you that low-budget productions are asking you to give them a chance to be taken seriously. You have to participate in order to make them real, otherwise all you've got is 'an inverted ice-cream cone'. Looking at the whole culture industry from this perspective, you begin to descry its machinery.

Isn't it just the same for 'cool' productions, too? Isn't this the emotional sub-structure of standardisation and mechanical reproducibility? By bringing up the '*Spargel*'[8] for discussion, Zappa's Cheapness unmasks the libidinal investment employed by culture industry to give its goods an aura of reality. If the audience's libido is itself part of the culture industry—as Adorno and Horkheimer argued in *The Dialectic of Enlightenment*[9]—Cheapness opens a vulgar crack in the circularity of production and consumption. Realising how capitalism administrates desire, Zappa learned lessons from Cheapness. Though basically mass-deception, culture industry is a *belle dame sans merci*, and Zappa found his own way to cause her some dismay. In so doing, Zappa's music resembles Adorno's gloomy prognostications of mass manipulation: a necessary step to find appropriate weapons to beat capitalism, not a sad way to give up the fight because it's all over now, Baby Blur. Zappa's entire *oeuvre* is an attempt to make the listener conscious of his/her own libidinal involvement in the productive machinery.[10] Crucially, it's not what Zappa thinks or says about this effect that is interesting, rather the way his art entertains our *id* and produces activity on the part of the listener. If beauty is a trademark of oppression and order, deformity is the aesthetical precognition of revolution. This is borne out by the Latin word *monstrum*, which originally meant 'wonder', no less than 'horrible shape'. Capitalism gives birth to monstrous categories, those used in Marxism and Negative Dialectics, a logic of disintegration (*Logik des Zerfalls*[11]) which enables us to name the 'new', something critical thought and action can't do

Fig. 39: Godzilla

without. That's why revolution can find appropriate expression only in *monstrosity* (i.e. a polemical overthrow of manipulation), rather than the usual depressive paranoia of leftist intellectuals. Critical thinkers who don't want to know about the monsters inside their own souls, are not only deluding themselves, but also castrating hidden wonders.

For his part, Zappa cunningly describes the sad impotence of the critical theorist unable to take part in the event criticised. In *Uncle Meat,* Don Preston is worried about Phyllis' weird love for the monster, and works out some cheap psychoanalytical explanation, looking for some trauma in her childhood: 'It must be, uh, her mother and father probably told her that she's real ugly and awkward and dumb and everything... And so she relates to people that are ugly, dumb and awkward.' After that, Don is driven to sociological conclusions: 'And our young society today goes to all these monster movies, and they see them on television night after night ...' Phyllis: 'It's so terrific to be with the monster!'. Don: 'We're raising a new generation of *monster lovers* ...'[12] As a matter of fact, a genuine sociological explanation of this phenomenon had been finely and cynically proposed by Adorno years before. As he pointed out in *Minima Moralia*, the giant creatures

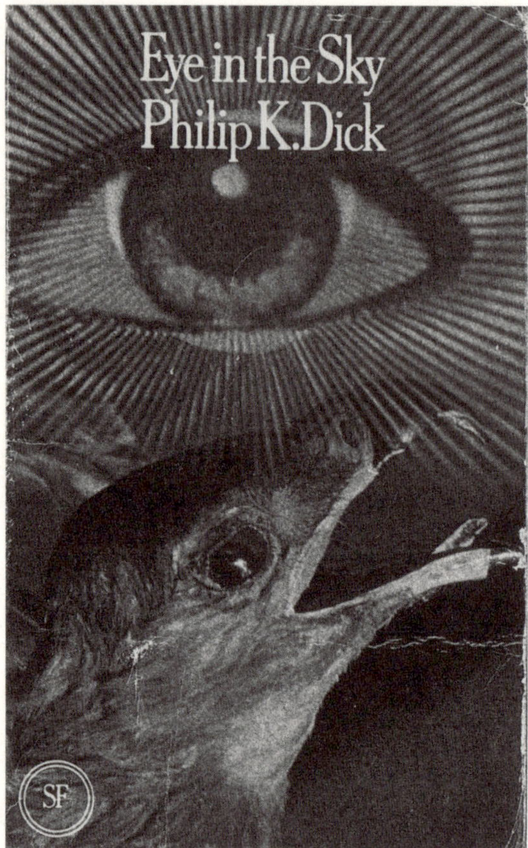

Fig. 40: *Eye in the Sky*

of the popular imaginary like the Loch Ness monster are 'collective projections of the monstrous total State. People prepare themselves for its terrors by familiarising themselves with gigantic images. In its absurd readiness to accept these, impotently prostrate humanity tries desperately to assimilate to experience what defies all experience.'[13] The desire to see those prehistoric creatures in action once again reveals the secret hope 'that animal creation may survive the injustice Man has perpetrated on it and produce a better species who could finally make it.'[14]

Adorno's insights also elucidate the *Animé Manga* of Go Nagai, another artist inspired by 50s science-fiction. In his stories, planet earth is attacked by monsters that embody the revolt of repressed nature against culture.[15] As well as alluding to our mineral and biological origins, "The Ocean is the Ultimate Solution"[16] presents genocide as the negative image of redemption on the earth, while the connection between fear of otherness and hidden desire of self-destruction is immortalised in the aftermath of "Spider of Destiny": 'Eat the earth people! Eat them, and chew them, and brutally stomp on what's left, and then report to me. For the conquest of earth and the moon and the stars and the space in between, all the comets and stuff, will be ours!'[17]

Here Drakma shows the inner mechanics of identity thinking: the very prospect of otherness generates the desire to destroy it, because identity can only find satisfaction in reaching its totalitarian goal, fulfilling its demand for absoluteness, annihilating every residue.[18] If identity thinking is to perform its 'circular motion' there must be no 'outside'.[19] In this respect, monster movies are indeed a sort of second-hand 'mythology' that articulates, like every mythology before it, a dialectic of fear and desire.

But this is just one side of the story, the negative, depressing one. To transform this obscure mythology into critical enlightenment, as Negative Dialectics indeed requires, we should take a look at Zappa's personal theology, as revealed on the cover of *One Size Fits All* and in related songs. Zappology has a better chance of grasping Conceptual Continuity if it's not too worried about Zappa's 'real' intentions and instead maps his unconscious clusters of imagery. Zappa persistently connected cheap science fiction to the prone posture of relaxation encouraged by the sofa. For example, in "Time is Money" on *Sleep Dirt*, Drakma the Queen of Cosmic Greed sings to the earth people from her *couch* in the sky; in "The Radio is Broken" from *Man from Utopia*, another song about 50s sci-fi B-movies, reference is made to 'the partially reclining G-force lawn furniture'; on *One Size Fits All* the cover shows outer space, but superimposed on it is a sofa. There's also the cheapest form of American furniture, a chrome dinette, a table and chair for eating at. This one is so cheap the yellow plastic seat has already torn, allowing the stuffing to extrude.

The concept of 'outer space' is linked via 'nothingness' and 'annihilation' to the idea of *emptiness*, another important element in Zappa's

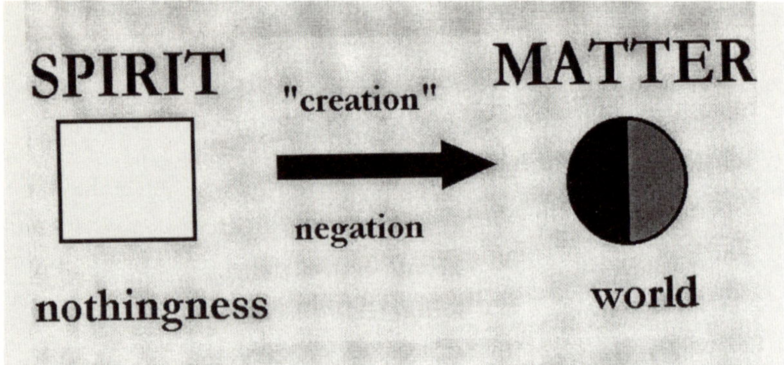

Fig. 41: Spirit/Matter

Conceptual Continuity since *Freak Out!*. The 'emptiness' attacked in songs like "Hungry Freaks, Daddy", "Baby Snakes", "Beautiful Guy" and "We're Turning Again" is clearly the moral and intellectual vaporisation of American culture. It implies the idea of something that's been emptied. The vacuum cleaner—a recurrent motif in the *oeuvre*—is the perfect symbol of such an emptying force. It's with the Sofa routine, though, that 'emptiness' is attacked as a cosmological illusion, giving Zappa's moral disappointment its materialist urgency.

In Philip K. Dick's *Eye in the Sky* (1957), God is figured as a giant eye at the core of a heliocentric Solar System, according to a vision produced by the distorted mind of a religious fanatic. Zappa's speculations about God's sofa performs a critique of idealism, showing that the religious inversion of matter and spirit (*i.e.* the atrocious idea that matter is a product of spiritual activity) is an ontological perversion of truth. Putting a sofa—a manufactured object, the very symbol of middle-class intimacy—in the midst of a primordial nowhere is a cunning reminder of the actual thinker behind every metaphysical speculation. Far from being an innate, natural idea, this 'nothingness' is manufactured by human mind—no less than a sofa; it's nothing but the persistent, active negation of the sensuous world.

Although Zen Buddhism may have led Zappa out of Catholicism[20], he was aware that repressive 'emptiness' is something religion can't do without, even if it doesn't force you to believe in *ex nihilo* creation. As already pointed out by William Blake in his prophetic work *Urizen* (1794), this primordial emptiness is

Unknown, unprolific,
Self-clos'd, all-repelling. What Demon
Hath form'd this abominable void,
This soul-shudd'ring vacuum?[21]

Appropriately sung in German, "Sofa" works like a materialist critique of idealism.[22] Adorno, though himself a German philosopher, refers to this kind of sterile contemplation in his 'Amnerkungen zum philosophischen Denken' using an English phrase: 'armchair thinking'.[23] It is precisely the absurdist interaction between abstract 'emptiness' and the banality of the sofa which gives Zappa's song its critical charge. It begs comparison with Hegel's *Science of Logic*, notoriously an account of God's thoughts before the creation of the world. In his attempt to describe the becoming of reality as a consequence of God's mental activity, Hegel starts with utter emptiness reaching out for the determination of solid things through a conceptual method known as 'speculative dialectics'. The very beginning of Hegel's *Logic* presents us the idea of pure Being, which soon reveals itself as an empty concept: in a word, Nothing. From its part, pure Nothing 'is simply equality with itself, complete emptiness, absence of all determination and content [...] it is, therefore, the same determination, or rather absence of determination, and thus altogether the same as pure Being'.[24] This dialectical overturn of pure Being into pure Nothing is, as a matter of fact, an attack on the idea of pureness and immediacy, as well as that of beginning. Marx took this Hegelian argument still further in his *Economic and Philosophical Manuscripts of 1844*, condemning philosophical 'abstraction' and the necessity of divine creation altogether.

> When you ask about the creation of nature and man, you are abstracting, in so doing, from man and nature. You postulate them as non-existent, and yet you want me to prove them to you as existing. Now I say to you: Give up your abstraction and you will also give up your question. Or if you want to hold on to your abstraction, then be consistent, and if you think of man and nature as non-existent, then think of yourself as non-existent, for you too are surely both nature and man. Don't think, don't ask me, for as soon as you think and ask, your abstraction from the existence of nature

> and man has no meaning. Or are you such an egotist that you conceive everything as nothing, and yet want yourself to exist?[25]

Hegel's line of reasoning clearly went far beyond his intention. It turns against the very idea that the world can be understood through a gradual self-determination of thought, that its structure can be disclosed by thought alone. This led to the famous *Theses on Feuerbach*, where Marx argues that philosophical thought is incapable of proving the reality of its concepts without engaging in political praxis, without actualising its ideas. The eleventh thesis ('philosophers have interpreted the world, the point is to change it') is commonly misunderstood and trivialised as banal pragmatism. Stalin's version of Marxism was a practical demonstration of the dangers of this theoretical mistake. Adorno made clear the difference between genuinely sexy Marxist theory and Stalin's repressive pragmatism. Adorno corrected Hegel's methodological mistake, suggesting that dialectic should begin with the turgid, complex, actual, dirty 'thing' rather than with pure Being. Otherwise it would idealistically misinterpret the world as a product of subjectivity before even starting to interpret it.[26]

The core of such dialectic is materialism: there can be no *Bestimmung* without the position of an existing, material world. The concrete is already there, and every effort to jump to some pure 'origin' is a hidden negation of the world, a pointless attempt to deny it. Adorno learned his lesson from Marx and recognised 'the poverty of philosophy', its desperate attempt to grasp the 'world' as a mere logical category.

> Is it surprising that everything, in the final abstraction [...] presents itself as a logical category? Is it surprising that, if you let drop little by little all that constitutes the individuality of a house, leaving out first of all the materials of which it is composed, then the form that distinguishes it, you end up with nothing but a body; that, if you leave out of account the limits of this body; you soon have nothing but a space—that if, finally, you leave out of the account the dimensions of this space, there is absolutely nothing left but pure quantity, the logical category?[27]

Marx laughs at those 'metaphysicians who, [...] the more they detach themselves from things, imagine themselves to be getting all the nearer to the point of penetrating to their core'[28]. On the contrary, the more philosophical abstraction proclaims it's discovering some 'essence', the more it is just crawling over the surface of the world like a slug, unable to see the real processes involved in it. Having conceived the world as a product of logical abstraction, it's no mystery that thought can find infinite satisfaction in thinking itself, as suggested in Aristotle's *Metaphysics.* [29] That's why the Mystery Man want us to 'reach Nirvana tonight'.[30] He 'ain't really made for bein' out in the street'.[31] The result of abstraction is inanity, as shown by another poem by William Blake: 'The Human Abstract'.[32]

And now: the philosophical Mumbo Jumbo you all were waiting for, the Crux of the Biscuit and no mistake! If emptiness is no neutral space, rather an active, ontological negation of reality, so immobility is no neutral moral choice, rather a political negation of human praxis. Materialism is negation of idealism, which from its part is negation of the world, dressed up like scientific observation. That's why materialism, being the negation of negation, has an affirmative, practical charm. Ain't this boogie a mess?

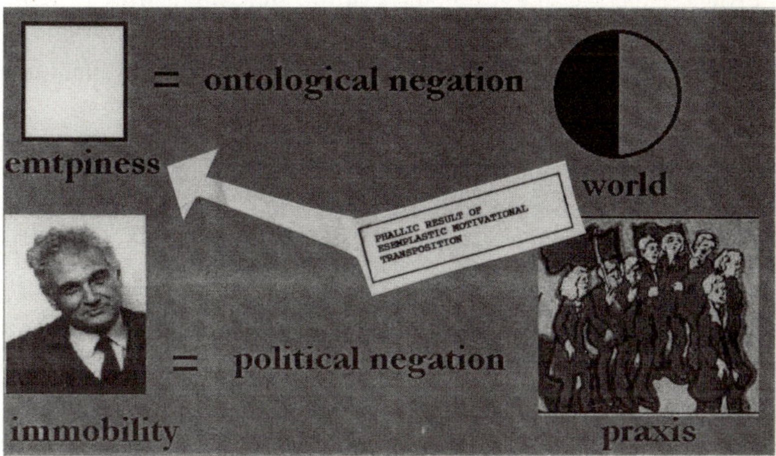

Fig. 42: Ontological Negation

Claiming to speak from the point of view of God—who presumably knows 'how things really are'—idealism blatantly tells us 'how things have to be'. Dreaming on his divine divan, the philostopher welcomes the world with all its misery and contradictions, as if nothing could change. The priest tells us, a change is gonna come, but not in this life. The artist is currently doing things, but for his own sake. The world has messed their mind up ... but was it the world, or was it the religion? As you see: philosophy, religion, art ... they all go together.[33] On the contrary, materialism knows there's no understanding without *transformation*: but 'action' is 'sensuous activity', as Marx called it, it means changing reality here and now.

Intellectual activity is neither an end in itself, nor the *Ursprung* dreamed of by transcendentalists. Recognising this, critical thought finds itself always *in medias res* (as Benjamin would say), with a world that's already going on: 'If you been/*Mod-O-fied*/It's an illusion, an yer in between.'[34] Zappa's critique of idealistic emptiness works very like the preposterous beginning of Mahler's *First Symphony*, itself a musical parody of Hegel's *Logic*. The symphony begins with a long pedal of harmonics, as if it was looking for some celestial, not-physical sound. The entire string-section—here come those screaming nylon strings again—is playing a single note, an 'A': which is the basic note in Anglo-American musical nomenclature, and also the first letter of the alphabet. Mahler wrote on the score: *wie ein Naturlaut*, 'like a sound of nature', as if he was, too, describing some kind of primordial birth.[35]

And yet, as Adorno recognised in his famous essay on Mahler, the cunning orchestration required to achieve that sound gives this romantic interpretation the lie. Itself a product of human technique, the mystical opening of the symphony suddenly slips into the mock banality of a fanfare, a "Regyptian Strut." This eruption, this 'bursting in' as Adorno calls it, reveals the falsity of that cosmic beginning. That's why Adorno calls it a 'curtain',[36] the eternal trick of bourgeois *decor* seeking to hide its 'nylon strings'. A literary equivalent is Zappa's account of creation in "Once Upon a Time" or "The Poodle Lecture". The resounding words 'In the beginning ...' are followed by absurdities, lumpy gravies smeared over on the smooth canvas of bourgeois cosmic abstraction. Absolute beginners are stupid and kitsch.

Fig. 43 & Fig. 44: Poodle Breeding Techniques.

Moreover, 'the end of everything that stands' is also, notoriously, 'a beautiful friend' and, therefore, a lie. By contrast, Zappa's music knows no beginning and no end, and yet it doesn't deny becoming, meaning, hope: *i.e.* the possibility of *action*. Like Darwin's theory of evolution, Zappa's music ruins the yuppie dream of immortality, but not the underclass desire for revolt and change. Darwin's insight was materialistic and dialectical because it revealed how order, complexity and beauty of the world—which had been always seen as a result of divine intervention—was originated by the activity of a not-conscious, self-moving matter. "The Ocean is the Ultimate Solution", with the irregular twists of the rhythmic guitar and its boiling drum/bass section, recalls Darwin's concepts of life and evolution as struggle rather than as a single, linear, rational, transparent development. Zappa's musical rendition of this idea should be contrasted to the slow crescendo of "Würm" by Yes—named after the famous theorist of the glacial era—at the closing section of "Starship Trooper", a song which connects science fiction to the origin of life on earth in the manner of De Palma's mediocre *Mission To Mars*.

The contingency of the human race is a source of desperation and immobility only for those who can't live their present. Actually, religious people are so frightened of the fact of contingency—the sheer improbability of human existence—that they invent a God in order to make our miserable little incidental planet the centre of creation. They want the world to have a 'meaning' so that they can contemplate its 'beauty'. They don't want to be reminded to the fact that the world is a 'fucking bloody mess' and 'ugly as sin', because, otherwise, there might be something they needed to do about it: 'They stand still, they shut up, then they don't do nothing out of the nowhere'.[37] They're the Nowhere People. On the other hand, us Esemplastic Zappologists at this conference—we're the Apes from Utopia.

1. Frank Zappa, "Cheepnis", *Roxy & Elsewhere*, 1974.
2. *Ibid.*
3. Frank Zappa, "Flambay", *Sleep Dirt*, 1978.
4. Frank Zappa, "Beauty Is A Lie", *You Are What You Is*, 1981.
5. Theodor Adorno, 'Vers une musique informelle', *Gesammelte Schriften*, Frankfurt am Main: Suhrkamp, 1997, Vol. 16, p. 502; translated Rodney Livingstone, *Quasi Una Fantasia: Essays on Modern Music*, London: Verso, 1994, p. 280. Readers may be surprised that I have characterised Adorno—widely admired in some circles as Defender of the Fragile Soul, the Guardian of *Innerlichkeit*, the Sylent Knyght of Decaying Subjectivity—as an *anti*-subjectivist. The point is that Adorno was a Marxist, not a fucking romantic existentialist. So he (partially) defends anti-subjectivism in music as the good (*bestimmte*) negation of fake subjectivity (this of course doesn't make him a stupid Stalinist denying the validity of individual experience).
6. Frank Zappa, "Cheepnis", *Op. Cit.*.
7. After that, cars would probably 'crash all over the place/As a result of people with Hawaiian shirts on .../Lookin' up to see her face', Frank Zappa, "Drowning Witch", *Ship Arriving Too Late to Save a Drowing Witch*, 1982. All in all, reality is far more stupid than its pale cinematic copy.
8. Frank Zappa, "Shall We Take Ourselves Seriously?", 1982, *You Can't Do That on Stage Anymore Vol.5*, 1992.
9. 'The attitude of the public, which ostensibly and actually favors the system of the culture industry, is a part of the system and not an excuse for it.' Theodor Adorno and Max Horkheimer, *Dialektik der Aufklärung*, 1944, *Gesammelte Schriften*, Vol. 3, p. 143; translated John Cumming, *Dialectic of Enlightenment*, London: Verso, 1979, p. 122.
10. 'People are usually aware when the government's hand goes in their pocket; they're not usually aware when the government's hand reaches for other erogenous zones on their body, or covers their eyes up.', Frank Zappa to Jim Ladd, US interview radio broadcast produced by Bill Levy, transcribed in *Nuggets*, April 1977, p. 17; reproduced in Michael Gray, *Mother! Is The Story Of Frank Zappa*, London/NY: Proteus 1985, p. 152.
11. Theodor Adorno, *Negative Dialektik*, 1966, *Gesammelte Schriften*, *Op. Cit.*, Vol. 6, pp. 148-149; *Negative Dialectics*, translated E. B. Ashton, London: Routledge and Kegan Paul, 1973, pp. 144-6.
12. Frank Zappa, "Uncle Meat Film Excerpt Part I", *Uncle Meat*, 1969/87.
13. Theodor Adorno, §74 'Mammoth', *Minima Moralia*, 1945; translated Edmund Jephcott, *Minima Moralia*, London: Verso, 1974, p. 115.
14. *Ibid.*
15. See Marco Maurizi, 'Ecce Robot: How To Philosophise with an Atomic Punch', *Soundscapes—online journal on media culture*, ISSN 1567-7745, Vol.5, February 2003.
16. Curiously enough, the previous title of this song was "One More Time for the World".

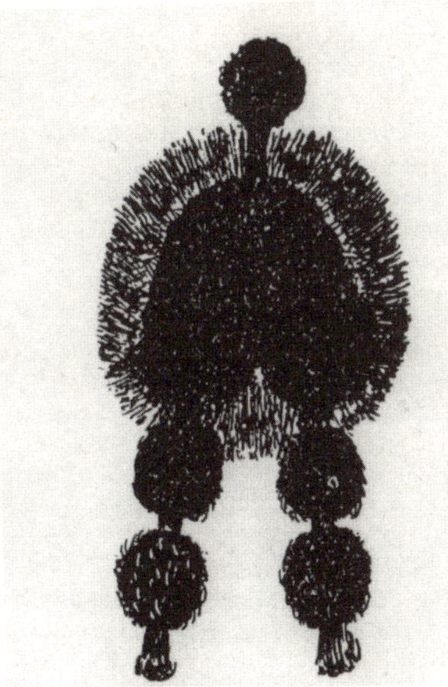

Fig. 45: Poodle From Rear.

17. Frank Zappa, "Spider of Destiny", *Sleep Dirt*, 1979.
18. By the same token, it's the desire to destroy that manages to find its enemy, according to Adorno's and Horkheimer's interpretation of anti-semitism. See Theodor Adorno and Max Horkheimer, *Dialektik der Aufklärung*, *Op. Cit.*, pp. 192-234; *Dialectic of Enlightenment*, *Op. Cit.*, pp. 168-208.
19. Frank Zappa, "Nanook Rubs It", *Apostrophe(')*, 1974.
20. Michael Gray, *Op. Cit.*, p. 24.
21. William Blake, *The Book Of Urizen*, 1794, p. 1; London: Thames and Hudson, 1978, p. 44. Blake's vision steams with 'sulphurous foams' and vile liquids, getting very near to Zappa's imaginary. He also calls 'woof' that 'infinite labour' woven round the Void: i.e. 'science'. The role of apostrophe and zero as images of 'omission' and 'absence' are explored by Ben Watson, *Frank Zappa: The Negative Dialectics of Poodle Play*, London: Quartet, 1994, pp. 253-259. For another interesting use of nullity, see John Lydon's 'nothing, a void, zilch, zero, nought, nothing, vacuum', "Fodderstompf", Public Image Limited, *First Issue*, 1979.
22. See Ben Watson, *Poodle Play*, *Op. Cit.*, pp. 261-271; Ben Watson, 'Phänomenologie des *One Size Fits All*: Georg Wilhelm Friedrich Hegel und Frank Zappa', a paper delivered at Zappanale #14, Kamptheater, Bad Doberan, 25 Juli 2003 available on <*www.militantesthetix.co.uk/zappo/OSFAweb.htm*>.
23. Theodor Adorno, 'Stichworte', *Gesammelte Schriften*, *Op. Cit.*, Vol. 10/2, p. 603.
24. Georg Wilhelm Friedrich Hegel, *Science of Logic*, § 132-133.
25. Karl Marx, 'Private Property and Communism', *Economic and Philosophical Manuscripts of 1844*, translated Marco Maurizi; *Early Writings*, translated Rodney Livingstone, London: Penguin, 1975, p. 357.
26. Theodor Adorno, *Negative Dialektik*, *Op. Cit.*, p. 139; *Negative Dialectics*, *Op. Cit.*, p. 135.
27. Karl Marx, 'The Metaphysics of Political Economy', *The Poverty of Philosophy*, 1847, Moscow: Progress, 1975, pp. 98-9.

28. *Ibid.*
29. Aristotle, *Metaphysics*, §7, 1072 b18-b30 which Hegel cites at the end of his *Encyclopaedia of Philosophical Sciences*, §577.
30. Frank Zappa, "Cosmik Debris", *Apostrophe(')*, 1974.
31. Frank Zappa, "Yo Mama", *Sheik Yerbouti*, 1979. "Pojama People" and "Muffin Man" are other good examples of imbecile inanity.
32. William Blake, 'The Human Abstract', *Songs of Experience*, 1794; *Complete Writings*, edited Geoffrey Keynes, Oxford: OUP, 1966, p. 217.
33. As the Central Scrutinizer puts it at the start of Act II of *Joe's Garage*, 1979.
34. Frank Zappa, "A Token of My Extreme", *Joe's Garage*, 1979.
35. Gustav Mahler, 'Titan', *Symphony No. 1 in D Major 'Titan',* New York: Dover, 1998, p. 1.
36. Theodor Adorno, *Mahler: Eine musikalische Physiognomik*, 1962; translated Edmund Jephcott, *Mahler: A Musical Physiognomy*, Chicago: UCP, 1992, p. 4. *Editors' note:* Recall the leering mockery of 'The residual echoes from the giant explosion/Where they said it beginned', "The Radio is Broken", *Man from Utopia*, 1983: a direct hit at pseudo-materialist, existential awe before the findings of natural science. This awe, incidentally, curses post-Cagean musicology (*e.g.* Douglas Kahn's postmodernist rehabilitation of theosophist composer Dane Rudhyar: 'a vibrational logic extant in Cage and, indeed, still audible somewhere between the avowed quantum behaviour of "microsound" and echoes reverberating off the Big Bang', 'Ether Ore: Mining Vibrations in American Modernist Music', *Hearing Cultures: Essays on Sound, Listening, and Modernity*, edited Veit Erlmann, Oxford: Berg, 2004, p. 127); Zappa's 'they said'—siting cosmic knowledge in mundane power relations—evinces precisely the skepticism about metaphysical beginnings and endings which Maurizi finds in Adorno.
37. Frank Zappa, "I Come from Nowhere", *Ship Arriving Too Late to Save a Drowning Witch*, 1982.

Poodles: a Zappological Reading of *Ulysses*

Gamma

A Note from the Editors

Esemplastic Zappology attempts to complete Empirical Zappology by smashing the alienation and oppression of bourgeois individualism and/or celebrity fixation, and thereby finding manifestations of conceptual continuity in the 'object' as well as in the 'project', in the *Quod Aliquo Mundane* as well as the hermetic *oeuvre.* As a living embodiment of Practical Zappology (which Gamma calls 'speaking Zappanese'), Gamma is the biscuit-crucial antidote to idealist tendencies within the Esemplasm. He is well-known to audiences at Muffin

Men concerts throughout the land, and has supplied accommodation to Jimmy Carl Black when he was in town.

Living in the Martian Embassy, a font of extra-terrestrial gratification hidden in the commodius curve of Oseney Crescent in Kentish Town, North London, Gamma holds court on a bench in Cantelowes Park, where he plays with Tami's big black poodle Jake and drinks impressive amounts of Strongbow cider. A squeaking squeezy plastic potato named 'Bobby' has been a recent intermediary between man and dog. The indecipherable mumblings of various stumbling men and women—*aka* the local winos and dogwalkers—are word-surfed by Gamma into rhapsodic zappological constructs of considerable artistic complexity, not to say complex artistry. Gamma interprets Zappa's output macrostructure as a blueprint (or excuse) for a sensuous existence outside the realm of the ordinary, and as such plays havoc with the, um, *pretensions* of a purely theoretical Zappology, always in danger of reducing the *oeuvre* to a chest-of-drawers of interpreted finitudes. The systematic anti-system of Gamma's life and opinions—intimate, personal, telephonic, answer-phoned, mini-disced, radio-broadcast, written (big letters in black felt-tip), reported or recalled in fond recollection—must be experienced to be understood, but the following tries to inkle a blotch or two from the dark Quink of his desiring. Gamma brought Jake the Poodle to ICE-Z, along with the sculptor Mick Bonfield, who also brought Sammy the Lapdog. The entry of these four in the mid-afternoon raised the level of the conference from the merely abstract to the canine level.

Late at night, unable to quell the fomenting inkenstink of his rampant connectivitis, Gamma has a habit of reading vast swathes of James Joyce's *Ulysses* out loud to Tami, a text which in his mouth becomes chocker-block with conceptual-continuity clues and devices. We thought maybe we could get some of this stuff out beyond the realms of Kentish Town, and suggested he curate an event titled 'Poodles: a Zappological Reading of *Ulysses*' at ICE-Z. However, in accordance with a persistent tendency within Zappanese to deviation (Democritus: 'the atoms however *swerve*'), we didn't get what we expected. Instead of the reading of *Ulysses* we'd been promised, Gamma read us 'General Field Theory' from *Freedom is a Two-Edged Sword*, a collection of essays by John Whiteside Parsons edited by Cameron and

Hymenaeus Beta for New Falcon Publications in Tampe, Arizona in 1989, the initial publication in their Oriflamme series.

Parsons' paper begins with the highly Zappological insight that

> in *homo sapiens*, intellect has grown to the point where it is equal to or even more powerful than instinct in regulating certain basic forces.[1]

Some conference delegates found the text's attention to the formation of power relations in *groups* relevant to Zappa as band leader and employer of technical staff, others to the socio-dynamics of the Esemplasm itself. The self-consciousness about group-formation in the situationist-tinged Paris section (Les Fils de l'Invention) was hence reflected in a text by a member of the Agape Lodge of Aleister Crowley's *Ordo Tempi Orientis.* Gamma concluded his reading with the following brief extemporisation:

> John Whiteside Parsons was born in 1914. He was a rocket scientist, and he died in 1952 because he was playing with rockets. [*laughter*] Yeah, I know. Keep smiling. And Bush wants to go to Mars!—ha ha ha. Anyway, Jack wrote all this stuff down here. Ben asked me to read *Ulysses*, and I thought to myself yesterday, that's the one: *Freedom is a Two-Edged Sword*!

The repercussions of Gamma's promise of a reading from *Ulysses* didn't stop with this deviation, but instead resounded yet further down the *Ewigkeit.* When we came to post the above account of Gamma's deviance on the ICE-Z section of the Militant Esthetix website, we received the following e-mail (readers who would like to see another example of Gamma's genius, please refer to the appendix, where the text for his contribution to MERZ NITE has been reproduced):

> My name is Calvin Krogh. I'm a young Zappa fan from Norway, who is just starting to get into *Finnegans Wake*, after getting an excellent lecture about it in school. I have read your (Mr. Watson's) book *Negative Dialectics*. Perhaps I understood one tenth of what I read, but I liked it. It's informative, entertaining and mind-boggling (isn't that the word?). I also saw *Finnegans Wake* mentioned under Bibliography in *The Complete Guide to the Music of FZ*. What

> I'm dreaming of now is a book, or at least a paper, that deals with the relationship (or whatever) between Zappa and Joyce (especially *Finnegans Wake*). And: I must admit, I was a little disappointed to see that there was no 'zappological reading of James Joyce's *Ulysses*' as promised at the International Conference of Esemplastic Zappology.[2] It's an interesting topic. If such a book is ever released, no matter who writes it (almost), I'll be first in line to buy it.
>
> Sincerely, Calvin K. 25 February 2004

Everything has a significance, and the closer you get to the dark pestle of your own most misfortunate longings, the deeper the correspondences tinkle in the mortuary: symmetry under a cemetery wall. If you are reckless enough to expose the contents and discontents of your mind on a website, chances are that cybergliders will zip by with their casual, street-ballet insouciance and let slip glib questions or requests, some of which will gradually work you into a läther. Such a foam-flecked response is festering below, Laid-ease and Genital-men, a blobulent outgrowth of speckled speculation prompted by this electronic *communiqué* from Calvin Krogh.

Already, by virtue of his name—a suave, latinate, north-french conscience diving into the icycled mouth of a terminal viking loch (it's not the Kyffin, it's the boffin they bump you off in)—Calvin Krogh is a worthy constituent of the rewritten scarscape which rips like weasels through the esemplastic uncalculus, and whose twinkling canopy stretches like the Duke of York's broomhandle between Stonehouse & Lancaster, Bromley & Hillsborough, Earshape & Eyewurzle, Amen & Omen, a mixed-metaphorical schema making a counter-angle to the fine dotted line between Muzak & Dyoublong?.

Fictional Response to Meister Krogh

The only way Out To Lunch could deal with the pustulent, pushing, seminal, seminiferous, ludicrous, criss-crossed, litter-strewn, letter-raving *literary* energies unleashed by such a missal, so reminiscent of his own ominous encounter with *Finnegans Wake*, aged fourteen, in the school library, was to go to his sickbed and watch the gristle grow porter. Using the excuse of a gastric flu from Birmingham (named in the *Evening Standard* of 2 March 2004 as Small Round-Structured Virus, or SRSV) which was taking down the London radical intelligentsia like so many ten-pin skittles (no *Pudel*, this SRSV!), OTL cancelled all engagements and, hugging a copy of *Finnegans Wake*, locked the door, switched on the answerphone, dowsed the house lights and wrapped himself in the rank sheets of an enseamèd bed. He would *read* his way through the problem ...

The *Wake* fell open at the Shem chapter, which Out To Lunch read in its inkish entirety, his reading of its guiltridden *exposé* striated with comments overheard from female adolescents smoking empty rizla papers in the communal hallway and talking about ginger girls dying their hair to avoid the nasty comments, their random urban chatter helping to dispel the nuisance of a mono-reading imposed by having listened repeatedly to an LP of Cyril Cusack reading these pages back in 1972. Sleep after the *Wake* was characterised by a grinding compounded of greenish drops of unnamed proclivities, the furnace-traction roaring and clunk-clinking of the metabolic rate, Rabelaisian lists, port-hole scratchings, parallax funnelled into thunderous brow-clenched argument, the pennyweather bellshirts of Ken-Fox-like unpreplanned physico-*verité* ejaculations, Tim Allen-style lists, winter grease, merry varlets, coshed quotatoes, disinterred monuments, burnished plop plops, schystlike micas, incredulous incas, jesuits squirted the wrong way, blobules of mercury, excess'n'excess'n'excess, zappaesque weren't-beenie bouquets strung on anti-catholic wireless immanent critiques, and wasp stings. The hurt wound of nonstopping torture, the punishment machine of Kafka's penal colony which your comfy moralism merely upholsters (Raoul Vaneigem out of Frances Stracey), the unholstered pistols shooting sex signs at the starlets, pop! pop!, the grim grey grind in the back of the tooth and the continual black pump of the heart, no lentsome ventilation or the dove pigeon peace pledge, no blue skies courtesy Microsoft Corp., no knowberry boots at the back of the store. Hard hard hard in the body of the mind. Like Dallas Boner said of Maxayn Lewis, true funk gets the machines back into the body, plays a keyboard ripple on the vertebrae, makes me know the electro-spark of nerve tissue. Helter Mass Skeleton Endroit! I'm an ident-fix of the human *imago*, better see what the others are doing by writhing here on this my couch of foolskin flusick bedmento.

The licksmoothies' amorphous cheese of disorganised nomad protoplasm can't take the crunch and splinter of the bone itself: the rigour of our phallicism is a merely a reminder of the bonehard *splendide* within this our living corpse. To be alive we must know our very bodiness and place-mat, our ortal actuality. Bonney bony elbows in the face of every Bloomsbury pusillanimity!

Let's say the names and place them toe to toe, as if on a deathslab:

```
F r a n k  Z a p p a
J a m e s  J o y c e

G a i l  S l o a t m a n
N o r a  B a r n a c l e
```

That frigging fits. What more do you want, a catachism? A catamite schysm? A dynamited parliament and a catachistic strokeback, a cat-o-nine-tails waved in your features?

```
U l y s s e s
W e a s e l s?
```

It must be admitted that

```
F r a n k  Z a p p a
F r a n z  K a f k a
```

is more spookily congruous, a coincidence wreathed in esemplastic ectoplasm, and no doubt explains why Franz Kafka's 'In the Penal Colony' is the only piece of modern literature referenced on a Zappa album. But (another *aperçu* of Dallas Boner's) all those 'avant' pop-music wankers who drop heavy names (on their broken toes!) in *Wire* interviews are just so much tiresome chestphlegm and nuke-us mucous: the testament must be written INTO THE METHOD OF THE BODY OF THE WORK. No flashes on readymade images confirming a commercial imaginary! No icons plugged into the power circuit of temporary illusion! No exploitation of semiotic triggers which will look quaint-as-Victorian-fairyporn when the next wave of image-change splashes on the bitchhead! No collusive inclusion of 'sexy pics' like a Sonic Youth LP cover... no Roger Deanesque fantasy lanscape like Edgar Quinet rhapsodizing the scentladen florist's array ... no chiffon to sneeze on, no baby hooks (the 'drazy hoops'? does anyone out there believe the lyric sheet on the *Trout Mask* CD?) to bleed on, no streets left for dummies to jog on or doggies to god on. MATERIALIST ESTHETIX, baby, as inexpensive as plea song! No mystery, gnome history, no images, no references, no tuned-up Bowie-esque sing-song and pouting, no *moral*: a cavalcade, a cornucopia, a barrelload, a garbage truck, a sorghum pipe, an icing'n'ointment utensil fully-charged with STUFF STUFF STUFF, all from somewhere, scintillated and wriggling with its torn-from vectors, a velcrose-fastened *animé* ball comprising a bit of everything from whatever bin (and *gwine* be, I hear), seething and weaving and frothing and spuming into a monstrous garish *collage*nikov mock abstract on the freeway TEN FEET TALL! How like your dreams...

Er, more specifically... Zappa and Joyce are cultural subversion cranked up to multispeed, where impediments to the artist's megalomaniac will to put anything next to anything have become a persistent itch whose scratching rends the body of the work so it no longer 'works', it's all over the place ... but *what a place*! Both were medievalists contesting a puritanical rationalised logico-commodity system imposed by the Protestant Worth Ethic, reacting against repressive Roman Catholic upbringings and schoolings, but saving the good part: the yearning for a universal world picture. But instead of an inert ecclesiastical myth designed to prevent the masses noticing their chains, Zappa and Joyce turn the rosy esemplastic holographic wonderment of the Chartres effulgence into a begargoyled beast at the beck-and-call of anyman or woman brave enough to walk by hissside. It hisses at cowardice and snarls at censorship and sniffs at repression, electrically sensitive to the BULLSHIT surrounding SOCIAL OPPRESSION.

People who write about *Finnegans Wake* without reading it (most-people) forget how OBSCENE and SHOCKING and ANGRY and RAW and NAKED it is. Folding everything into the thumping rhythms of a few favorite prose passages whose style he loved but whose content he disdained, Joyce evaded the British wartime censors (the same ones who'd pooped on *Ulysses*) by producing a book of 'incomprehensible gibberish'—incomprehensible to every 'educated' person, that is, who's forgotten that everything written is merely a transcription of something said in lust or anger or accountancy or pure punning fun. Joyce catches the words in their spastic automatic splenetic shapescule before they've had time to settle into orderly grey-ruled narrow-feint monosense. *Finnegans Wake* is the best book of the twentieth century. It has of course has been roundly condemned and squarely rejected as 'unreadable' or 'difficult' by politicians, academics, journalists and mass-media spokepersons who wish to keep alive the desiccated, non-lived, duped and BORING spectacle of life supplied to us by those who rule. But the *Wake* has been celebrated and pored-over and disputed and read—read read RED—by all true REVOLUTIONARIES, SURREALISTS, BEATS, POETS, FREE IMPROVISORS, ZAPPA FANS & COCKROACH-FANCIERS as the bible of Post-Capitalism, our glimpse of a humanist democracy beyond war, exploitation, media manipulation and the money form, where MATERIALIST RECOGNITION OF OUR ACTUAL LIVES (what the *Communist Manifesto* called facing with sober senses our real conditions of life and our relations to our kind[3]) becomes the open swinging-bar door on a limitless realm of play, adventure, learning, social contact and sexual bliss.

Biographical Trivia

When Frank Zappa was born James Joyce was still alive: Joyce died on 13 January 1941; baby Frank was born just 23 days before. The list of names in *Freak Out*—which includes James Joyce (just after Charles 'Merry Christmas Baby' Brown)—are arranged in eight columns of *23 lines* each.[4] Although the names of Joyce and Zappa do fit the same lettrist grid, their boehmic syllababbles waft very different aromas. James is soft, the repeated 'J' is soothing, the sounds around his name invoke amiable joy and soulful high spirits (*âme* is 'soul' in French, 'Oi!' is a Jewish ejaculation used in London's East End); Frank Zappa is a weird abutment of northern Germanitude ('Frank' rather than Frances or Francesco) and the southern Italianate (in Italian 'zappa' means a primitive garden implement). 'James Joyce' is soft on the tongue, juicy, kiss-like, smooth on the ear: 'Frank Zappa' is staccato, a shock, a joke, a poke in the eye. In the 60s, ignorant of Italian words for primitive garden implements, most fans thought Zappa's name was a put-on, a perverted brandname-style misspelling of 'zapper', *i.e.* 'one who zaps' ('Zap!' being a word like 'Pow!' and 'Wham!' used by post-war comic strips to describe the impact of ray-guns, or the sound sound of righteous fists meeting well-shaved chins).

As associations accrete around them, words develop meanings. Since the special area of artists is, as the Danish painter Asger Jorn put it, 'fascinations, their elaboration and interplay' (*The Natural Order*, Report No. 1 of the Scandinavian Institute of Comparative Vandalism, 1962[5]), the names of artists are especially conducive to such accretions. Nevertheless, the fact that Joyce was a pacifist and humanist born into an era of wars and one successful revolution, and that Zappa was a brash self-promoter born into an era of wars and consumer booms and failed revolutions, should not extinguish the extraordinary congruence of their project/objects. Both made vast works which require inhabitation by the reader/listener. Joyce acts like a summary of everything the book and reading can do, Zappa like a prediction of everything recording media can and will do. Only reader/listeners who are sensitive to what they have in common can understand what makes them tick unique. Zappa was a *saboteur* in the face of the mass-media spectacle, a font of lacerating poetry who relentlessly criticised hype, lies and manipulation. His emphasis on the detail and surface of his art (so unlike the mysterious promises of hip lurking behind the folk modes and echoic shimmer of the Velvet Underground) links him straight to Kurt Schwitters and James Joyce. Zappa's art doesn't speak by provocation, positioning or reputation (Duchamp, Warhol, Koons) but in the grain of its maximalist mediation. It's not good because it shocks the art world, it's good because it improves MY world.

Far from being a bookish retreat from modernity, *Finnegans Wake* is set in a public house with a TV-set playing (a device yet to be inflicted on the masses when Joyce wrote), though this TV-set is generally ignored in favour of the psychic reality of those in the pub (which include the landlord's family and children upstairs in bed or seated on the stairwell staring down through the banisters). Joyce's prose evades the repression of literature and the responsibility of the concept, and proposes instead a universal humanism in recognizing the quaint proclivities of the human animal. Zappa recognised that the superficial 'immediacy' of the mass media was in fact the same spectacular oppression which Joyce found in official knowledge. They both had a thing about knickers. Different social poisons: same radical-subjective antidote.

The *New York Times* didn't take kindly to the links between Joyce and Zappa made by my *Frank Zappa: the Negative Dialectics of Poodle Play*[6], interpreting them as a claim that Zappa was a 'wordsmith on a par with James Joyce', as if I wasn't aware Zappa turned out albums not books. But since it irritates the brokers of cultural value so much to be reminded that Joyce took literature down to the dregs, to the left-behinds, those who aren't afraid to say what's on their minds, to the stumblers down in the dew, let's look at this STUFF—even though it comes out as something that looks like 'nonsense' to you, oh my bourgeois brothers.

Dropping into the *Wake* is so like listening to Zappa, it's pitiful how few critics have remarked upon the similarity. You are buffeted by powerful hot winds full of acrid scents you cannot name but which you know promise strange and wondrous feasts (in pots!). It's like landing on the roof of an alien factory in the midst of the arrival of an important shipment of off-planet ores while also drinking meths with the winos in a bivouac made of discarded rocket fins, moon rocks and space rubbish. The poor saddoes who believe that sorting out each little 'reference' will clarify the *oeuvre* miss the point: only readers/listeners who are prepared to drop 'getting the point' and experience the prose/music as a sensual, below-the-belt *massage* will ever get the point. This is not to deny the fun to be had in Joyce Studies and Zappology, which in the right hands (skeptical, materialist, interested, un-star-fixated, collective, Marxist) can use the objectivity of their projects to develop a holistic, dialectical (esemplastic) interpretation of history and cosmos, a science that (unlike positivism) has desire in it, and a desire that (unlike postmodernism) has science in it. But we HEARD the 'meaning' of the *Wake* and we SAW the 'meaning' of *Weasels* as soon as we jumped with joy to experience such willful, artful, SINFUL transgressions of the norm-oriented artifacts pumped at us down the culture shoot. The lack of ostensible here's-the-hero, boy-meets-girl, I'm-a-bright-guy, here's-a-sad-song 'meaning' was our Orghast, our Persephone, our Citron Peel of Lebanon. What did Joyce and Zappa want, an audience of FREAKS??! Yes indeed, sir.

Shem and Frank

Allah 'n' Fang Ist Schweppes ... logically enough, the chapter begins with Shem's origins:

> Shem is as short for Shemus as Jem is joky for Jacob. A few toughnecks are still getatable who pretend that aboriginally he was of respectable stemming...[7]

But this narrative logic is directed at a cipher. Who is 'Shem' anyway? We've never been introduced. The first whole sentence of the *Wake* (a *leitmotif* perpetually recycled in variant versions throughout the book, a list of events) is followed directly by:

> Rot a peck of pa's malt had Jhem or Shen brewed by arclight and rory end to the regginbrow was to be seen ringsome on the aquaface.[8]

Nearly Shem, but not quite. This is Joyce's assault on the written word as an inadequate transcription of sound, and nowhere is this more apparent in *names*, which resist the homogeneity imposed by national, codified languages and force people to pay attention to 'accent', a term for linguistic residues and tongue habits of subaltern tribes and communities. Think of all the problems which southern English people have with spelling the 'Micks' and 'Mikes' from up north correctly, or the extraordinary discovery made by Mick (or was it Mike?) Dougan from Pudsey, when he visited Derry and heard Eamonn McCann address his partner Goretti: we'd all been fooled by the gaelic spelling into pronouncing her name—which was obviously 'Gerty'—in McCann's Irish brogue!

Finnegans Wake is not simply about the dissolution of sense as the poststructuralists and postmodernists would have us believe. The rot in the malt is *yeast* and it makes alcohol, leading to drunkenness and conviviality (a wake, as in the booze-up after a funeral). The dissolution of sense has a positive outcome. The *Wake* is a highly motivated and charged satire on English as a definitive tongue, stretching its syntax to include the variants and nuances of its future worldwide users. It reads less like literature than as a transcript of the ravings of a stand-up comic:

> he was an outlex between the lines of Ragonar Blaubarb and Horrild Hairwire and inlaw to Capt. the Hon. and Rev. Mr Bbyrdwood de Trop Blogg was among his most distant connections...[9]

The residual Anglo-Saxon letters preserved in aristocratic names are mocked as stuttered pomposity. The social resentment in *Finnegans Wake*—against an England whose first imperialist foray was the subjugation of Ireland—is relentless, raging and violent, and only academics have the 'training' to blot it out of their analyses. It corresponds very precisely to the resentment in Zappa versus the 'beautiful people', the blonde pupils with surf boards who lord it in Californian high schools, condemning brunettes, wops, dagos, Mexicans and blacks to lower levels of the social hierarchy.

Shem was a sham, so low that, like Keith Richards, he preferred tinned salmon to the real thing. Beefsteak is rejected as the feastmeal of the English oppressor, who'd wrecked Irish peasant life, and reduced the land to a desolate green meadow for the rearing of cattle.

> None of your inchthick blueblooded Balaclava fried-at-belief-stakes or juicejelly legs of the Grex's molten mutton or greasilygristly grunters' goupons or slice upon slab of luscious goosebosom with lump after load of plumpudding stuffing all aswim in a swamp of bogoakgravy for that greekenhearted yude! Rosbif of Old Zealand! he could not attouch it.[10]

This is a good example of the 'the subaltern grandiloquence', which according to Paul Sutton in his paper in this volume 'has been particularly noted of Black and Irish verbal culture' (p 103). The hungry tend to wax big on food (*cf.* Louis Jordan's "Beans & Cornbread"). It's not exactly what Sutton calls the 'mincing but menacing' style of Zappa's 'the sterile canvas snoot of a fully charged icing anointment utensil' ("A Little Green Rosetta"), where a parodic techno-fetishism adds a surface of gleaming chrome to farinaceous-fatty facetious presentness, but compared to Henry James or Virginia Woolf, it's close (Sutton also contends that the famous, swooning conclusion of

Joyce's short story 'The Dead' is not sublimity but kitsch, a piss-take of the hypocritical sentimentality of the appalling Gabriel; by putting in question the only known locale of unalloyed sublimity in Joyce's *oeuvre*, Sutton brings Joyce still closer to the 360°-parody of Zappa). Such is the zinging compatibility of Zappa's attitude with the poetry of the colonised—speaking English, but without inhabiting it—that he could recite Dylan Thomas at the Hammersmith Odeon without anyone guessing it wasn't Zappa's own text.[11] The 'weird correspondences' between Joyce and Zappa noted by readers/listeners result from the fact that they *really* opposed—right into the grain of their artistic production, right into the body of emotive truth—the 'oppression' which all good liberals tut-tut about.

This holds true for concepts of the New World in their work. As an ideology for the comfortable middle class, postmodernism—postcolonial studies and all—totally misconstrues colonisation, blaming the 'whites' *in toto* for crimes against 'blacks'. Actually, the colonisers of New Zealand, Australia and America were the oppressed and marginalised of the first world countries, hounded out of their allotments by the capitalist enclosures. As an Irishman, Joyce never ceased to think about the New World where so many of his compatriots were forced to flee: the *Wake*'s first whole sentence, by putting 'North' in front of 'Armorica' (an ancient kingdom subjugated by Julius Caesar) invokes America; the sentence also mentions the 'stream Oconee', which any world atlas will reveal as the river in the United States on the banks of which there's a town called 'Dublin', founded by Irish refugees.

There have been exhaustive attempts to nail singular meanings in *Finnegans Wake*. Honest attempts to register its effects generate insights unheard-of in idealist literary criticism. Yet Joyce's puns and jokes and linguistic sabotage refute definitive interpretation. Nevertheless, in its whirl of random detail and association-by-wordsound, *Finnegans Wake* digs a ditch totally unlike the high-culture modernism of the American modernist poets with whom he is associated, T.S. Eliot and Ezra Pound. They came to Europe to escape American 'vulgarity' and learn about 'European culture', which in the United States is a synonym for the rights and privileges of the top stratum of society. Joyce, on the other hand, dragged literature down into a morass of oral wit and song and repartee, drinksodden and jovial, to which no amount of classical learning can ever provide a key. Yet everybody to whom you read a sentence of the *Wake* will provide some information from their own particular walk of life which will illuminate your understanding—of the *Wake*, of themselves, of us, of the world. Frank Zappa's *oeuvre* works just like that: you can't look up the meaning of 'crab-grass' or 'sexual harassment in the workplace' or 'why does it hurt when I pee?' in a reference book. Ask your neighbour instead. It's amazing how much people know. This discovery of infinity in the mundane—the Romantic concept of a life as a perpetual unfolding, an ongoing hail-fellow-well-met metropolitan metamorphosis and *omnium gatherum* (or Esemplasm)—was deliberately fostered by Zappa as a counter-blast to the vain, isolated, adolescent mindset of rock, which wants a heroic, superman ideology ('I have stared into the abyss!'... no, you've stared at *your failure to get a date!*) circumscribed by a couple of books (one by Kerouac, the other by Greil Marcus) and a few soundtracks (the Doors and the Velvet Underground).

Shem's proclivities are enumerated in the *Wake*—not only is he a sham, but he's addicted to drink, especially a

> rhubarbarous maundarin yellagreen funkleblue windigut diodying applejack squeezed from sour grapefruice[12]

The phrase 'fancy you're in her yet' becomes the name 'Fanny Urinia'. Female peepee, the taste of which all men secretly thirst for: the sexual reductionism used by both Joyce and Zappa as their weapon against pomposity and hierarchy.

Finnegans Wake is a book, but it must be read aloud or you won't get it:

> shaking the worth out of his maulth[13]

It's when you say 'worth' you realise how close it actually is to 'words'; a 'maul' is a hammer, and putting it inside 'mouth' makes you realise how slight a movement of the tongue is needed to add 'l' to 'th'. *Wakese* makes your tongue work, you splutter and gargle, making all those barbaric sounds which ignorant and unreflecting people say foreign languages are full of. This is anti-chauvinism below the level of morals, it's entered the grain of speech itself, it's *physical*. After this immersion in polysyllabic macaronic, it's the transparent discourse of the upper classes which appears cruel and oppressive:

> some wellwishers, vainly pleading by scriptural arguments with the opprobrious papist about trying to brace up for the kidos of the thing, Scally wag, and be a men instead of a dem scrounger, dish it all[14]

'men' for 'man' and 'dem' for 'damn' mock the clipped accent of the stiff-upper-lipped British Imperialist.

Joyce indicts the racist prurience with which whites project their repressed desires on the behaviour of black folk. Like Zappa's "Brown Shoes Don't Make It" and *Thing-Fish*, this is achieved *via* unchecked wallowing in the regressive murk of their secret fantasies and desires:

> Darkies never done tug that coon out to play non-excretory, anti-sexuous, misoxenetic, gaasy pure, flesh and blood games, written and composed and sung and danced by Niscemus Nemon, same as piccaninnies play all day, those old (none of your honeys and rubbers!) games for fun and element we used to play with Dina[15]

Joyce got this past the British censors because he staged *Finnegans Wake* as a flow of gibberish rather than realism: a continual commentary on what it's like to reads something where the text is only what it is, and never gives itself over to a narrative suitable for Broadway or Hollywood.

Like Zappa, Joyce indulges in self obsession to the point where his *oeuvre* becomes the entire world. The Situationists coined the term 'radical subjectivity', but they never gave anyone outside their time and place (Paris 1958-69) opportunities to experience it. Joyce and Zappa explode the boundaries of bourgeois *politesse* and a rational public order sustained by legal contracts between supposedly equal citizens. They reveal the actuality of lust, greed and lies beneath the bourgeois veneer. Shem is Joyce's self-portrait as a writer, and echoes his own biography:

> He even ran away with hunself and became a farsoonerite, saying he would far sooner muddle through the hash of lentils in Europe than meddle with Irrland's split little pea[16]

Fig. 47: Gamma

This self-portrait sits inside *Finnegans Wake* like the scene in *200 Motels* where Ringo Starr, dressed up to look like Frank Zappa, composes music by rubbing the magic lamp, switching on a transistor radio at random and spilling black coffee on his manuscript: it's an illusory moment of self-reflection because artistic subjectivity has already swallowed the universe, and there is nothing that isn't drenched in the artist's personality.

> his Ballade Imaginaire which was to be dubbed *Wine, Woman and Waterclocks*, or *How a Guy Finks and Fawkes When He Is Going Batty*[17]

'Ballade Imaginaire' puns together a play by Jean-Baptiste Molière (*La Malade Imaginaire*) and the traditional Irish ballad which the *Wake* sometimes imagines it is. But as Zappa pointed out in the Central Scrutinizer's preamble to "Watermelon in Easter Hay" on *Joe's Garage*, imaginary art only exists 'in the imagination of The Imaginer' (this is what the Central Scrutinizer actually says, it's transcribed wrong in the lyric sheet). '*Wine, Women and Waterclocks*' substitutes a Roman method of measuring time—the waterclock—for 'song' in the list of life's pleasures for men; this is because it sounds like 'waterclosets', or toilets, and Joyce's fascination for women pissing and chamber pots is legendary. Joyce's art is poised on the same ludicrous brink of absolute indulgence as Zappa's, and therefore begs similar questions about freedom in a society where free competition is meant to resolve every issue.

Guy Fawkes was the Catholic rebel who attempted to blow up the English Parliament: Joyce's battiness/madness was to believe that bourgeois representative democracy was not the summit of human history. As he wrote to his brother Stanislaus:

> You have often shown opposition to my socialistic tendencies. But can you not see plainly from facts like these that a deferment of the emancipation of the proletariat, a reaction to clericalism or aristocracy or bourgeoisism would mean a revulsion to tyrannies of all kinds? (*c.* 12 August 1906)

> If the Irish question exists, it exists for the Irish proletariat chiefly. (25 September 1906)

Joyce detested *Sinn Fein* because they campaigned against English imperialism using reactionary sexual politics, accusing them of 'venereal excess'.

> I am nauseated by their lying drivel about pure men and pure women and spiritual love and love for ever: blatant lying in the face of truth. (13 November 1906)

Born in a period when Stalinism had tarnished the hopes of the early twentieth century, Zappa declared himself neither a Marxist nor a socialist—indeed explicitly opposed them—yet throughout his life vilified the hypocrisies of bourgeois public figures and politicians in a Joycean manner. Both Joyce and Zappa perceived Englishmen as responsible for global oppression (first the British Empire, and then the United States—in both, the top layer of society originates from England). Their art revels in reducing the English language to rubble. The *Wake*'s self-descriptions could work as descriptions of *Thing-Fish*:

> he would wipe alley english spooker, multaphoniaksically spuking, off the face of the erse[18]

Like Zappa, Joyce's heavy use of collage and parody made him unpopular among critics wedded to conventional notions of artistic originality and genius. Both show that artistic materials are not invented out of thin air by the isolated individual, but are social products.

> Who can say how many pseudostylic shamiana, how few or how many of the most venerated public impostures, how very many piously forged palimpsests slipped in the first place by this morbid process from his pelagiarist pen?[19]

The extra 'e' makes 'plagiarist' refer to Pelagius, the fifth-century heretic. Pelagius insisted that human will is capable of good without divine grace and denied the doctrine of original sin. He was attacked by St Augustine. In 418 AD, he was excommunicated by Pope Zosimus. The materialist view of culture is fundamentally anti-religious, since it demystifies ultimate meanings, making them something we can all play with (not just priests). Sexuality is the holy orifice available to everyone, and oppressive religiosity, mystical bullshit and bad rock music all stem from sexual frustration.

Like Zappa, Shem sports a moustache:

> anna loavely long pair of inky Italian moostarshes glistering with boric valine and frangipani[20]

Like Zappa, ("Montana", "Excentrifugal Forz", "Porn Wars", "Tiny Sick Tears"), Shem loves to talk about masturbation:

> *Handmarried but once in my Life and I'll never commit such a Sin again ... This is the Way we sow the Seed of a long and lusty Morning*[21]

And he's accused of it by his enemies:

> ...every day in everyone's way more exceeding in violent abuse of self and others... the worst, it is hoped, even in our western playboyish world for pure mousefarm filth[22]

In a fantastic list of the contents of Shem's room, there are at least two Zappaesque motifs:

> worms of snot... globules of mercury[23]

"Let's Make the Water Turn Black" (*We're Only In It for the Money*) is about a boy called Ronnie who smeared his nasal mucous on a window; *The Real Frank Zappa Book* reports '... blobs *of mercury*. I used to play with it all the time. The entire floor of my bedroom had this "muck" on it, made out of mercury mixed with dust balls. One of the things I used to like to do was pour the mercury on the floor and hit it with a hammer, so it squirted all over the place. I lived in mercury.'[24] Metal which is liquid at room temperature; the perfect element for Heraclitean dialecticians (the *Wake* begins with 'riverrun', referencing Heraclitus's famous *dictum* 'no man goes down to the same river twice'; "Baby Snakes" is (hera)clitoral).

Like Zappa, Joyce indulged in furious scatology ('your scatchophily'[25]). They both took as much delight in the body and its products as any infant. Both had problems with propriety and property: obscenity and copyright laws.

> he shall produce nichthemerically from his unheavenly body a no uncertain quantity of obscene matter not protected by copriright in the United Stars of Ourania[26]

The motif of the mad professor in Zappa may be derived from 50s monster movies, but it nevertheless stands for the alchemist: Doctor Faustus at work in his study/laboratory. Zappa and Joyce both wanted to create *oeuvres* which would include everything and be conceived as a single entity: esemplastic artists at the very edge of their technique who find in self-exploration the key to the cosmos.

> this Esuan Menschavik and the first till last alshemist wrote over every square inch of the only foolscap available, his own body, till by its corrosive sublimation one continuous present tense integument slowly unfolded all marryvoising moodmoulded cyclewheeling history[27]

Zappa said he conceived of time as a 'spherical constant'.[28] Both Joyce and Zappa understand that linear time is a social oppression, and that when human consciousness conceives *everything*, time is circular. This is what analytical philosophers call 'mysticism', but never before has mysticism been proposed by such funny and bullshit-free thinkers (unless it was Giordano Bruno).

Justius accuses Shem of antisocial behaviour:

> you, who sleep at our vigil and fast for our feast[29]

Zappa's eccentric sleep patterns are well-documented (he prefered night time, when there weren't so many people 'doing bad things ... *scurrying*'[30]): he hated Thanksgiving, complaining bitterly when his children prepared turkey and cranberry sauce and forced him to sit at table with them.[31]

Shem likes fire and explosions:

> the dynamitisation of colleagues, the reducing of records to ashes, the levelling of all customs by blazes, the return of a lot of sweet-empered gunpowdered didst unto dudst[32]

As a schoolboy, Zappa was obsessed with explosives; his art was likewise a firestorm, breaking rules and incinerating customs.

Justius's speech compounds all the misery and mystery which religion and the judicial bureaucracy inflictd on the oppressed. Joyce's satire on officialdom brings the *Wake* into the orbit of Zappa and Kafka:

> O, by the way, yes, another thing occurs to me. You let me tell you, with the utmost politeness, were very ordinarily designed, your birthwrong was, to fall in with Plan, as our nationals should, as all nationists must, and do a certain office (what, I will not tell you) in a certain holy office (nor will I say where) during certain agonising office hours (a clerical party all to yourself) from such a year to such an hour on such and such a date at so and so much a week *pro anno...*[33]

Justius winds up calling Shem insane:

> Sh! Shem, you are. Sh! You are mad![34]

One of the contentions of the Mad Pride civil rights movement is that capitalism—*i.e* poverty, alienation, lack of personal recognition in a celebrity culture—drives the poor and oppressed crazy. We take heart

Fig. 48: Starmap with Shelves

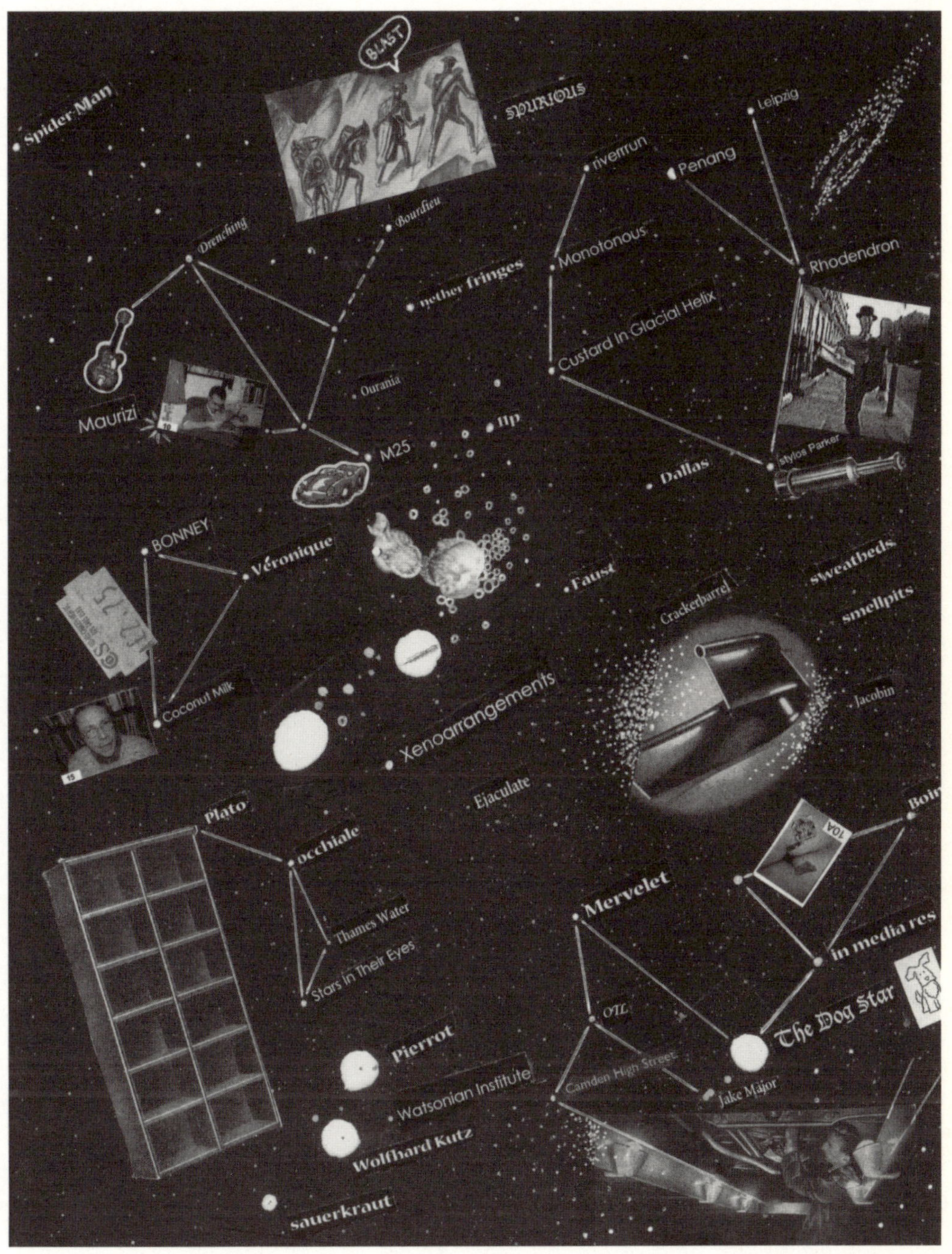
BLAST
Spider-Man
Drenching
Bourdieu
nether fringes
Maurizi
Ourania
M25
flp
riverrun
Penang
Leipzig
Monotonous
Rhodendron
Custard In Glacial Helix
stylos Parker
Dallas
BONNEY
Véronique
Coconut Milk
Faust
Crackerbarrel
sweatbeds
smellpits
Jacobin
Xenoarrangements
Ejaculate
Plato
occhiale
Thames Water
Stars In Their Eyes
Mervelet
in media res
The Dog Star
OTL
Pierrot
Camden High Street
Jake Major
Watsonian Institute
Wolfhard Kutz
sauerkraut

from the fact that during economic slumps and social revolutions, when money suddenly wields no power, it's the turn of tycoons and bankers to go crazy.

There is an outbreak of guilt at the end of the Shem chapter and a running into mother's arms[35] which is not Zappaesque at all. Zappa kept faith to his delinquent distrust of guilt and sentiment all his life.[36] The point of this essay is not to claim Joyce and Zappa were identical as personalities, that would be ridiculous (besides, such arguments belong to the twilight world of gossip). The point is, that as rebels against the Roman Catholicism they were born into, Joyce and Zappa had an extraordinarily keen understanding of how religious oppression works. They understood how an honest recognition of one's own sexual impulses can liberate people from religion, nationalism and fascism. For them, art—joy-in-words in Joyce's case, joy-in-music in Zappa's—wasn't something 'high' and 'uplifting', the kind of secular replacement for religion it is in W.B. Yeats and T.S. Eliot, but a *weapon* for improving society and vanquishing its ills. Anyone who understands Joyce and Zappa in this way this has a duty: to help foment a left culture which is as brave, subversive and progressive as theirs. And as funny!

1. John Whiteside Parsons, *Freedom is a Two-Edged Sword*, edited Cameron & Hymenaeus Beta, Tampe: New Falcon Publications, p. 85.
2. Yes, in some ways it was a pity Gamma chose to read John Whiteside Parsons rather than James Joyce at ICE-Z, although it did enable him to have a go at rocket science and George Dubya, all that Nazi technology required for the US empire. If Gamma wrote books, who'd need to write anything else? ... *blow your harmonica, son.* This paper is dedicated to Calvin Krogh, and also to Gerry Fialka, who has long insisted on connections between Zappa and the *Wake*, and made them real by answering the phone for Barking Pumpkin in the early-90s whilst simultaneously leading a *Wake* reading-group at Los Angeles Public Library—and also to jwcurry, who sees things our way too. Go Fialka! Go curry!! Go Krogh!!!
3. Karl Marx and Friedrich Engels, *The Communist Manifesto*, 1948; translated Samuel Moore, 1888; edited David Fernbach, *The Revolutions of 1848*, London: Penguin, 1973, pp. 70-1.
4. Are the strange coincidences noticed by Poodle Play articles of faith, mnemonic devices or simply jokes? We're still not sure. The jury (a terrifying dream team consisting of my mother Katherine, my brother Oliver, J.H. Prynne, Tony Cliff, Esther Leslie, Charles Fort, T.H.F. Drenching, Paul Sutton, Vladimir Vernadsky, Andrew Greenaway, Raya Dunayevskaya and Eleanor Crook) is still out. Benjamin called such spurs to the poetic imagination 'constellations'. It's a useful analogy. There's no astronomer who didn't start by recognising the Plough, but from an extra-terrestrial point of view, the constellations are arbitrary projections on random clusters: as arbitrary as my excitment with the numerological/Burroughsian/Mittonesque favourite '23'. Giordano Bruno—who

speculated that the universe was infinite and the sun just another star, thus breaking out of astrology into astronomy proper—made his living outlining 'world pictures' to rich noblemen and courtiers. These weren't simply inaccurate versions of the diagrams at the front of your world atlas (those which show the milky way, the earth's crust, the world's religions and pork production), they were *mnemonic devices*, prototypes of the personal computer and the personal organiser. Science without mnemonic devices—recognition of the thinking subject—is undialectical, unteachable, unreal. Poodle Play rejects postwar surrealism as it sank into a slowsand of individualised art-production, astrology and magic, but follows Marx in refusing to accept knowledge frozen at the moment of Thomas Hobbes, when 'knowledge based upon the senses loses its poetic blossom' and 'passes into the abstract experience of the *geometrician*' [Karl Marx and Friedrich Engels, *The Holy Family*, 1844; translated Richard Dixon and Clemens Dutt, Moscow: Progress, 1975, p. 151]. Microsoft's *Encarta* has something wrong epistemologically: it stuns with facts about everything under (and above) the sun, but it doesn't lead you to understand why the facts are there and why you're looking at them. Those who dismiss the 23 day overlap between Zappa and Joyce as 'irrelevant' know nothing about the internal motivation of either: this 'fact' would've made both of them improvise a facet or motif! Deprived of the fascinations which buzz about them like fireflies, 'facts' about artists disintegrate into historical dust so dry and boring only reference books can contain them. What is the point of *quantifying* the qualitatively-defined achievements of art? *Encarta* has a reply, and one dear to the heart of Bill Gates: historical importance, or *sales figures*! The Microsoft view of knowledge—like that of a purely Empirical Zappology—is boring because, like all bourgeois thought, it really only understands marketing, not the world. Such reference works are only brought down from the bookshelves to 'settle disputes' (dictionaries for Scrabble players). Poodle Play doesn't doubt the need for positive fact (the 23-day overlap *is* a positive fact!), but alerts the reader to the unconscious repressions and gratifications involved in being subjected to 'facts'. Louis Althusser did a great disservice to Marxist theory, when, dimly plodding in the wake of the French Enlightenment's critique of Catholicism, he portrayed Marxism as 'objective science' versus 'popular ideology'. In Britain, a country where the denial of personal experience has long been the commonsense of the bourgeois scientific system, Marxism should pack a shocking emphasis on the experiential and contingent. We's been feeling this way for a long time now, and we wants ARTICULATION! When facts flash from the rubble of the centuries, it's because they speak to desires that require satisfaction: powerful mnemonics require psychoanalytical and historical investigation. The astro-physicist who can't name the constellations will not be able to explain the universe to a child under a night sky. Education de-linked from the senses is abstract and authoritarian, idealist and neo-Kantian, seamless and scriptural, boring and bookish, however 'true'. A truth which cannot be tested by the person who's told it is an article of faith, not of science. Repression of the desirable scrambles of pleasurable thinking makes knowledge professional, unchanging, hieratic—in short, religious. Constellations matter because they ensure we recognise that knowledge is a historical product. The astronomer who says star names are 'arbitrary' and 'irrelevant' erases the Arab world's contribution to 'European' knowledge, and will be more susceptible to historical nonsense in debates about Islam. Good Golly, Cheb Alghol!

5. Asger Jorn, *The Natural Order*, translated Peter Shield, Adldershot: Ashgate, 2002, p. 63.
6. Ben Watson, *Frank Zappa: the Negative Dialectics of Poodle Play*, London: Quartet, 1994, p. 559.
7. James Joyce, *Finnegans Wake*, London: Faber and Faber, 1939, p. 169.
8. *Ibid*, p. 3.
9. *Ibid*, p. 169.
10. *Ibid*, pp. 170-1.
11. See *Poodle Play*, p. 478.

12. James Joyce, *Op. Cit.*, p. 171.
13. *Ibid*, p. 172.
14. *Ibid.*
15. *Ibid*, p. 175.
16. *Ibid*, p. 171.
17. *Ibid*, p. 177.
18. *Ibid*, p. 178.
19. *Ibid*, pp. 181-2.
20. *Ibid*, p. 182.
21. *Ibid*, p. 176.
22. *Ibid*, p. 183.
23. *Ibid.*
24. Frank Zappa with Peter Occhiogrosso, *The Real Frank Zappa Book*, New York: Poseidon Press, 1989, p. 19.
25. James Joyce, *Op. Cit.*, p. 190.
26. *Ibid*, p. 185.
27. *Ibid*, pp. 185-6.
28. *Zappa!* from the publishers of *Keyboard and Guitar Player*, Miller Freeman: San Francisco, 1992, p. 64.
29. James Joyce, *Op. Cit.*, p. 189.
30. Frank Zappa with Peter Occhiogrosso, *Op. Cit.*, p. 250.
31. *Ibid*, p. 252.
32. James Joyce, *Op. Cit.*, pp. 189-90.
33. *Ibid*, p. 190.
34. *Ibid*, p. 193.
35. *Ibid*, pp. 193-5.
36. Of course, Zappa would ensure that there'd be an exception: "Solitude", a tune written for his wife, left alone at home with the kids as he toured and consorted with groupies.

Addendum: The Negative Dialectics of *Arf*-Enlightenment[1]

Daniel DiPaolo

The boundaries between high art and mass culture have become increasingly blurred, and we should begin to see that process as one of opportunity rather than lamenting loss of quality and failure of nerve.

Andreas Huyssen[2]

Relationship of art to life? Well, I told you before, what I'm doing is entertainment. Choose between an entertaining life or the other kind—or the 'art' life. The answer becomes obvious.

Frank Zappa[3]

Frank Zappa's art is vast and difficult to categorize. Never content to behave within normative categories that delimit artistic output, the composer loathed by the United States Senate and admired by the likes of Pierre Boulez and Kent Nagano, wrote in many contexts, ranging from relatively straight-forward rock'n'roll to films such as the bizarre techno-documentaries *Uncle Meat, 200 Motels* and *Baby Snakes.* Frequently dismissed as a crank, Zappa was the next in line in a venerable tradition of American 'cranks' from Charles Ives, Henry Cowell and Harry Partch through to John Cage and John Zorn. Unlike his American predecessors, however, who—despite the sometimes eccentric or ludicrous nature of their music—have been relegated to the sphere of 'art', Zappa was and is considered a popular artist, a rock'n'roll singer and guitarist. As such, his demonstrable innovations, of a kind wholly unfamiliar to his counterparts in the rock realm, cast our attention not only to his art, but to the cultural and sociological apparatus in which it is enclosed—a scenario from which Zappa never wished to escape. At every point in his career he would refer to his music—confusingly—as 'entertainment'.

Since Zappa's compositions self-consciously resist analysis as mere examples of pre-existing genres or types, and are in this manner quite irreducible, the desire to read him as 'modernist' is justified. That this occurs in the guise of rock'n'roll is particularly iconoclastic. In the past decade, there has been a wave of emerging literature on Zappa, most of it focused on aesthetic and political debates in German philosophy. The impetus, of course, was Ben Watson's *Frank Zappa: The Negative Dialectics of Poodle Play*, in which he tropes Theodor Adorno, and especially his powerful but too often over-looked Marxist strain, to tease out the authenticity and truth in Zappa's music. Despite Zappa's petit-bourgeois lifestyle, Watson and others have continually shown that Zappa's music can be enlisted to the critical-socialist cause, and, just as importantly, that it is precisely Zappa's location within the pop sphere that allows him to question it and its grotesqueries.[4] In seeking to avoid the blunders of other more 'affirmative' considerations of pop culture at face value, the present examination will proceed from these premises, as well as that of Adorno's 'Culture Industry'—analysis in its proper form.

Even though Zappa occasionally expressed enthusiasm for the traditional classical concert hall during his various direct run-ins with high culture (most notably with the London Symphony Orchestra, the Ensemble Modern and Boulez's own Ensemble InterContemporain), the fact remains that Zappa was a rock composer, whose means of distribution necessarily aligned with those of other rock artists. In the same way as other popular artists, Zappa relied upon record sales and touring to sustain himself both as an artist and a citizen. The production of albums and tours throws Zappa's work into the arena of 'mechanical reproducibility' and Walter Benjamin's famous thesis.[5] Any account of art that involves the consequences of technology yet nevertheless swims in the stream of traditional art as well must acknowledge Benjamin's vital optimism in this area. Adorno's position on the matter of art's mingling with technology stands in contradistinction to Benjamin's more enthusiastic stance. This debate is of great relevance for thinking about Zappa, as many of the artists and types of art which find themselves in the crossfire between the two philosophers bear significant similarities to Zappa. The work of Bertolt Brecht and the Dadaists are perhaps the two most obvious examples. Moreover, Adorno's concept of the Culture Industry is every bit as useful today as it was then. Of course, while multi-national CEOs and Republicans are not fascists in the literal sense, the unambiguously market-driven character of contemporary Western society demands that we not discard Adorno's insights.

Discussing Zappa in light of the Adorno/Benjamin debate is not new. Connections are frequently drawn between Zappa, the Dadaists and Brecht. While it is doubtlessly necessary to understand Zappa's connections with his European antecedents, it is just as important to understand how he differs, which will help point towards what makes Zappa's music so special. Implicit in the evocation of Adorno and Benjamin is the distinction between high art and low art—modernist elitism and proletarian mass-populism—or, as it sometimes called, the Great Divide.[6] Although many attempts have been made to close this distance, Huyssen rightly reminds us that, 'these attempts have never had lasting effects. If anything, they rather seem to have provided, for a host of different reasons, new strength and vitality to the old dichotomy. Thus the opposition between modernism and mass culture has remained amazingly resilient over the decades.'[7] Contrasting Zappa with a few such attempts, along with several brief analyses of specific works, will hopefully demonstrate that Zappa puts an entirely new spin on this matter, and poses a devastating affront to the high/low rift never before imagined.

A major contributing factor to Zappa's special position in the high/low dichotomy is the fact that he openly acknowledged his place in the 'low' cultural sphere. Quite simply, Zappa is the only major popular artist on either side of punk to involve a critique of their own means of distribution into their art. Zappa gave the following response to *Telos* in a discussion of music's role in society:

> Volpacchio: When you hear, let's say, a Rolling Stones song promoting a commercial product, what does that say about the inherent properties of modern composition or song writing if music can be appropriate for such ends?
>
> Zappa: Well, if you think of a Rolling Stones song as a modern composition, you could bemoan the fact that it winds up being used in a commercial. But I believe that at the time most of that material was manufactured, the goal was to make money not to create an anthem for a generation.[8]

Here we see quite clearly Zappa circumscribing his sociological notion of music within the concept of the Culture Industry. The 'Culture Industry', it is worth remembering, is Adorno's famous formulation of the state of affairs any art must deal with in the twentieth century. For Adorno, society's economic base had colonised its cultural superstructure. Therefore, the logic of the commodity and its fetish-character rules; artistic products are divested of their original use-value, which is supplanted by that of universal exchange. Adorno was also allergic to any piece of culture that resembled ('Identity') any component of the Culture Industry, since any such product could be absorbed, reconstituted and sold back to the very people whom it sought to exploit.[9] Someone who believes that 'popular' music—that is, music whose commodity status does not bother it—can be a source of authentic social representation, and therefore accepts popular culture at face value, is in danger of succumbing to the fetish-character inherent in music designed specifically for dissemination within the market. Zappa correctly points out that with the supposedly 'revolutionary' character of a Rolling Stones hit, the relations of production—that this song or any song like it are only money-generating objects whose phenomenological form happens to resemble music—have been obscured. Those whom the song is meant to represent are simply the objects of economic calculation. Popular culture, Zappa realizes, works in the opposite direction from the one suggested by the notion of 'popular'.

Surprisingly, Adorno's own statements on authentic music frequently coincide with Zappa's compositional approach. Though a tireless defender of high art esotericism (Schönberg, Beckett, Joyce), Adorno did at times acknowledge that potential for lower forms existed. He famously wrote to Benjamin of autonomous and mass-mediated art that, 'Both bear the stigmata of capitalism, both contain elements of change... Both are torn halves of an integral freedom, to which however they do not add up'.[10] Adorno criticized society from the perspective of what he thought to be its potential. This sometimes gets overlooked, his pessimism deemed circular rather than revolutionary. As such we can understand his comment to mean—contrary to his characterization as a cantankerous elitist—that even he recognised the value of lower forms. He would later write:

> To the detriment of both, it [*i.e.* the Culture Industry] forces together the spheres of high and low art, separated for thousands of years. The seriousness of high art is destroyed in speculation about efficacy; the seriousness of the lower perishes with the civilizational constraints imposed on the rebellious resistance inherent within it as long as social control was not yet total.[11]

Adorno registers the devastation the Culture Industry has wrought on artistic expression, but withholds categorical denunciation of the lower regions because he, too, realizes that even the masses are entitled to proper art; it is only a matter of how to get there. Zappa derived aspects of his style from the Stravinsky-Varèse lineage. This 'externality', or free play with 'blocks of sound', encompassed an extraordinary breadth of styles. In Zappa's *oeuvre* the myriad possibilities for intersection boggle the mind—rock meets Varèsian noise, Stockhausen's pointillism, Webern's dissonant sparseness, Dadaistic tape-spliced sound montage, lounge-jazz sleaze and Broadway kitsch.[12] Moreover, many of Zappa's compositions, particularly the mid-1980s works for Synclavier, feature wildly imaginative rhythmic ideas paired with freely atonal pitch content.[13] Their paradoxically 'disciplined-sounding' freedom answers Adorno's call from *Philosophy of Modern Music.* Sensing the potential of the rationality of twelve-tone technique to double over on itself, Adorno wrote:

> ...the survival of music can be anticipated only if it is able to emancipate itself from twelve-tone technique as well. This is not to be accomplished, however, by a retrogression to the irrationality which preceded twelve-tone technique... It is rather to be achieved through the amalgamation and absorption of twelve-tone technique by free composition—by the assumption of its rules through the spontaneity of the critical ear.[14]

There is no better description of this dimension of Zappa's creativity.

In seeking to re-integrate the every-day, and highlight it via advances in artistic production, Benjamin, Brecht and the Dadaists provide further windows of understanding. The re-integration of the lived experience into art constituted the avantgarde's assault on what Peter Bürger calls the 'institution' of art.[15] Up to that point, economic and technological modernization in society existed separately from bourgeois art. The theatre, the concert hall, the novel, painting and sculpture all sustained internal growth without any conspicuous contributions from the realm of technology. The avantgarde radically transgressed this boundary and began infiltrating art with technological means. Fragments of the every-day in photo montage function quite differently than the seamless, organic bourgeois work of art. They invited a totally new response, calling upon the observer to recognise the familiar fragment and integrate it into their own flow of consciousness and 'relate it to sensuous-material experience.'[16] Walter Benjamin's category of 'authenticity' embraced this:

> Benjamin commends the incorporation of fragments of lived experience. These shards comprise art's 'authenticity'. Or rather they break with traditional notions of art and undercut representation

> by spurning representation in favour of the presentation of actuality.[17]

Zappa's music, which he himself refered to as 'junk sculpture'[18], embodies this principle. His lyrics depict comedically yet realistically the grittiness of actual life untouched by bourgeois artistic representation. On the 1976 album *Zoot Allures,* Zappa positioned the microphone so close to his mouth that not a single cigarette-rotted throat vibration or spit crackle goes undocumented. Zappa believed real life to be stranger than any fiction and, though at times thoroughly fantastic, his subject matter is always firmly grounded in the brute realness of experience.

Joe's Garage is the apotheosis of the Benjaminian Zappa—Brechtian theatre meets stereo vinyl.[19] The triple-LP, double-CD work is a concept album in the form of a drama. It tells the story of Joe, an aspiring young guitarist from a quiet, suburban town in the United States. The narrator is the Big Brother-like Central Scrutinizer, which is nothing more than Frank Zappa's extemporized whispering into a megaphone. In the Central Scrutinizer's introduction, we learn that the U.S. Constitution is being modified to accommodate new changes in the law that haven't been passed yet, such as the pending illegality of music. The first song—the eponymous "Joe's Garage"—is ostensibly a simple rock number in which Joe and his friends form a low-budget garage band (everything in Zappa is low-budget and 'calculatedly second hand'[20], but only as the result of Zappa's own extremely high budget production value). Joe's band eventually gets gigs around town and attracts the attention of the area's young females. The rest of the work chronicles Joe's trials in the music indistry and confrontation with the law.[21] This is as close to Brecht as Zappa ever got. The combination of the concept rock album with drama is his own *Umfunktionierung.* Small local touches such as authentic *Schlager* styling (Joe attends a disco and chats up a very sexy robot *auf Deutsch*) and stock rock chord progressions (always made self-conscious through variation processes and a virtuoso composer's touch atypical of rock—another form of Zappa's externality) display a mastery of vernacular idioms very reminiscent of the practice of Brecht and his composer partner Kurt Weill. Zappa invokes *Verfremdungseffekt* in his own manner by means of spoken interruptions—the Wet T-shirt Contest emcee, The Central

Scrutinizer, L. Ron Hoover of the Church of Appliantology[22]—of a predominantly sung format; the spoken sections undercut the smooth flow of 'The Rock'n'roll Album'. Insofar as *Joe's Garage* is committed art, it is clearly an early manifestation of Zappa's political activities in the 1980s.[23] It deals with government suppression of artists, censorship, rightwing-style Big Brother tactics and the lunacy (as well as greed and extensive influence) of evangelists. Although poignent, *Joe's Garage* does not go for the political jugular as Brecht sometimes does, especially in his *Lehrstücke*, and is far too absurd to be a true representation of life in precisely the same sense.

Much has also been made of Zappa as Dadaist. His documentation of real life includes an emphasis on its unsavoury fringes; his inclusion on live recordings of pre-song statements ('this has go to be the one with all the right notes on it'[24])—these are all constant reminders of the music's material presence in real life, and real life's presence in it.[25] However, a closer look at *Joe's Garage* reveals the significant *differences* that exist between Zappa, Brecht and Dada, despite all that has been made of their similarities. Brecht sustained his critique of ideology from within high-art theatre itself. Unlike Zappa, Brecht confined himself to re-directing bourgeois enlightenment against itself, and on its own turf. Brecht may have interrupted the normative theatre experience, but it remained a theatre experience. *Joe's Garage* confuses the issue of rock music and drama altogether. As drama, it is sustains a narrative and builds characters' personalities but is anti-uniform and distorted.[26] As a rock'n'roll album, its dramatic content questions its status as rock'n'roll. In addition, danceable tunes are interrupted with asymmetric metres, displaced jazz improvisation abounds, and Zappa's ingenious use of musical diegesis puts to shame other rock'n'roll character-representational techniques that involve only lyrics or changes in the singing voice. It is avantgarde in its ironic appropriation of the every-day, and modernist in that its overall form and presentation is rigorously self-defined and particular to itself.

Joe's Garage's musical devices also serve to separate it decisively from Dada. If we acknowledge that Dada's mission was to challenge the very institution of art, it becomes readily apparent that *Joe's Garage*, and most of Zappa's entire catalogue for that matter, constitute nothing of the sort. One begins to notice details in Joe's Garage that testify to modern art's 'pointless' delight in its own purposelessness. The first song proper, 'Joe's Garage', is based on a very simple I-VI-IV-V chord progression in E major that does not change harmonically throughout the song's six minutes. Ordinarily, this suffocating constraint on harmonic motion would repel a listener expecting invention. But Zappa self-consciously reflects on the humble rock'n'roll status of Joe's anthem by altering the texture of every single verse; nearly imperceptible instrumental layers, vocal backings, percussion emphases and even a diegetic 'wrong' rendition representing Joe's actual garage band become sources of invention for the song. "Catholic Girls" is another ostensibly 'stupid' song but it, too, cannot resist beautiful artistic diversions, beginning as it does with two bars of 9/8 (divided 2+2+2+3) followed by two bars of 7/8. This pattern is 'idiotically' repeated the expected four times, thus muting its lack of belonging within the banal confines of a I-V-IV [*sic*] pop song. Easily the dirtiest song on the album is 'Keep it Greasey', and even this is imbued with invention. Its second verse and xenochronic guitar solo[27] (a convenient technique for defying conventional structures) are underpinned with a virtually uncountable 21/16 pattern (with variations) unleashed by drum wizard Vinnie Colaiuta.[28] The artistry in mixing the lurid content of the lyrics with this blistering rhythmic virtuosity is unmatched in rock'n'roll. Thus, in contrast with Dada but similar to Brecht, Zappa actually believes in art, despite any objections he may have to its role in a divided society.[29] This division, in fact, becomes the focal point of some of the most interesting aspects of Zappa's *oeuvre.*

That there exists a split between high and low art in today's society can be accepted without contestation. Having withstood various threats from Pop Art, Jeff Koons and jazz, this gulf remains as strong today as it ever has been. The relative peace in the First World following the World War II created a situation in which the validity of political institutions was no longer questioned the way it had been in the first half of the twentieth century. This comfort zone relegated challenges such as Dada and Futurism to history (the 'historical avantgarde', as Peter Bürger puts it in *Theory of the Avantgarde*). We now gaze contemplatively at Duchamp's *pissoir* as if it were a da Vinci. In this manner, the logic of the high/low mentality has sustained a healthy hegemony over the societal role of art. Unlike orchestral performances of Pink

Floyd, the monotony of minimalism or the uncritical repetition of commodity culture on its own terms of Pop Art, Zappa's music is not an idle challenge to the high/low gap; it is an assault on dualistic thought itself. Like Marx's prose, Zappa's music causes 'turbulence at the level of the concept'.[30] The way Zappa stages the high/low split is uncompromisingly creative and, while society itself has not yet bowed from the pressure, Zappa's music is a powerful affront to the line of thinking that says certain artistic materials belong over here and certain ones belong down there.

Zappa's interest in the music of Edgard Varèse has already been noted. The other antipode in Zappa's compositional dialectic is American Black music—blues and R&B. This unusual mode of cross-breeding is emblematic of Zappa's belief on the division of art:

> Volpacchio: Yet in your music, despite the overlapping influences, you do consciously maintain a separation of styles and musical forms. Do you see a distinction between high and low art?
>
> Zappa: Or any art at all?[31]

Zappa's music does indeed recognise a division between high and low—all seams intact—yet their shocking confrontation in his *oeuvre* is an ironic reflection of a social situation he does not endorse. If you believe Ben Watson, who reads straight through Adorno's 'torn halves', Zappa's elementary building blocks—Varèse and Black music—actually belong together. It is only the social division that upholds any 'differences'. Watson writes:

> ...Varèse's futurism is not in a different world from Black music: both are responses to the city, both celebrate the vital 'primitivism' of the metropolis ... The assumed divide between 'high' and 'low' culture of course makes any such comparison preposterous—especially given classical music's genteel imagine (an image Varèse cordially hated) and the assumed irrelevance of funk ('feet music') to philosophy ('head music').[32]

Zappa's ironic representation of the presumed social roles of differenr musics forms a strong pillar of his style—the nuts and bolts of which have gone relatively unnoticed, as Zappology has so far tended to attract philosophers and literary critics rather than musicologists. Certainly the above examples from *Joe's Garage* could serve as illustrations of Zappa's synchronous appropriation of conflicting musical materials, but there are many others that perhaps go further. The following brief analyses should further elucidate this potent *Mischung*.

Zappa always presents his more intricate material as being accessible to his audience. This is crucial for his project of demystifying the flatulence, not of high art itself, but of the social apparatus that upholds its status. On a macro-level, this is easily achieved by relying on rock and jazz instrumentation. Though some of the material may be abstruse and confusing, the mass listener will not be alienated by 'classical' or 'avantgarde' instrumentation. But this is observable on a micro-level as well. During 1988 live performances of "Catholic Girls", Zappa would highlight the asymmetry of the opening metrical patterns such that it would be less intimidating.[33] After the introduction, the song quickly sinks into the blandness of the verse. The 'chorus' incorporates jazz sleaze, but the middle of the performance features an Albert Wing tenor sax solo over the asymmetrical pattern from the opening. However, Zappa satirizes the complexity of this musical task (soloing over 9/8-9/8-7/8-7/8) by shouting 'everybody!' just before the solo. This invitation to dance or sing along is totally uncalled for but is effective at dissolving the difficulty of the music.[34] A performance of "Any Kind of Pain" demonstrates another mode of this technique.[35] The song is in the style of pop-Broadway cheese and its lyrics deal with bogus media-manufactured feminine glam. The mindlessness of television beauty is spared no ridicule. The chorus remains locked in an oppressive 4/4 metre but breaks out at a crucial moment. When the lyrics say 'Yes she hasn't got a brain/let me just explain/any kind of pain...', the music suddenly but silently shifts into 7/8 with stresses falling on 'Any KIND of PAIN/LET me JUST exPLAIN'. Zappa's artistic twist, again involving asymmetrical beat patterns, is satirized the moment it appears. Percussionist Ed Mann hammers home the point in the final chorus with clown-like horn squawks on the seventh beat of the 7/8 bars, a momentous piss-take on asymmetric metrical complexity.

This aesthetic principle can also be found on the level of improvisation. Zappa's musicians were, of course, granted the freedom to improvise their own solos and fills, but they were always made to fit Zappa's compositional scheme. The little unscripted, improvised fills were referred to by Zappa as the 'eyebrows' of a piece.[37] "Ship Arriving Too Late To Save a Drowning Witch" is regarded one of Zappa's most difficult compositions to perform.[38] The opening section depicts monster movie trash while discussing a witch who has mutated and become '50-feet-tall' after sitting at the bottom of American's highly-polluted waterways. After an unexpected *Rite of Spring* quotation to the words, 'ritual sacrifice', the music explodes into a flurry of notes. Non-stop semi-quavers and constantly shifting metre produce an extraordinarily intricate texture. Once this passage ends, a short vamp sets up Zappa's guitar solo. However, in order to eliminate the slightest whiff of high-art transcendence, keyboardist Alan Zavod seizes the moment and inserts an atonally-inspired chord, which he twists with the pitch-bender to create the musical equivalent of dizziness—perhaps seasickness resulting from the witch's struggle in the ocean. Zavod's astute grasp of Zappa's aesthetic allows once again for the music—intelligently—to deny its own intelligence.

This, if anything, is the kind of technologically-based shock Benjamin would have admired. But it is not enough to discuss modern music's use of technology as if it were still the year 1925. The point of Benjamin's thesis was the newness required to jolt people into questioning things. 'The conventional is uncritically enjoyed,' he complained, 'and the truly new is criticized with aversion'.[39] By forging a new aesthetic based on ironic virtuosity, Zappa rattles the listener's consciousness into questioning the social basis which supplies the irony for Zappa's art. Zappa disturbs our sense of high and low by rearranging the very relations of production. Are these serious musicians playing stupid material or vice versa? How is a *rock* band playing that? How is a rock band playing *that*? How are his compositions so intellectual, intricate and detailed, and yet so corporeal, hilarious and ironic? The mind cannot make sense of these questions given the intensity of Zappa's compositional montage—but that is precisely the point.

It seems appropriate to conclude with a small discussion of Adorno. Adorno's Marxist musicology is too explosive to be confined merely to the domain he himself operated in. It would therefore be desirable to chip away at Adorno's edifice to allow into his theory music that doesn't necessarily refer to itself as 'modernist' or 'avantgarde'. Peter Bürger has suggested that Adorno's one-sided conception of musical composition rests on the notion that an age contains only one essential path on which musical material most travel. Obviously, at the time Adorno was formulating his theory this was the language of the Second Viennese School. However, as we have seen, implicit in Adorno's own formulation is the undoing of the dichotomous thinking that prevents absolute musical freedom. As a counter to Adorno's surprising tunnel vision on this matter[40], Bürger has proposed an extension of modernism that permits a sustained critique—an eclectic continuation of the modernist project of resistance, aesthetic innovation and integrity without devolving into the banal, affirmative nature of the 'anything goes' postmodernism. He writes:

> Instead of propagating a break with modernism under the banner of the postmodern, I count on its dialectical continuity. That means that aesthetic modernism must also recognize as its own much that it has until now rejected. That is, no more tabooing of tonality, objectivity, and traditional literary forms; but at the same time distrust of this material and of the appearance of substantiality which emanates from it. The recourse to past stocks of material must be recognized as a modern procedure, but also as an extremely precarious one.[41]

Bürger uses this concept to rescue Brecht and Stravinsky, but in fact Zappa is better suited to the task than Stravinsky. The latter's neo-classicism very often 're-did' truthful music. Recomposing—and claiming as your own—the music of Pergolesi and the Second Viennese School is not revolutionary, it is arrogant. Frank Zappa, an artist in America, a nation where the bourgeois musical tradition has not left the same historical residue, chose a different path. Instead of 'distrusting' the art of the past and then reproducing it in the very same medium, Zappa refuted the conventional social role of classical music. He not only played creatively with old forms, but viciously reconstituted them in a hitherto unimaginable blend of both musical wit and stupidity. Zappa is not afraid of polluting his genius with the sordid world of commodities and he realized that this was the proper place to start. Andreas Huyssen suggests that the 'utopian hopes' of the avantgarde live on 'desperately' in mass culture.[42] Given the depoliticization of the historical avantgarde and the academic sterility of high modernism in the current stage of advanced capitalism, perhaps Zappa's ironic reflection of society is the best hope there is to challenge the reified, class-based thought that underpins our culture.

1. This essay was first published in *Naked Punch* #3, December 2004. We would like to thank the editors for permission to reprint. For further information about this terrific magazine, visit <www.nakedpunch.com>.
2. Andres Huyssen, *After The Great Divide: Modernism, Mass Culture and Postmodernism*, Bloomington: Indiana University Press, 1986, p. ix.
3. Frank Zappa cited in Ben Watson, *Frank Zappa: The Negative Dialectics of Poodle Play*, London: Quartet Books, 1993, p. 545.
4. Typical would be Marco Maurizi, 'Theses on ('Bis er spritzt') Feuerbach, or, Why Zappa Fans and Rock Academics are Two Halves of an Integral Whole which, under current Social Conditions of Exploitation and Injustice Cannot Add Up ...', Leipzig, 29 January 2002, posted on <www.militantesthetix.co.uk/zappo/MARCO.html>. It would appear that Adorno's insistence on the inseparability of form and content in philosophy has found a new home in Zappology. *Editors' note*: 'Yes indeed, here we are! At Saint Alfonzo's Pancake Breakfast...'.
5. Walter Benjamin, 'The Work of Art in the Age of Mechanical Reproduction', 1936; translated Harry Zohn, *Illuminations*, London: Fontana, 1992.
6 Andres Huyssen, *Op. Cit.*.
7. *Ibid*, p. *vii*.
8. Florindo Volpacchio, 'The Mother of All Interviews: Zappa on Music and Society', *Telos* No. 87, Spring 1991, p. 127.
9. This goes to the heart of Adorno's aesthetics. Non-identity (or 'high-modernist abstract ultra-weirdness'), very much in the manner of Adorno's own prose, was the only way of asserting an artist's fortitude in the face of the Culture Industry—or not selling out, you could say. Only by rationally working out its own 'material', Adorno contends, can the work of art show up the external world for the lie it is: the freedom of the artistic subject negatively reflects the unfree world we inhabit.
10. Theodor Adorno, 18 March 1936, letter to Walter Benjamin; *Aesthetics and Politics*, edited Ronald Taylor, London: Verso, 1977, p. 123.
11. Adorno, 'Culture Industry Reconsidered', 1963; *The Culture Industry*, edited J.M. Bernstein, London: Routledge, 1991, p. 85.
12. A far cry from the postmodernist 'anything goes' mentality, what is most striking is Zappa's (mostly) authentic re-creation of these styles. Although there is no better word than 'external' to describe the overall aesthetic, his 'internal' knowledge of how these styles work is what makes his music so compelling.
13. See especially: Frank Zappa, *Jazz From Hell*, 1987; *Meets the Mothers of Prevention*, 1985.
14. Theodor Adorno, *Philosophy of Modern Music*, 1948; translated Anne G. Mitchell and Wesley V. Blomster, New York: Continuum, 1973, p. 115.
15. Peter Bürger, *Theory of the Avantgarde*, translated Michael Shaw, Minneapolis: University of Minnesota Press, 1984.
16. Jochen Schulte-Sasse in Bürger, *Op. Cit.*, p. xxxix.
17. Esther Leslie, *Walter Benjamin: Overpowering Conformism*, London: Pluto Press, 2000, p. 117.
18. Ben Watson, *Op. Cit.*, p. 93.

19. Frank Zappa, *Joe's Garage Acts I, II & III*, 1979.
20. Max Paddison, 'Zappa, Frank', *Grove Music Online*, edited L. Macy (accessed 15 September 2004), <*www.grovemusic.com*>.
21. It is rather like *Clockwork Orange*, as Joe emerges from prison 'cured' but eerily lobotomized.
22. This chap, who encourages Joe to attend the machine-fetishist disco, is a parody of Scientologist L. Ron Hubbard, who has somehow managed to convert countless celebrities and jazz musicians—including the great Chick Corea—to his superstitious, white collar cult. Religious leaders, and particularly evangelists, were always a target for Zappa, an opponent of any structure that impeded the ability of the ordinary person to think unobstructed and rationally for themselves.
23. 'Committed art' refers to Benjamin's argument that, at the time he was writing, emancipatory art required explicit political content—hence, his fondness for Brecht. Benjamin stressed that correct politics and proper literary technique were necessary conditions for one another. Of course, Adorno believed just the opposite—that artistic parable does no justice to the horrors of the real world it depicts, an imbalance which, in turn, impinges on a work's status as art.
24. Frank Zappa, 'Be-Bop Tango (Of the Old Jazzman's Church)', *Roxy & Elsewhere*, 1974.
25. The most extensive effort in this direction is Ben Watson, 'Frank Zappa as Dadaist: Recording Technology and the Power to Repeat', *Contemporary Music Review*, 1996, Vol.15, Part 1.
26. Much to everyone's relief, there is virtually no trace of Wagnerian leitmotiv.
27. This term refers to Zappa's habit of using live guitar solos and superimposing them onto studio backtracks. Interestingly, all solos on Joe's Garage are of this type with the exception of one that occurs only in Joe's mind, found in the song 'Watermelon in Easter Hay'. Thus all 'real' guitar solos are imaginary, and the one 'imaginary' guitar solo is real.
28. This unbelievably intricate pattern was somehow deciphered through a collaborative effort between the author and the brilliant drummer/Zappa-fetishist from the Royal Academy of Music, Alexis Nunez.
29. Zappa's music may actually align better with Surrealism as described by Jürgen Habermas, 'Modernity: An Unfinished Project', *The Post-Modern Reader*, edited Charles Jencks, London: Academy Editions, 1992, p. 165.
30. Ben Watson, 'Why Marx Matters for Artists', paper delivered at the Kings College Society for the Study of Marxism, 17 March 2004, p. 6; printed in *Naked Punch* #2, May 2004.
31. Florindo Volpacchio, *Telos, Ed. Cit.*, p. 127.
32. Ben Watson, *Contemporary Music Review, Ed. Cit.*, p. 131.
33. Frank Zappa, "Catholic Girls", *You Can't Do That on Stage Anymore* Vol.6, 1992.
34. There are numerous such invitations in Zappa's live output. On the same volume, but in a different performance, this one from 1978, Zappa counts in the song's diabolical 13/8 metre before south Indian violin virtuoso L. Shankar launches into a brain-bending Lydian-based solo. As in the Karnatic practice of beat counting, the way he sings '12 123 [quick] 1 2 3 4 [long]' makes it easy to grasp the metre as a kind of melodic phrase.
35. Frank Zappa, "Any Kind of Pain", *Broadway the Hard Way*, 1988.
37. Frank Zappa with Peter Occhiogrosso, *The Real Frank Zappa Book*, London: Picador, 1989, p. 164.
38. Originally on *Ship Arriving Too Late To Save a Drowning Witch*, 1982, but here a combined 1982/1984 performance from *You Can't Do That on Stage Anymore* Vol.3, 1989.
39. Walter Benjamin, *Op. Cit.*, p. 234.
40. *Editor's Note*: As a spritzer to this discussion, the editors suggest we all go dig up Adorno's 'Vers une musique informelle', 1961 (translated Rodney Livingstone, *Quasi Una Fantasia: Essays on Modern Music*, London: Verso, 1992) where the old 'dogmatic' modernist sounds

like he's calling for Absolutely Free Improvisation in the Esemplastic Sense (*i.e.* with everyday life—*a.k.a.* Gamma—onboard). However, we recognise that there is a problem with the institutionalised avantgarde which uses Adorno as its patron saint, especially in Germany.

41. Peter Bürger, 'The Decline of the Modern Age', translated David J. Parent, *Telos* No. 62, Winter 1984-5, p. 129.
42. Andres Huyssen, *Op. Cit.*, p. 15.

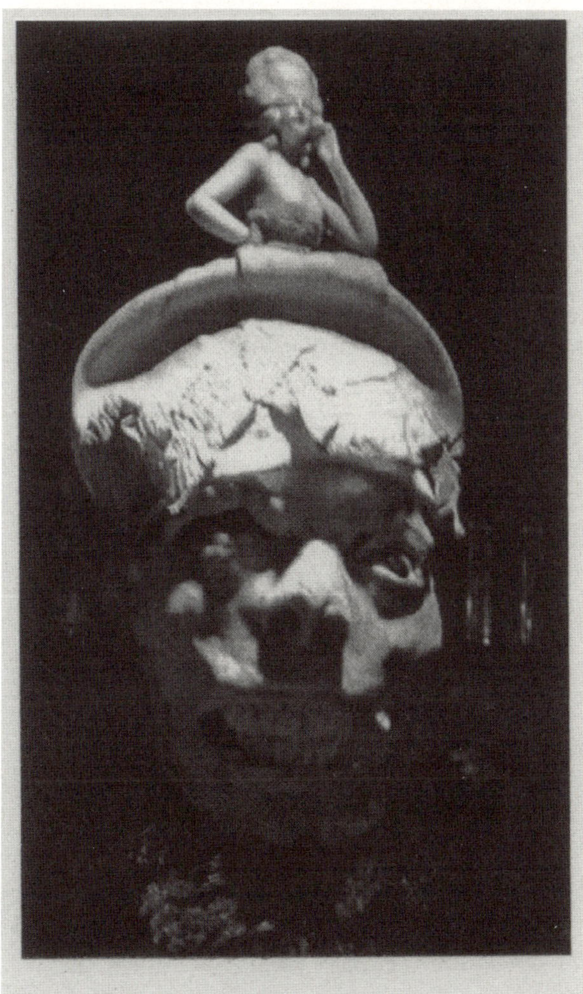

Moustache installation, or, what happens when you remodel a garden-centre Venus de Milo while listening to Frank Zappa.
by Eleanor Crook

Notes On Contributors

Sean Bonney's recent books of poetry are *Notes on Heresy* (Writers Forum, 2002) and *poisons, their antidotes* (West House, 2003). Currently, he's working on a synthesis of Marxist theory, hardcore porn, documentary observation and random insult. He lives in south London.

Daniel DiPaolo was born in Albany, New York and earned a BA in music from the University of Rochester. He escaped New York amd got to London, where he gained a MMus in historical musicology at King's College in 2004. He is currently enrolled in the MA/PhD programme in music theory at the Eastman School of Music, back in Rochester, New York. In addition to Frank Zappa and Zappology, Dan is interested in counterpoint, tonality, Brad Mehldau, Keith Jarrett, Romanticism and free improvisation. He likes it when music analysis and social criticism click. When away from school, Dan plays "The Black Page #2" on his electric keyboard and waits for Napoleon Murphy Brock and Ike Willis to call.

T.H.F. Drenching is an improvisor, composer, call-centre worker and SWP member living in Levenshulme, south-central Manchester. With Sonic Pleasure he runs Fenland Hi-Brow Recordings <*www.fenlandhibrow.co.uk*>, a mail-order label dealing in free improvisation, *musique concrète* and disastrous related ephemera. He also publishes poetry under the preposterous name Stuart Calton, two books of which have been published by Barque Press. He is one fifth of Derek Bailey's Limescale (see Incus CD56) and one half of the Dictaphone and bricks duo Pleasure-Drenching Improvers. Free Palestine.

Gamma wouldn't be here if not for an accident. His childhood was spent in the north Yorkshire countryside before dropping into The Smoke in 1967, where he gradually mutated into a science fiction geek. Now resides in Kentish Town with Jake the Poodle Dog where he is redesigning the walls at the Martian embassy and instructing alien students in Martian etiquette. First memory of Zappa was him being on *Juke Box Jury* as the mystery guest, "It Can't Happen Here".

Francesco Gentile was born in Rome in 1963. He worked for IT companies for 15 years 'and never find any Zappaphile around!'. So until the early 90s he just shared his momomaniacal FZ freakness with a few friends in Rome. Eventually, thanks to the Internet and to Debra Kadabra, the Italian FZ Appreciation Consortium <*www.debrakadabra.com*>, he met many Zappa fans. He's been involved with DK since 1994, editing itz sumptuous fzine and planning various obnoxious events. In 1999, he helped with the first Italian FZ conference *Frank Zappa Domani*, organised by Gianfranco Salvatore. He wrote an annotated phonography and videography for a book with the same title published in 2000. In 2000 and 2003 he participated in two FZ radio specials broadcast by RAI Radio 3. Recently he wrote two articles in English, both available on the Internet: 'Cruising with *YCDTOSA*' <*web.tiscali.it/effeg/cwy/cwy.htm*> and 'What I Do is Composition', a tentative biography of FZ <*www.obst-music.com*>.

Jürgen Gispert was born in Worms on the Rhine in 1959. He's a social anthropologist specialising in Armenian culture (special field: memorial culture of Armenia). Presently living in Leipzig, formerly communist East Germany now under West German protection. It seems that he has a taste for the bizarre. He first encountered FZ's music at the age of eight. He lost contact for nine years, but then tasted the *madeleine* again, *with a bullet.* Since then he's sampled and studied FZ's stuff without getting into symbiosis. He likes mimesis. He's of the opinion that THE BOOK on FZ hasn't been written yet and that THIS BOOK you've got in your hand now is THE BEGINNING OF REAL ZAPPOLOGICAL HARDCORE SCIENTIFIC HUMOROUS SHAMELESS VOLUPTUOUS WORK!!!! It will transcend globalisation (another word for imperialism) and replace it with intercultural understanding! The secret word for tonight is: 'Forget to vote, begin to think'.

Richard Hemmings is known to some as Evil Dick and lives in Leicester. Contrary to his unofficial biography, which states he took up composition after becoming disillusioned working as an human ashtray in a lesbian S&M parlour, Richard Hemmings developed an interest in writing music at the tender age of two, when he discovered innovative sounds could be made by chipping the ivory piano keys on his parents' up-right piano with the edge of a wooden rule. Still unable to form a proper sentence, let alone write one down, music notation proved too much for the Evil infant, and his desire to compose was put on hold. By the age of three he had developed a unique way of hitting the piano with his fists; he liked the way it sounded, but more importantly, he liked the way it annoyed his older sister. Music, although still a mystery, was working its familiar magic on the toddler. Two months later... *<www.polemicmusic.com>*.

Dominique Jeunot was born on 25 June 1959 in Paris, could sing "Only You" at the age of 2 and "Masters of War" around 6. Got acquainted with FZ music through *Hot Rats* in '72, then *Overnite Sensation*. First saw Frank in Paris in September '74. Co-founder in '95 of the non-profit FZ French society known as Les Fils de l'Invention (The Sons of Invention). Co-wrote with Guy Darol *Zappa from Z to A* (Le Castor Astral, 2000). Dominique died unexpectedly in his sleep in 2004.

Esther Leslie was born in 1964 in the suburbs of north London, where she enjoyed a comprehensive education. A fanatical obsession with the best and worst of European culture—Karl Marx and the Nazis respectively—led her to learn German and write a book about Walter Benjamin, published by Pluto Press in 2000. Abortive efforts to get to California 'for research purposes' spurred the next work on Walt Disney and the European avantgarde. During the years of researching *Hollywood Flatlands* (Verso, 2002) she was drip- and force-fed Bruce Bickford and *The Simpsons* by the Zappa obsessive who shares her bed and bathwater, and gradually she was inculcated into the Zappological tribe. Heretical within the Esemplasm, she has been known to ejaculate: 'I prefer live Muffinz to Zappa on disc'. Together with Ben Watson she runs the website <*www.militantesthetix.co.uk*>.

Born in Rome on 28 June 1974, **Marco Maurizi** is a philosopher and electric guitarist infected with Adornoite lycanthropy. In 2001, he initiated a longterm project on the history of dialectics at Leipzig University. He's currently working on Nicholas of Cusa at the Tor Vergata University in Rome. His publications include *Adorno e il tempo del non identico* (Rome: Jaca Books, 2004). He played in several rock bands in the 90s, and in 2001 with drummer Cristiano Luciani founded the improvisation duo LENDORMIN (Out To Lunch divined a contraction of LENin-aDORno-benjaMIN, but it's actually the name of a brand of sleeping tablets). In 2003, Lendormin was selected by Wallace Records for their compilation *PO Box 52.4* (Wallace44), and collaborated with DBPIT (Der Bekannte Post-Industrielle Trumpeter) for the concept album *The Outstanding Story of Mr Mallory* (Sweet Farewell, 2004). When Marco's fingers get stuck, he writes Marxist articles in order to make our environment less *ostile* to dreamers. When his mind is blowing, he picks up his guitar and makes himself ostile to his environment. He's among the founders of the art/performance group Amnesia Vivace. In April 2004, he helped stage Amnesia Vivace's *Scrivere l'Es* conference in Rome. His domestic life is devoted to Agnese and several extraordinary dogs.

Simon Prentis has spent the last 50 years unsuccessfully attempting to come to terms with this thing we call life, a process further retarded by the habit of living for extended periods in other countries and cultures—most conspicuously in Japan, where he studied Aikido and Zen for several years. Currently resident in London, he somehow makes a living as a translator, interpreter and producer of rancid TV programmes. Since 1982 has assisted the ZFT in sundry capacities as translator, archivist, intermittent exegetist and sometime 'semantic scrutinizer'.

Keston Sutherland was born in 1976 and currently produces essays and poems. Edits the fugitive journal *Quid* and co-edits Barque Press

<*www.barquepress.com*>. Has recently completed a long study of the poet J.H. Prynne. Lectures in twentieth century literature and critical theory at the University of Sussex.

Paul Sutton was born in 1968 and, in 1984, having already miraculously acquired a passion for Shakespeare at school, he heard "Peaches en Regalia" on TV (*The Friday Rock Show*). Accordingly, two years later he resigned his paper round, and devoted his retirement to Zappology and the study of the bourgeois canon, largely under the not always gracious patronage of the DSS. In 1998, Sutton moved to London where he bagged a brace of little bo-peep diplomas and began attending the Klinker. He is currently practising Zappology full time, though his enemies at the Job Centre have other ideas.

Ben Watson was born in 1956 south-west London, where he suffered a public school education. He became obsessed with Frank Zappa in 1975 when he discovered that the initial letters of *One Size Fits All* were an anagram of 'sofa'. His initial forays into Zappology were published in small-press literary mags inspired by the Marxist counter culture of the late 60s and early 70s, a scene forced underground in the Thatcherite 80s. In 1994, *Frank Zappa: the Negative Dialectics of Poodle Play* (Quartet) brought these texts overground. *Derek Bailey & the Story of Free Improvisation* (Verso, 2004) attempted to bring another phalanx of cultural subverts to light. In 2003 he was presented with the Order of the Green Muffin at Zappanale #14. Watson earns a crust indexing and proof-reading for various publishers. He's convinced that the music of T.H.F. Drenching, Paul Minotto, Ian Stonehouse and Evil Dick would change the world, if only the bastards in charge would let people hear it.

Appendix

Proto-Zappology

In 1945 the poet and surrealist Aimé Césaire warned: 'modern science may be nothing but the ponderous verification of a few wild images thrown up by poets'. This appendix includes a few wild images thrown up by Ben Watson in the late 70s, which may—or may not—prove useful for the burgeoning (if not ponderous) science of Esemplastic Zappology. The first five pages—hubristically and thrasonically entitled 'The Ultimate Piece on FZ'—were a contribution to a new rock magazine proposed, founded and edited by Jonathan Romney in 1976. They were rejected as 'too idiosyncratic'. 'Puck', 'Hand Press with typical "V" raise Tool' and 'Wax' were one-off constellations of images and words contrived in the years 1978-9, photocopies of which were handed to Nick Kimberley at his poetry bookshop Duck Soup. Help was not forthcoming for these psychotic episodes.

We conclude the appendix with 'MERZ NOTES', five sides of manuscript paper written by Gamma for his performance at MERZ NITE under the dome in the Victoria & Albert Museum on Friday 25 January 2002. It omits the improvised exchange (Heckler: 'Dada!' Gamma: 'Mama!' Heckler: 'Dada!' Gamma: 'Mama... Mother of Invention!') which was in some ways the culmination of the piece as performed, but the original score is nevertheless of great anthropological, not to say zappological, interest... it has been embellished with some fragrant fragmenta deriving from the Esemplasm.

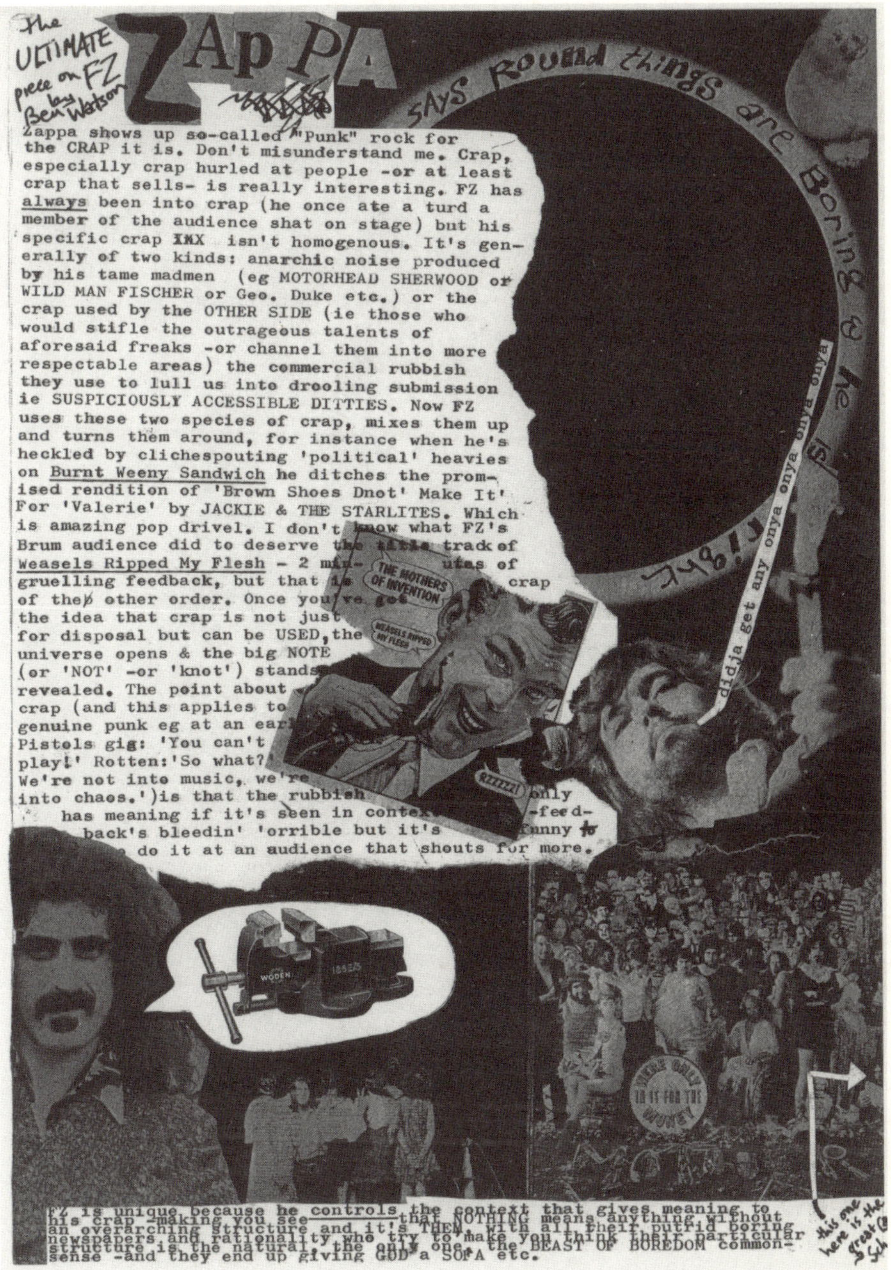

Zappa shows up so-called "Punk" rock for the CRAP it is. Don't misunderstand me. Crap, especially crap hurled at people -or at least crap that sells- is really interesting. FZ has always been into crap (he once ate a turd a member of the audience shat on stage) but his specific crap XMX isn't homogenous. It's generally of two kinds: anarchic noise produced by his tame madmen (eg MOTORHEAD SHERWOOD or WILD MAN FISCHER or Geo. Duke etc.) or the crap used by the OTHER SIDE (ie those who would stifle the outrageous talents of aforesaid freaks -or channel them into more respectable areas) the commercial rubbish they use to lull us into drooling submission ie SUSPICIOUSLY ACCESSIBLE DITTIES. Now FZ uses these two species of crap, mixes them up and turns them around, for instance when he's heckled by clichespouting 'political' heavies on Burnt Weeny Sandwich he ditches the promised rendition of 'Brown Shoes Dnot' Make It' For 'Valerie' by JACKIE & THE STARLITES. Which is amazing pop drivel. I don't know what [FZ's] Brum audience did to deserve the title track of Weasels Ripped My Flesh - 2 min- utes of gruelling feedback, but that is crap of the other order. Once you've got the idea that crap is not just for disposal but can be USED, the universe opens & the big NOTE (or 'NOT' -or 'knot') stands revealed. The point about crap (and this applies to genuine punk eg at an ear Pistols gig: 'You can't play!' Rotten: 'So what? We're not into music, we're into chaos.') is that the rubbish only has meaning if it's seen in contex[t] -feedback's bleedin' 'orrible but it's [f]unny to do it at an audience that shouts for more.

FZ is unique because he controls the context that gives meaning to his crap -making you see that NOTHING means anything without an overarching structure and it's THEM, with all their putrid boring newspapers and rationality who try to make you think their particular structure is the natural, the only one, the BEAST OF BOREDOM commonsense -and they end up giving GOD a SOFA etc.

In the City of Cambridge
FREAK-OUT!
The Mothers of Invention
FREAK OUT!
states that you on 12th March, 1976
in the said City
not carry:
(a) one lamp showing to the fr
(b) one lamp showing to the rear
visible from a reasonable dista
Contrary to Section 74 and Secti
You are summoned to appear
at the hour of 10.30 a.m. befo
House, Guildhal
Road Traffic Act, 1972.
26th April, 1976
urt sitting at the Court
Justice of the Peace
FRANK Z
THIS - HAZ NO MESSAGE
"It's more conservative. Every beat the playlist gets shorter. Pretty soon there will be only two records to play, both punk."
the word concealed here is 'song'
HENCE conceptual continuity to emphasize PLACEMENT rather than mere existence. IT'S WHERE the details come that matters (like sex it's WHERE you come that matters, not THAT you come) not so much the details 'seen in themselves' because that's only a way of saying that you accept society's methods of placement instead of being able to control them. This is where punk tends to collapse -its significance is read onto it by the media as conventional rock 'n roll excess -Rotten the lovable cockney urchin (a new Tommy Steele) etc I'm saying that unlike FZ Punks aren't in control of their crap -it's a kind of diarrhoea (& hence the nappy pins...)
flower power sucks
HOT RATS
MOTHERS
ZAPPED
ROCK star Frank Zappa went to court yesterday to hear a track from one of his records.
Zappa yesterday

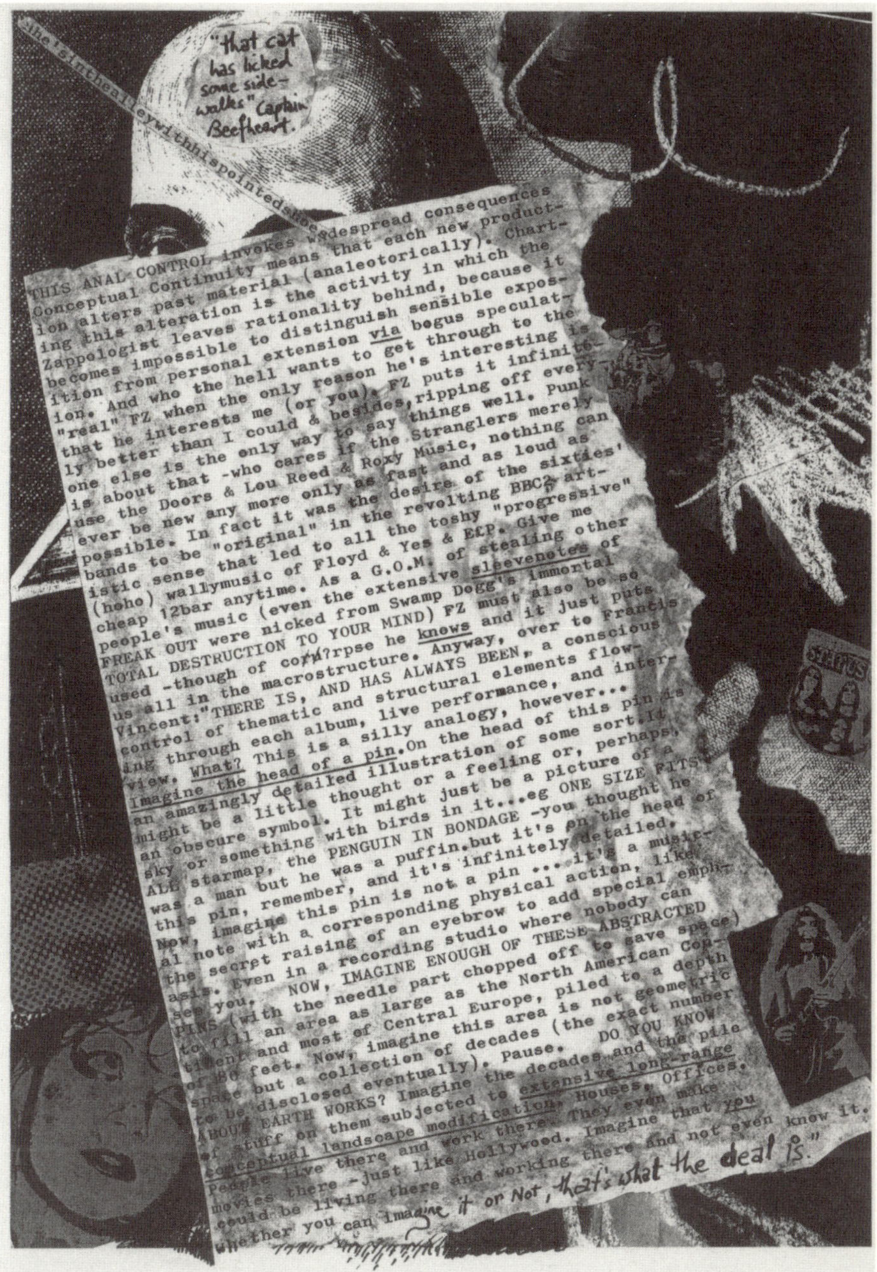

THIS ANAL CONTROL invokes widespread consequences
Conceptual Continuity means that each new production alters past material (analeotorically). Chart-
ing this alteration is the activity in which the
Zappologist leaves rationality behind, because it
becomes impossible to distinguish sensible exposition from personal extension <u>via</u> bogus speculation. And who the hell wants to get through to the
"real" FZ when the only reason he's interesting is
that he interests me (or you). FZ puts it infinitely better than I could & besides,ripping off everyone else is the only way to say things well. Punk
is about that -who cares if the Stranglers merely
use the Doors & Lou Reed & Roxy Music, nothing can
ever be new any more only as fast and as loud as
possible. In fact it was the desire of the sixties'
bands to be "original" in the revolting BBC2 artistic sense that led to all the toshy "progressive"
(hoho) wallymusic of Floyd & Yes & E&P. Give me
cheap 12bar anytime. As a G.O.M. of stealing other
people's music (even the extensive <u>sleevenotes</u> of
FREAK OUT were nicked from Swamp Dogg's immortal
TOTAL DESTRUCTION TO YOUR MIND) FZ must also be so
used -though of co?rpse he <u>knows</u> and it just puts
us all in the macrostructure. Anyway, over to Francis
Vincent:"THERE IS, AND HAS ALWAYS BEEN, a conscious
control of thematic and structural elements flow-
ing through each album, live performance, and interview. <u>What?</u> This is a silly analogy, however...
<u>Imagine the head of a pin</u>.On the head of this pin is
an amazingly detailed illustration of some sort.It
might be a little thought or a feeling or, perhaps,
an obscure symbol. It might just be a picture of a
sky or something with birds in it...eg ONE SIZE FITS
ALL starmap, the PENGUIN IN BONDAGE -you thought he
was a man but he was a puffin.but it's on the head of
this pin, remember, and it's infinitely detailed.
Now, imagine this pin is not a pin ... it's a musical note with a corresponding physical action, like
the secret raising of an eyebrow to add special emphasis. Even in a recording studio where nobody can
see you. NOW, IMAGINE ENOUGH OF THESE ABSTRACTED
PINS (with the needle part chopped off to save space)
to fill an area as large as the North American Con-
tinent and most of Central Europe, piled to a depth
of 80 feet. Now, imagine this area is not geometric
space but a collection of decades (the exact number
to be disclosed eventually). Pause.   DO YOU KNOW
ABOUT EARTH WORKS? Imagine the decades and the pile
of stuff on them subjected to <u>extensive long-range</u>
<u>conceptual landscape modification</u>. Houses, Offices.
People live there and work there. They even make
movies there -just like Hollywood. Imagine that <u>you</u>
could be living there and working there and not even know it.
whether you can imagine it or Not, that's what the deal is."

This page is in columns as I'm told a WHOLE page of print is too diffikult two reed. I continue to quote FZ as I'm half asleep

FZ: "What I'm trying to describe is the type of attention given to each lyric, melody, arrangement, improvisation, the sequence of these elements in an album, the cover art which is an extension of what is recorded, released, and/or performed during a concert, the continuity or contrasts of material album to album, etc., etc., etc.,....all of these detail aspects are part of the Big Structure. The project/object (maybe you like event/organism better (sure do ed.))incorporates any available visual medium, consciousness of all participants (including audience), all perceptual deficiencies, God (as energy),The Big Note (as universal building material), and other things. WE MAKE A SPECIAL ART IN AN ENVIRONMENT HOSTILE TO DREAMERS."

If you think I made all this up go and look up IT no.115, 1971.

THE CONSEQUENCES of this unique macrostructural control are too extensive to document in anything approaching responsible totality here, but I shall chart a few peculiar "coincidences".

When asked, in 1969, which way he thought his music would go, FZ replied "It will probably get more obscure". Though most people would agree with this prediction up to THE GRAND WAZOO (1972) few would be willing to argue for any degree of complexity in the albums since the appropiately titled OVERNITE SENSATION (1973). That record and the coup in Chile were the two atrocities of 1973. Taken without regard to Conceptual Continuity OS is either a driving and hilarious tour-de-force or a particularly unpleasant and Chauvinistic piece of sell-out vulgarity. But of course it is neither of these. Look at its placement: straight after FZ's most "arty" efforts, HOT RATS/WAKA-JAWAKA & THE GRAND WAZOO. The "respectable" music critics loved these last two. Joachim Berendt in The Jazz Book: "It has become apparent that Zappa's many records with small groups were only anticipations of his big-band productions of the seventies...Most critics feel that with the album THE GRAND WAZOO Zappa's music reached its culmination so far." (p.363) As FZ, in his conceptual persona of super-fashionable-teenage-punk-band-leader, says: "the overall impact of that group would be that it was between pseudo-Jazzette and cranial" (NME Apr17 '76). I can just see the enthusiastic Berendt rushing out to buy APOSTROPHE because it has his "discovery" Jean-Luc Ponty on it, only to find the new jazz star's contribution reduced to delineating the "fidget" of the "mystery man" —one bar of Cosmik Debris. OS is in fact one of FZ's most complex and difficult records: it concerns REVERSAL. To explain what I mean I shall have to resort to ripping off other people's words. The cover shows a mirror, right? The point is that WE are inside the mirror, not what is portrayed (the beercan on our side has reversed lettering)ie. FZ

POJAMA
PEOPLE
make you sleepy
with the things they might say
If she reverses the Albert Hall decision I'll even give her a backstage pass!

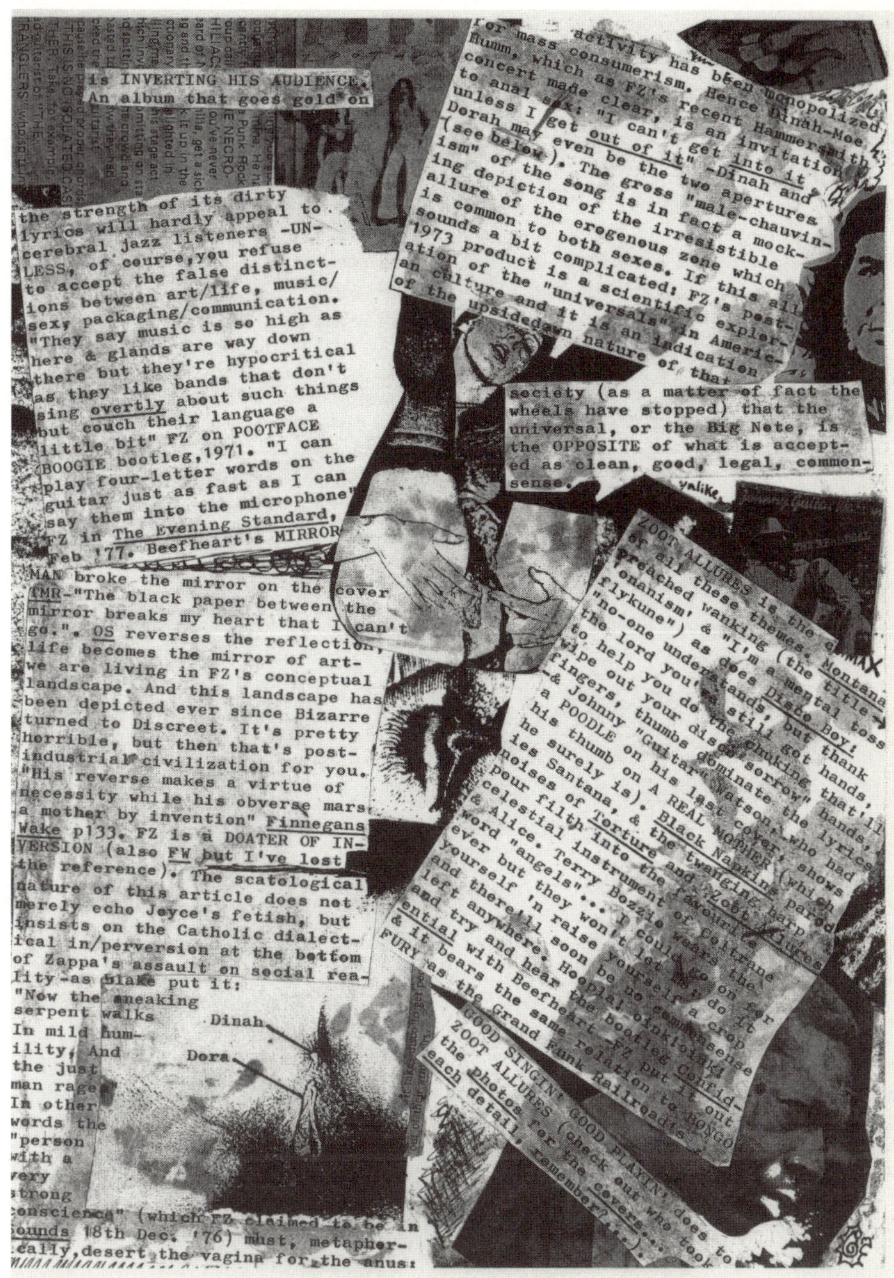

is INVERTING HIS AUDIENCE. An album that goes gold on

the strength of its dirty lyrics will hardly appeal to cerebral jazz listeners -UNLESS, of course, you refuse to accept the false distinctions between art/life, music/sex, packaging/communication. "They say music is so high as here & glands are way down there but they're hypocritical as they like bands that don't sing overtly about such things but couch their language a little bit" FZ on POOTFACE BOOGIE bootleg, 1971. "I can play four-letter words on the guitar just as fast as I can say them into the microphone" FZ in The Evening Standard, Feb '77. Beefheart's MIRROR MAN broke the mirror on the cover TMR-"The black paper between the mirror breaks my heart that I can't go.". OS reverses the reflection, life becomes the mirror of art- we are living in FZ's conceptual landscape. And this landscape has been depicted ever since Bizarre turned to Discreet. It's pretty horrible, but then that's post-industrial civilization for you. "His reverse makes a virtue of necessity while his obverse mars a mother by invention" Finnegans Wake p133. FZ is a DOATER OF INVERSION (also FW but I've lost the reference). The scatological nature of this article does not merely echo Joyce's fetish, but insists on the Catholic dialectical in/perversion at the bottom of Zappa's assault on social reality-as Blake put it: "Now the sneaking serpent walks In mild humility, And the just man rages" In other words the "person with a very strong conscience" (which FZ claimed to be in Sounds 18th Dec. '76) must, metaphorically, desert the vagina for the anus:

Dinah

Dora

activity has been monopolized for mass consumerism. Hence Dinah-Moe Humm, which as FZ's recent Hammersmith concert made clear, is an invitation to anal sex: "I can't get into it unless I get out of it" -Dinah and Dorah may even be the two apertures (see below). The gross "male-chauvinism" of the song is in fact a mocking depiction of the irresistible allure of the erogenous zone which is common to both sexes. If this all sounds a bit complicated: FZ's post-1973 product is a scientific exploration of the "universals" in American culture and it is an indication of the upsidedown nature of that

society (as a matter of fact the wheels have stopped) that the universal, or the Big Note, is the OPPOSITE of what is accepted as clean, good, legal, commonsense.

yalike.

ZOOT ALLURES is the CLIMAX of all these themes. Montana preached wanking (the title 'onanism' & "I'm a mental toss flykune") as does Disco Boy! "no-one understands, but thank the lord you've still got hands, to help you do the choking that'll wipe out your disco sorrow" hands, fingers, thumbs dominate the lyrics & Johnny "Guitar" Watson, who had a POODLE on his last cover, shows his thumb on A REAL MOTHER (which he surely is). Black Napkins parodies Santana, & the twanging harp noises of Torture and Zoot Allures pour filth into the favourite celestial instrument of Coltrane & Alice. Terry Bozzio wears the word "angels"... I could go on for ever but they won't let me, do it yourself 'n raise yourself a crop and there'll soon be no commonsense left anywhere. Hoopla! oinkloiaki! and try and hear the bootleg Confidential with Beefheart -FZ put it out & it bears the same relation to BONGO FURY as the Grand Funk Railroad's GOOD SINGIN' GOOD PLAYIN' does to ZOOT ALLURES (check out who took the photos for the covers... each detail, remember?...)

if you thought Mårten's question about Stravinsky's <u>Soldier's Tale</u> was abstract, try this (the present situation IS abstract) -:

PUCK

discreet discipline in the frozen wasteland

Cube Fitting

this is the flat india-rubber DISC used for a ball in bandy or ice-hockey; it is also a bird, known variously as the NIGHTJAR, GOATSUCKER or WHIP-POOR-WILL. The last of these is the popular name in the US & Canada for one particular species, <u>antrostomus (Caprimulgus) vociferus</u>. It also means to strike or hit, and is the name for a mischievous demon, and in Middle English was identified with the DEVIL himself. Sucking at udders by night, the Puck is a male sexual demon, Vampire or Incubus (the Zomby putting the <u>warp</u> in <u>woof</u>): the nightjar derives its name from the peculiar whirring noise which the male makes during the period of INCUBATION. Milton used the word 'incube' to mean 'fix in a cube' -BOXING the dog, huh. Sleeping in a jar, watch mum and dad fuck through a door which is not a door but AJAR (the jarring noise of the adult male goatsucker), watch Frunobulax come in the cave. This puts us in a PUCKER (a state of agitation or excitement) and our RICTUS gets PUCKERED (drawn into wrinkles, small folds, cockles or bulges). Open the box, eat the apple.

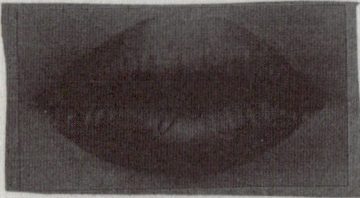

ECO DAMP PUCKERED RICTUS

1348 the year of the plague, Black Death sweeps Europe: wind up working in a gas station, extracting gold from the mouths of the victims before they're sent to the chambers. We are traveling across the wasteland toward a huge hydro-electric dam. Dynamo hum increases as we near it. As Hart Crane said: "the velvet hummed of dynamoes, where hearing's leash is strummed" Poodle audience clap, two paws sticking up. mONtANa, be a mental toss fly coon and play with yourself like Johnny Guitar: transcen dental meditation, those deadly Jaws. Hotcha!

OUT TO LUNCH

Black Puck No 2

Dirty Paws GRITLESS HAND CLEANSER

FAN BELTS

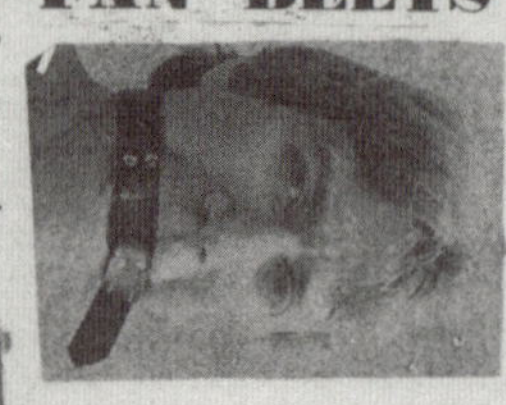

OUT TO LUNCH

Hope you liked BREEDING FROM YOUR POODLE & the PHAEDO -show it to Bubba.

Hand Press with typical "V" Raise Tool

That voice was a lamentation. Calmer now. It's in the silence you feel you hear. Vibrations. Now silent air. Bloom ungyved his crisscrossed hands and with slack fingers plucked the slender catgut thong. He drew and plucked. It buzzed, it twanged . . . Thou lost one. All songs on that theme. Yet more Bloom stretched his string. Cruel it seems. Let people get fond of each other: lure them on. Then tear asunder. Death.

BRITOOL STUD EXTRACTORS

James Joyce Ulysses p358

T. & J. EXPANDING PILOT REAMERS

Under its heather mask the quag allures, with an allurement not all mortals can resist. Then it swallows them up or the mist comes down.

Who is Studebaker Hoch? what does it mean?

COOL APSE AT THE BOTTOM OF THE CRYPT/ALL SECRETS YEARN FOR ANALYSIS

SILVER SLAVER
IN A HALF-DUG
CRAVE

from the COMPASSES to the bistouri, and from that to the ZITHER

CRUX VOBISCUM

Never utter a note which is atvariance with the tensions and relaxations and percussions and other affections of the strings out of which the body is composed

LISTEN TO THE SIRENS OF VARESE which is now neutralized to become the wistful longing of the passer-by

AT EACH BLOODY RIOT SHE BLOSSOMS
FORTH FILLED WITH GRACE AND TRUTH

NESTHILL PETROL SQUIRT

Curtains and draperies. Soft and enrapturing notes. Even the organ. As soon as there is no more nerve current and the blood in the veins is no longer hot, the SINFUL BODY, this seat of universal LUST, becomes a corpse and the souls can converse unhindered about peace, love and flowers.

RITE OF SPRING or THE RITUAL DANCE OF THE CHILDKILLERS
the enthronement of a mechanical factor as authority or ms pinky
a danse macabre around the fetish character of consumer goods by
a mutant industrial vacuum cleaner.

comparable torpid state is adopted during
in the cooler parts of the world, mating

AUTHENTICITY GAINED SURREPTITIOUSLY THROUGH THE DENIAL OF THE SUBJECTIVE POLE or THE NIGHT OF THE IRON SAUSAGE

aversion to the total syntax of music?

THE CRAVING OF THE CRAVEN

OTZ.

Continental vespertilionids recorded from
nts. Inconspicuous and innocuous, they
cept perhaps when a colony in a church or
and, in any event, these often disperse with
nal weather. Bats are, indeed, the
ge nocturnal world. often unheeded

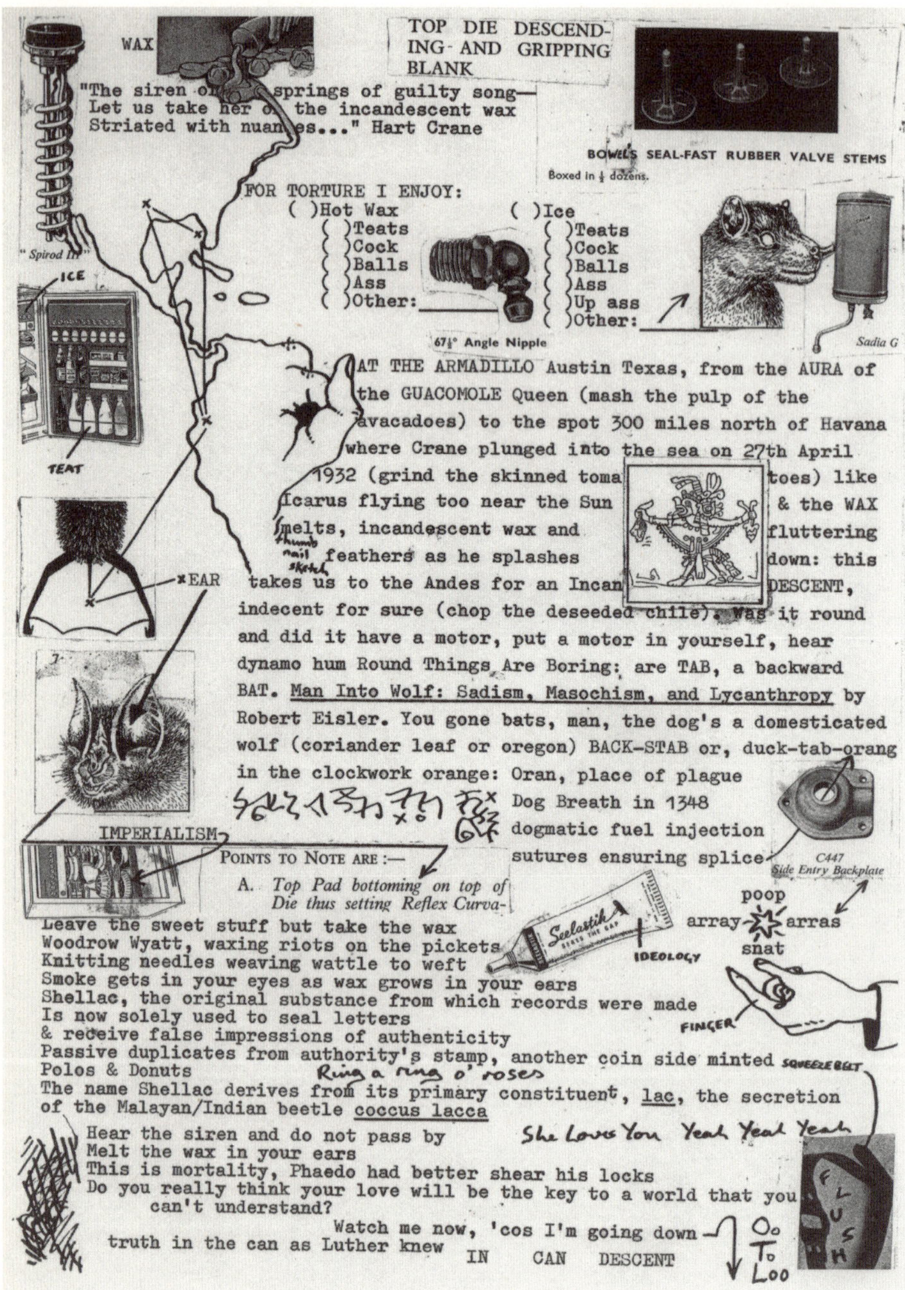
WAX
TOP DIE DESCENDING AND GRIPPING BLANK
"The siren of springs of guilty song—
Let us take her on the incandescent wax
Striated with nuances..." Hart Crane
BOWEL'S SEAL-FAST RUBBER VALVE STEMS
Boxed in ½ dozens.
" Spirod II"
FOR TORTURE I ENJOY:
( )Hot Wax
( )Teats
( )Cock
( )Balls
( )Ass
( )Other:
( )Ice
( )Teats
( )Cock
( )Balls
( )Ass
( )Up ass
( )Other:
67½° Angle Nipple
Sadia G
ICE
TEAT
AT THE ARMADILLO Austin Texas, from the AURA of the GUACOMOLE Queen (mash the pulp of the avacadoes) to the spot 300 miles north of Havana where Crane plunged into the sea on 27th April 1932 (grind the skinned toma toes) like Icarus flying too near the Sun & the WAX melts, incandescent wax and fluttering feathers as he splashes down: this takes us to the Andes for an Incan DESCENT, indecent for sure (chop the deseeded chile). Was it round and did it have a motor, put a motor in yourself, hear dynamo hum Round Things Are Boring: are TAB, a backward BAT. Man Into Wolf: Sadism, Masochism, and Lycanthropy by Robert Eisler. You gone bats, man, the dog's a domesticated wolf (coriander leaf or oregon) BACK-STAB or, duck-tab-orang in the clockwork orange: Oran, place of plague
Dog Breath in 1348
dogmatic fuel injection
sutures ensuring splice
thumb nail sketch
EAR
IMPERIALISM
POINTS TO NOTE ARE :—
A. Top Pad bottoming on top of Die thus setting Reflex Curva-
C447
Side Entry Backplate
poop
array
arras
snat
Seelastik
IDEOLOGY
FINGER
Leave the sweet stuff but take the wax
Woodrow Wyatt, waxing riots on the pickets
Knitting needles weaving wattle to weft
Smoke gets in your eyes as wax grows in your ears
Shellac, the original substance from which records were made
Is now solely used to seal letters
& receive false impressions of authenticity
Passive duplicates from authority's stamp, another coin side minted
Polos & Donuts
Ring a ring o' roses
SQUEEZE BELT
The name Shellac derives from its primary constituent, lac, the secretion of the Malayan/Indian beetle coccus lacca
She Loves You Yeah Yeah Yeah
Hear the siren and do not pass by
Melt the wax in your ears
This is mortality, Phaedo had better shear his locks
Do you really think your love will be the key to a world that you can't understand?
Watch me now, 'cos I'm going down
truth in the can as Luther knew
IN CAN DESCENT
OO TO LOO
FLUSH

MERZ NOTES.

3. minutes enuf
time2boil an oeuf?
an urf – an egg
time to fry
frying it

Cityful passing away
other cityful coming
passing away too:
other coming on – passing on
Houses
lines of houses
streets
miles of pavements,
piled up bricks, stones.
Changing hands
This owner, that

ticketmaster.
ticketmaster.co.uk
08705-344-4444 | 24 HOURS 7 DAYS
TICKET NUMBER : 14 9
DOWN UNRESERVED
MUSIC STAGE PROMOTIONS LTD
FRANK ZAPPA
WHEN WORLDS COLLIDE
AT OCEAN
£ 0.00 270 MARE ST, HACKNEY E8
SC WED 05-NOV-03 19:00-24:00
COMP SEAS02 28OCT3 13:03

Landlord never dies they say
other steps into his shoes
when he gets his notice ~~to quit~~
2 quit.
They buy the place up with GOLD
+ still they have all the GOLD
swindle in it somewhere.
Piled up in cities
worn away age after age
Pyramids in sand
Built on bread + onions
Slaves Chinese Wall.
BABYLON.
Big stones left.
Round Towers.
Rest Rubble
Sprawling SUBURBS
jerry-built

Kerwan's Mushroom houses
built of Breeze
Shelter for the Night.

No One is Anything
If you want to
Scramble yourself out there
every stale joke, fart, chew
sneeze & stomach rumble
If your trick no work
yu better RUN.
Everybody's doing it
they all scramble in together
& the populations of the URTH
just settle down
a nice even brown color.

Death needs time for what
it kills to Grow in.
Let the Dying Die
let the Lying Lie
let the Crying Cry.
Wait.
Time.
A landing field.
The Martians understand this very
well.
The definate article THE
The contains the implication
of one & only:
THE GOD
THE UNIVERSE
THE WAY
THE RIGHT
THE WRONG.
if there is another then
THAT UNIVERSE
THAT WAY IS NO LONGER
THE UNIVERSE

THE WAY.

EITHER/OR
TRUE OR FALSE
MOTHER OR FATHER

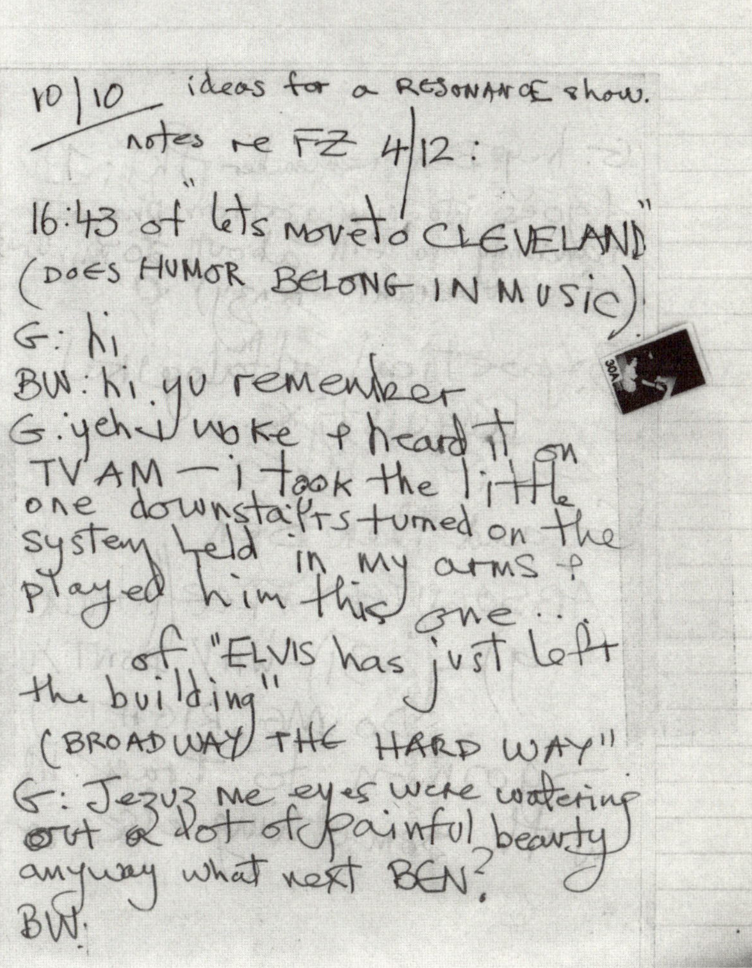
10/10 ideas for a RESONANCE show.
notes re FZ 4/12:
16:43 of "lets move to CLEVELAND"
(DOES HUMOR BELONG IN MUSIC)
G: hi
BW: hi you remember
G: yeh i woke & heard it on TV AM — i took the little one downstairs turned on the system held in my arms & played him this one..
of "ELVIS has just left the building"
(BROADWAY THE HARD WAY"
G: Jezuz me eyes were watering out a lot of painful beauty anyway what next BEN?
BW:

Discography

Freak Out! (1966)
Absolutely Free (1967)
We're Only In It for the Money (1968)
Lumpy Gravy (1968)
Cruising with Ruben & the Jets (1968)
Uncle Meat (1969)
Hot Rats (1969)
Burnt Weeny Sandwich (1970)
Weasels Ripped My Flesh (1970)
Chunga's Revenge (1970)
Fillmore East—June 1971 (1971)
200 Motels (1971)
Just Another Band from L.A. (1972)
Waka/Jawaka (1972)
The Grand Wazoo (1972)
Overnite Sensation (1973)
Apostrophe(') (1974)
Roxy & Elsewhere (1974)
One Size Fits All (1975)
Bongo Fury (1973)
Zoot Allures (1976)
Zappa In New York (1977)
Studio Tan (1978)
Sleep Dirt (1979)
Sheik Yerbouti (1979)
Orchestral Favourites (1979)
Joe's Garage Acts I, II & III 91979)
Tinseltown Rebellion (1981)
Shut Up 'N Play Yer Guitar (1981)
You Are What You Is (1981)
Ship Arriving Too Late to Save a Drowning Witch (1982)
Baby Snakes (1983)
The Man from Utopia (1983)

London Symphony Orchestra Vol.1 (1983)
The Perfect Stranger (1984)
Them or Us (1984)
Thing-Fish (1984)
Francesco Zappa (1984)
Mystery Disc 1 (1985)
Meets the Mothers of Prevention (1985)
Does Humor Belong in Music? (1986)
Mystery Disc 2 (1986)
Jazz from Hell (1986)
London Symphony Orchestra Vol.2 (1987)
Guitar (1988)
You Can't Do That on Stage Anymore Vol.1 (1988)
You Can't Do That on Stage Anymore Vol.2 (1988)
Broadway the Hard Way (1988)
You Can't Do That on Stage Anymore Vol.3 (1989)
You Can't Do That on Stage Anymore Vol.4 (1991)
The Best Band You Never Heard in Your Life (1991)
Make a Jazz Noise Here (1991)
You Can't Do That on Stage Anymore Vol.5 (1992)
You Can't Do That on Stage Anymore Vol.6 (1992)
The Yellow Shark (1993)
Civilization Phaze III (1994)
Ahead of their Time (1995)
Playground Psychotics (1995)
The Lost Episodes (1996)

Posthumous releases by ZFT

Läther (1996)
Frank Zappa Plays the Music of Frank Zappa (1996)
Have I Offended Someone? (1997)
Everything is Healing Nicely (1998)
FZ:OZ (2002)
Halloween: Live in NYC 1978 (2003)
Joe's Garage (2004)
Joe's Dommage (2004)
Quadiophiliac (2004)

Index

N.B. Entries in **bold** indicate illustrations